CALVIN

Baseball's Last Dinosaur

An Authorized Biography

Jon Kerr

Jon Kerr is a Minneapolis-based sports writer for United Press International. He has written extensively for the *Minneapolis Review of Baseball, City Pages,* and the *Twin Cities Reader.* Jon was active in the Save The Met organization dedicated to the renovation of Metropolitan Stadium and is a member of the Society for American Baseball Research (SABR). He holds a master's degree in American History from the University of Minnesota.

CALVIN

Baseball's Last Dinosaur

An Authorized Biography

Jon Kerr

 Wm. C. Brown Publishers

To true fans, both old and new.

CONTENTS

Contents

FOREWORD

On a spring morning in 1985, a reporter called Calvin Griffith's room at the Court of Flags Hotel in Orlando, Florida. The Washington Senators and their descendants, the Minnesota Twins, had been coming to Orlando for spring training since the 1930s, but this was the first time that a Griffith would not be in charge of the operation.

"Sure, come on up," Calvin said. "We'll talk."

The Court of Flags is a hotel with modest rates that caters to the tour bus crowd. The members of the Twins new regime had moved to fancier digs—expensive hotels and condominiums—for the spring, but Calvin continued to headquarter at the Court.

"I like it here," Calvin said. "They gave me the same suite, even though I don't own the ball club anymore."

Griffith had just moved in a couple days earlier, making the drive over from Melbourne, Florida, where he spends the winter in an oceanfront condo. Now, Calvin was roaming the room in his bathrobe, drinking a cup of coffee and peering into boxes. He was looking for a copper bracelet he wears to combat arthritis.

"Where did I put that danged thing?" Calvin asked.

There was a knock on the door. "Come on in," Griffith shouted, and in walked his twin brothers, Jimmy and Billy Robertson. Jimmy was wearing his trademark, red-and-white nylon cap and red windbreaker. Billy was wearing his traditional sports coat.

The Robertsons poured themselves a cup of coffee. They talked over any baseball news that had appeared in the morning newspapers, and they started telling stories about the early days in Orlando.

"When we first came here, the grounds away from town were sand," Billy said. "If you drove out Winter Garden Road to eat oysters at Lee and Rick's, one of you was going to have to move over to the side and let the other guy pass. When you did that, you'd get stuck in that sand and have to shovel yourself out."

"That's right," Calvin said.

The Twins were scheduled to play an exhibition game that night in the Houston Astros new complex at nearby Kissimmee. This reminded Calvin of the time in the '30s, when he was the general manager of the Senators Chattanooga farm club.

"We brought the Chattanooga team over to Kissimmee for an exhibition game that day," Griffith said. "Do you know what the gate receipts were for that game? Twenty-five cents. That's what it cost to get into the game, 25, and we had one fellow pay to get in. I walked over there and gave him his quarter back."

The stories of springtimes past in Orlando kept coming for the next two hours. There were many laughs, and there might have been a tear when the reporter excused himself with a final question:

"How did the family feel about being back for spring training and not having a Griffith in the office of team president for the first time in 64 years?"

There was a full minute of silence. Billy stared out of Calvin's picture window. Jimmy took a few puffs off his cigarette. Calvin crooked an index finger and dabbed at his eyes.

"It's tough," Calvin said.

A few months later, the same reporter dropped into the suite that belonged to Calvin at the Metrodome. The agreement Griffith signed when he sold the team to banker Carl Pohlad in September 1984 permitted him to keep possession of the suite—the one closest to home plate—for five years.

With most suiteholders, the deluxe atmosphere is used for entertaining highfalutin friends and customers. For Calvin, it was a place where he and his brothers, and their friends—John Lenke, the bartender, and Sherm Seeker, the cook, from the press room; Angelo Giuliani and Killer Kane, two oldtime baseball men from St. Paul—could watch the ballgame.

The amazing part of the Calvin Griffith story is that, despite being a member of such a powerful group as the major league baseball owners, he was able to retain such simple tastes. He would rather watch a ballgame with his brothers and a few blue-collar friends, people who share his passion for the sport, than the president of company who had bought eight season tickets.

Calvin was raised in baseball before anyone heard of public relations. The phrase "no comment" was never in Calvin's vocabulary. He said the first thing that came into his mind, and that was it.

In the fall of 1981, the Twins played their last game at Met Stadium. Rather than a nostalgic group of oldtimers, a large share of the crowd that showed up was a younger, T-shirt-wearing bunch that became increasingly raucous as the afternoon progressed. They trapped Calvin as he walked to the men's room during the game and he signed autographs for more than an hour.

"My hand went numb," Calvin said.

When the game ended, the Twins had a post-game ceremony in which the bases, home plate and the pitcher's mound were to be given away. The ceremonies were being conducted by vice-presidents Howard Fox, Bruce Haynes and Clark Griffith. Calvin was in the press room, adjacent to the visitors' clubhouse and behind the third-base dugout.

The crowd started to chant "Calvin, Calvin, Calvin." After 21 seasons, many of which he found himself being vilified as a cheapskate, it seemed as though Griffith finally had reached an audience—a young, rowdy group that saw him as the wonderful character he always had been.

When Griffith came ambling down the tunnel, into the dugout and then onto the field, bedlam erupted. It was a situation that cried for Calvin to offer a simple "thank you," to recall some of the great moments at the Met and then shuffle back to the press room to finish his vodka tonic.

That wouldn't be Calvin, though. He had to say what was on his mind. Calvin did say thank you, but then he gave the fans hell for not buying more tickets in years past, so economics wouldn't have forced his ballclub to move downtown to the Metrodome.

There was also Calvin's infamous speech in Waseca, Minnesota—off-the-cuff remarks that were reported by a visiting newspaperman from Minneapolis and construed to be racist, sexist and about ever other "ist" you can think of. During the question-and-answer portion, Calvin was asked about Jerry Terrell, a utility infielder. Terrell was a hero in that part of the country because he was raised three miles from Waseca, was signed from Twins tryout camp and made it to the big leagues.

Again, PR cried for Griffith to tell the crowd what a fine contributor to the Twins that Terrell had been, but Calvin had to say what was on his mind. He talked about how diluted baseball's talent had become with 26 teams and said it was a "damn disgrace" that a ballplayer with as little ability as Terrell had played so long in the big leagues.

Pure Calvin.

When I was a young baseball writer in the mid-'70s, trying to impress people with my hard-nosed journalism, I took considerable delight in ripping Griffith and the rest of the family over the tight-fisted manner in which they ran the ballclub. Calvin had a hide as thick as a rhinoceros. You could whip him in print, he would tell you off, and then it was forgotten.

Within a few years, I changed tactics on Calvin. I began to appreciate the fact this was an irascible, irreplaceable character on the national sports scene, and that we were lucky enough to have had him in our midst in Minnesota. To me, losing was a small price to pay for having a baseball man and baseball family running the local ballclub.

It's my opinion now—and it will be the day I hang up the typewriter—that the saddest day in Minnesota sports was September 7, 1984, when the Griffiths officially turned over their baseball franchise to a banker who didn't know Ty Cobb from corn on the cob.

What we couldn't do is allow Calvin Griffith and his family to get away without compiling their treasure chest of stories. Those stories are here!

Pat Reusse

FOREWORD

Jon Kerr has brought to print a baseball story that was asking to be written, preferably by somebody with a sharp sense of ownership values. It also could have been appropriately titled: *Inside Baseball*; or *One Man's Family, a Baseball Heritage*; or *A Name In The Game. Calvin: Baseball's Last Dinosaur, An Authorized Biography* embraces all of the above, with new revelations of boardroom politics, and life on the bring by a clubowner lacking the deep pockets of the new breed of baseball tycoons.

It abounds with subplots as well; with the struggles to keep alive in baseball the name of the Griffith clan and the pioneer spirit of its patriarch, Clark C. Griffith, a founder of the American League, hands-on owner of the Washington Senators and role model for Calvin Griffith in his commonsense efforts to keep the franchise and the family together over the generations.

In his own dedication to the book, Jon Kerr traipsed the nation to find support material for the story of Calvin Griffith; from former players, former managers, friends, newspapermen, and some enemies. He deals knowingly with the sadness of the family feud that sundered the family relationship of Calvin with his own son, who regarded his father as hopelessly old-fashioned in his baseball dealings, leading to their contempt for one another.

The story of the Griffith-owned franchises in Washington and Philadelphia owed its credibility in great measure to the full cooperation of Calvin Griffith in what is an all-out telling of the tale pulled together by Jon Kerr. It is spiced as well by Calvin's admitted malapropisms, exampled best by his 1982 comment that rookie outfielder Jim Eisenreich was "doomed to be a star."

It is the story of Calvin Griffith presiding and perspiring over the last of baseball's family-owned legacy franchises, first in Washington, later in Minnesota. It is a play-by-play Tale of Two Cities in which Calvin was booed, and loved, and booed again. Kerr, with Calvin's help, replays the seduction of Calvin by Minnesota's promise of greener fields, how he ditched his pledge to "keep the team in Washington as long as I'm alive;" how he became Minnesota's hero by delivering two quick first-division teams and, in the Twins fourth year, a pennant. How Minneapolis fans were spoiled by those early successes and how, later, there was trouble in Minnesota City. Both the team and the affection for Calvin soured.

For all his poor notices in other matters, Calvin did establish himself as the number one maven among all the clubowners in terms of evaluating players and stocking one of the best farm systems in the league.

But along came the monster of the free agency wrung by the players from the owners, and Calvin's mom-and-pop operation succumbed to the new rules of the game.

In vain he had led the fight against free agency, not only losing that battle but finally awakening to the truth of it after refusing Bill Campbell the $8,000 raise to $38,000 the pitcher sought at the end of the 1976 season. A few weeks later, Campbell signed with the Red Sox for $1 million.

It wasn't wholly pretty for the Griffiths at the finish when Calvin did agree to sell their 52 percent control of the Twins. Not only was Calvin saddened that the book closed on the Griffith name that had a 91-year run in the Major Leagues, he came to view the club's sale as a disaster in terms of how it was negotiated. Outwitted by the Minneapolis banker who bought the club, he relates, were his newly-reconciled son and his novice nephew to whom he left the dealing. There was perfidy, too, he claims by a long-time office associate and trusted friend who was sly about being on both sides of the deal. And at $38 million, he came to know he had sold cheaply. Within four years, the Baltimore franchise would go for $70 million. The authorized biography of Calvin Griffith keeps no secrets, one of its charms.

Shirley Povich

ACKNOWLEDGMENTS

Many debts of gratitude are due to those who have assisted or encouraged the writing of this book.

In particular I would note the assistance of the Baseball Hall of Fame Library in Cooperstown, N.Y., Wilson Library at the University of Minnesota, particularly the Inter-Library Loans division for their help in securing newspaper microfilms from many sources. The St. Paul Pioneer Press Library was also helpful, as were the Minnesota Twins.

Individuals of note include Jean Pieri, Ralph Neubeck, David Brauer, John Sheehy, Julian Empson, Jerry Farrell, Ken LaZebnik and the Minneapolis Review of Baseball, Mark Vancil, Pat Reusse, Charley Walters, Jay Weiner, Mike Augustine, Anthony Schmitz, Don Leeper, Gerald Moore, Tom Mee, and Margaret Youngquist.

My thanks certainly is extended to all of the numerous persons who agreed to interviews and often extensive questioning on subjects of distant or controversial past. Despite exceptions, I found that even in our public relations conscious society most honest persons still prefer to candidly address issues.

I would especially thank the Griffith and Haynes families for their openness in discussing some of their most private feelings and histories. Any family has its secrets and tender subjects. But the Griffiths and Haynes had a candor that generally exceeded expectations.

Of course their model was certainly exceptional. Calvin's candidness and depth of openness continues to amaze me. He was always willing to tackle even the most difficult subjects.

Certainly Calvin never had to be prodded to discuss baseball. I shall miss our discussions of the game and its history. Sitting across from him at his desk, in his home, or in his box at the stadium his love and respect for the game was always clear to the listener.

Chapter 1

THE GRAND FINALE

"The fans were really great. I've been hung in apathy before so I didn't know what to expect."

The skies were overcast and grey, not unlike the color of the Hubert H. Humphrey Metrodome's teflon roof, on the evening of June 23, 1984, as Calvin Griffith and Thelma Haynes met their banker at home plate. Baseball's last dinosaur was facing his own extinction.

A man at the same time reviled and loved for his single-minded devotion to his beliefs, Calvin tenaciously held on to the only way of life he had ever known. "I'll tell you one thing, I wouldn't let anybody push me," he says with a smile that contrasts with the firm edge in his voice. "If anybody started pushing me, I really got obstinate. I tell you the truth, I was really hard to get along with. I knew what I wanted to do and we were gonna do it that way because who was gonna take all the crucifixin' . . . er, get crucified was me."

But now the end had arrived in dramatic fashion. Over 20,000 fans witnessed the pre-game event as the brother and sister ceremonially signed over their family business for approximately $32 million to Carl Pohlad, whose corporate titles included the presidency of F&M Marquette Banks, the chairmanship of MEI Corporation, and enough other financial holdings to make him Minnesota's wealthiest man.

Now Pohlad's possessions would also include a piece of the national pastime, though formal contract signings and league approval would delay official sale of the Griffith's 52 percent ownership of the Twins for another two months.

Calvin tearfully began dabbing at his puffy eyes with a handkerchief almost from the moment he and his sister disembarked from their blood red convertible. It was apparent that there was more than money involved in this public display of emotion. With a characteristic innocence that betrayed his often gruff exterior, Calvin was suddenly face to face with the end of a way of life for not only himself and his family, but also baseball, and even his nation.

"You gotta weep at a time like this. This was the hardest day of my life," admitted the man who had almost come to embody controversy in his closing years of ownership.

Only afterwards would Calvin come to realize how hard the succeeding years outside baseball would be.

For nearly 65 years, the Griffith name had been a part of baseball ownership. Hall of Famer Clark Griffith, one of the American League founders, actually purchased his first shares of Washington Senators stock while still a player-manager in 1911. By 1920, the "Old Fox" had gained majority control of the franchise that he would operate in the nation's capital and eventually pass to his two adopted children at his death in 1955.

The team's move to Minnesota in 1961, further spread both the geographical and emotional significance of the Griffith name. Condemned as a heartless traitor in Washington and welcomed as a hero in his new home, the move was only one of many examples of Calvin's lifetime of controversy and love-hate relationships with the general public.

Minnesota baseball fans would react with mixed feelings to the signing ceremony 23 years later that ended the dominant role of the often controversial owner. Calvin, as recently as that spring, threatened to sell the team south to Tampa, Florida or elsewhere. In response, an organized ticket buyout had, while appearing to hold the Twins to their Metrodome lease, reinforced the widely held image of Griffith's petty greed.

Now as Calvin's recognized rotund figure moved slowly to the center of the Metrodome diamond for the brief round of speeches and the signing ceremony, he and Mrs. Haynes were greeted by a standing ovation.

Perhaps it was only good sportsmanship. But its intensity and later events would suggest real support, despite a history that included the 1969 firing of Billy Martin, the charges of racism after a 1978 speech at the Waseca Lions Club, the 1975 exile of Harmon Killebrew to end his playing days in another uniform, the loss of numerous free agent stars over the years, and Rod Carew's trade in 1979, among other unpopular moves.

"Calvin wasn't a person who went on the boards of directors of civic organizations or joined United Way. And then the ballclub was starting after the 1960s to decline and I think people sorta got down on Calvin," explains his friend and former Twins board member Wheelock Whitney.

"But after selling he was appreciated for what he tried to do and became a hero—not to the business community but to Mr. or Mrs. Joe Fan on the street, the little guy. Now he stands for what's right in the world," says Whitney.

Calvin wasn't enamored of such analysis at the time. But with a characteristic malapropism he remembers his feeling of appreciation and even some surprise. "The fans were really great. I've been hung in apathy before so I didn't know what to expect."

"I think I got quite an ovation. I didn't know what to expect," he explains. "You always get a jerk somewhere. Look at the President of the United States, the most powerful man in the country and he gets booed and every other damned thing."

While a scattering of boos and one banner proclaiming Minnesota "Free at Last," reflected Griffith's often stormy relationship with fans, media and players, most sentiments were kinder. Other more typical banners read "Thank You, Calvin," and "Thanks for the Memories."

Memories must have been flowing for the man born 72 years before as Calvin Robertson. Since joining his uncle, Clark Griffith, in Washington during the summer of

2

1922, the soon-to-be-fatherless ten-year-old had known nothing but baseball. His sister originally came along for the trip, but stayed to join in an almost lifelong partnership. Three younger brothers, Sherry, Billy, and Jimmy Robertson, eventually joined their siblings and helped run the operation together for over half a century.

But the changing economics of baseball caught the Griffith-Robertson organization increasingly short-handed. After glory years in the 1960s brought Minnesota a pennant in 1965 and division championships in 1969 and 1970, Twins fortunes began to fade on the field and at the box office.

Free agency and escalating player payrolls were financially and philosophically difficult to accept for a family that had been raised to spend only cash on the barrel head. Compared to the Steinbrenners, Autrys, Yawkeys, and Buschs with whom he had to regularly compete, Calvin was operating a ma-and-pa corner store battling against supermarket franchises. His response of refusing to adopt modern marketing and financing techniques would be part stubbornness and part conviction.

Calvin would never be timid about taking positions. "I have learned that if you run for a popularity contest you don't achieve things," Calvin would tell a reporter. "You must make a few mistakes in this world if you want to accomplish things. I must have made a few because I have been criticized pretty good. Overall, I think our organization has done a good job using baseball common sense," he said.

As corporate ownership came to dominate baseball, the hand-to-mouth Griffith organization became an anachronism struggling against the inevitable—and often with itself. Calvin often battled publicly with his son, Clark, while overlooking power struggles and intrigue among his closest advisors that could provide material for a Shakespearian tragedy.

Calvin's blunt speech and occasional verbal blunders added further material to the drama. "The way I expressed myself was how I was told," he recounts his instructions from his uncle. "Don't use a five dollar word when a 50 cent one will do . . . . You can't go out there and be Winston Churchill or Franklin Roosevelt and get out there talking to high school kids or kids in elementary school who are the ones who keep the game going. You gotta tell 'em the bare facts in the simplest way."

"My brother and I always have communicated very well," said Thelma Haynes at the time of the sale. "We agreed a long time ago that, if ever the time came when it made no sense for us to try to pay the salaries, we would sell. That time probably came a few years ago. It definitely is here now."

Calvin, who broke down sobbing at the end of the ceremony when greeted by Twins players and manager Billy Gardner, tried to be philosophical afterward. "It's not tough signing the club away," he said to then St. Paul Dispatch columnist Pat Reusse. "I don't have many regrets. You know, I met all the presidents from Coolidge through Ford. The only two presidents I haven't met are Reagan and Carter.

"I even met Castro one night at the ballpark in Havana, right before he lost the election to Batista," Calvin remembered of the Cuban leader who had once dreamed of being a Washington Senators pitcher. "How many people do you know who can say they have shaken hands with all those fellows?"

3

A man who sometimes placed undue trust in handshakes, Calvin was also a man trying to reconcile his private feelings at turning over to Pohlad not only the family business, but a team battling for first place in the American League West. The 1984 Twins would only fade from contention in the final days of the season.

But the nucleus of Kent Hrbek, Gary Gaetti, Kirby Puckett, Tom Brunansky, and Frank Viola who were all drafted or traded for by the Griffith organization would bring a world championship to Minnesota within three years. It was to be the first championship in the Senators/Twins organization since young Calvin Griffith had been a batboy for stars such as Ty Cobb, Walter Johnson and Babe Ruth in 1924. The dour 1987 manager, Tom Kelly, was even a holdover of whom Calvin had once counseled, "Go out and get yourself a goddamned bottle of whiskey and a strange woman and tomorrow you'll go four-for-four."

It was apparent that Griffith was shaken as he left the field after the ceremony marking his last public appearance as a Twins spokesman. Asked about his health by a concerned chauffeur, he reportedly again put up a strong front. "Get me a vodka tonic and I'll be okay."

But the man who was taken by a youthful twist of fortune from the depth of poverty to the top of the baseball world would later admit to Minneapolis Tribune reporter Paul Levy that the effects of the sale never left him. "The biggest thing was the night we sold," said Calvin. "Knowing you're no longer king. You're stepping down the ladder and letting the new king take over. It's like being President of the United States for two terms and knowing that you can't run for a third term."

Calvin's two terms had lasted longer than many men's lives and through much of the life of baseball. Touching many lives and issues of the sport, his personal history would be intertwined with baseball and society's struggle to cope with massive changes. His passing from the scene would also mark the passing of an approach to the sport, business and life that many would do well to reconsider.

Chapter 2

A NEW HOME IN WASHINGTON

"If Clark Griffith hadn't come along and taken me out of Montreal,
what would Calvin Griffith . . . What would Calvin Robertson be doing today?
What in hell would have happened to me?"

The only heights that the Robertson family knew in 1922 was Montreal's Mount Royale. Delivering newspapers up and down the narrow, icy streets in wintertime, hauling blocks of ice in the summertime, or working at whatever else James Robertson had lined up for survival for his family of nine didn't allow for a royal lifestyle.

As the eldest son, and second oldest child, 11-year-old Calvin learned to drive the horse and buggy in winter, bundled up as much as possible in blankets and furs. "But it was the biggest darn route in the city," he later remembered. "And let me tell you, in the god-danged wintertime it was cold. I don't never want to go back to that."

The Scottish-born James Robertson immigrated at an early age, first to Montana and later to Chicago, where he began work as a clerk in Marshall Field's department store. Through the intervention of his future brother-in-law, Clark Griffith, Robertson gained a tryout and a brief, though unsuccessful playing stint at third base with the Chicago Cubs organization in 1901. When that failed he became a baseball scout. His travels eventually took him to Montreal in 1908 where he met Jane Davies, a young seamstress, and grudgingly realized that his days on the diamond were ended.

Though he seldom discussed it, perhaps the disappointment of his baseball failure never left Robertson, who also quickly found himself responsible for a succession of children that included five sons and two daughters. The second in line was Calvin Robertson, born in Montreal on December 1, 1911.

James Robertson's health began to fail while he was still a relatively young man, with alcohol the chief suspected cause (despite the disagreement of Mildred, Calvin's older sister). "He was an alcoholic. That was it," insists Calvin of his father. "When a person is an alcoholic he has a tough time, that's all there is to it. I used to have to sneak down to the corner bar and see if he was in there. If he was in there I'd have to ask somebody to carry him up to the house 'cause his wife was waiting for him to have dinner or something like that."

Calvin's description of his natural father makes clear the obvious distance between the two. "He never encouraged me to do anything," remembers Calvin. "We never talked about anything. The only thing he did was get me to work. A father and son relationship never existed, I guess."

Even more painful are Calvin's memories of hiding in his closet or under his bed at night for fear of what might happen when his drunken father returned home. "I was the oldest boy so I was the one that he thought he had to make a show with so he could let the other ones know what the hell could happen to them if they did anything he didn't like."

Despite their father's background, baseball was largely overlooked in the Robertson household. "He (James Robertson) didn't teach me nothing about baseball," says Calvin, who grew up playing broomstick hockey in a courtyard behind their rowhouse. "I was a pretty good skater. I think that's why when we came out here (Minnesota) I was the only one who didn't fall on his ass right away."

Calvin does remember an occasional stop to sell newspapers outside Montreal's old minor league ballpark. "I didn't know too much about it," he remembers his brief glimpses of games. "They caught the ball and hit the ball, threw the ball. I didn't have any idea about the rules or why they did this or that. But you'd get enthused over the fans and get excited when they did. They could really make a lot of noise."

Even at an early age Calvin was more concerned with day-to-day survival. "It was tough," he says of his Montreal life. "I don't even know if we ever had Christmas, the family was so poor. But you didn't know it most of the time. You took everything for granted. Your father just wasn't capable. He'd finish the paper route and go to the corner bar."

Not surprisingly, Calvin had his own social adjustment problems. "I was a mean sonofabitch in Montreal," he admits. "I used to have fights all the time and couldn't get along with anyone. Even when I came to the U.S. I used to get into fights all the time---I'd go from one playground to another."

The problems continued at school as Calvin was often forced to take recess with the girls because he fought too much with the boys. His troubles even included a visit from truant officers when a humilated Calvin took to skipping school. "I was a bad student, real bad," he recalls. "About all I remember of class up there in Montreal was singing 'God Save The King.'"

While the Robertson children grew up playing in the streets and learning "Pig French," as Calvin called it, from their neighbors, their mother acted as the family's stabilizing force, as well as a part-time seamstress. "My mother was just a damn good woman, that's all there is to it," he summarizes with brevity. "An understanding woman."

In later years, Calvin would witness his mother's quiet willpower in other areas. "She was one of the greatest baseball fans we ever had. She had a seat in Washington. She used to go and sit in the upper deck over the vomitory (exit) where nobody could walk in front of her. She walked all the way up there every day."

Jane Robertson's effort to maintain a family in Montreal was even more of an uphill battle. "It was a struggle," says Calvin of life in their second-floor duplex. "But we were so bad off I don't even think we had a bathtub or running water up there in those days. We used to get washed up in the living room right by the pot-bellied stove. That was our heat," he describes, with a scar on his stomach from an accidental burn as a reminder.

With a post-World War I economic recession making jobs scarce, and James Robertson growing increasingly ill, it was apparent that the family needed help. The birth of twins Jimmy and Billy in 1921 meant there was an even greater excess of mouths to feed in the Montreal home. "We were all on the doorstep," Thelma says, now able to joke at what was then a near-desperate situation.

Help came in the summer of 1922 when James Robertson's sister and Clark Griffith's wife, Addie Griffith, came to visit from Washington and ended up changing the lives of the entire family. Little is known about the exact circumstances and timing of the visit. But Addie must have been appalled at the family's situation in Montreal. "I just remember she (Addie) did a lot of talking with my mother," says Calvin.

Out of that conversation came the idea of a visit to Washington, first for young Calvin and later his younger sister Thelma. It would soon become permanent. Whether intentional or not, the childless Griffiths had acquired future heirs to their recently acquired Senators baseball franchise.

Ironically, Calvin was not at all anxious to leave his family in Montreal, an attitude that resulted in Thelma's companionship on the trip to Washington. "I don't know why they chose me to go," he says, perhaps a bit naively. "They needed me (in Montreal). I was the oldest son. I took care of the horses and delivered the papers. I was the one that did most of the goddamn work. I don't know why it was me.

"But if I was going, I didn't want to do it alone," says Calvin. "It was a new world. I said 'I had to have someone to talk to.'"

Thelma remembers Calvin insisting that she also come. "They really wanted to bring Calvin back for a vacation," remembers Thelma. "Calvin wasn't very anxious to go alone, but I wanted to go, I was always wanting to go someplace. So we came together. It was just one of those things that was meant to be."

At ages 11 and 9, Calvin and Thelma had spent their last days in the same house with their brothers and sisters. Staying behind was Mildred, who, as the eldest girl, was expected to help her mother, and brothers Bruce, Sherrod, and the twins Jimmy and Billy.

It was a decision none would ever regret. But at the time, the prospect must have been frightening to the young brother and sister who had little knowledge of the outside world. "All I'd ever seen was the St. Lawrence River, where we got our ice for the summertime," remembers Calvin.

The nearly two-week automobile trip to Washington was full of eye-opening experiences for the towheaded pair. "It was very interesting stopping at those hotels on the way down," Calvin recounts with a shake of his head. "You'd walk in there and all of a sudden you'd see a big, old black bear standing there in the lobby. I'd never seen one before, and you'd get astonished. Hell, everything was new to me."

Just as important was the psychological impact of that trip. "Maybe that's when I got acquainted with myself," says Calvin, pausing for a moment of introspection. "I realized that there is something in this world besides working all the time."

7

Still awaiting them in Washington was the experience of meeting their uncle, Clark Griffith for the first time, at least in Calvin's memory. "I was told I'd met him. Thelma seems to think she'd met him on a train someplace, or called out the window to him. But I don't remember any of that stuff."

Griffith Stadium was their first stop in Washington, Calvin remembers distinctly. "We got in for the last game of the season. We drove into the ballpark the last part of the game. I didn't know what was what. But that was when I met Clark Griffith. He put his arm around me and said he was glad to see me and Thelma. He made me feel real comfortable."

Compared to life in Montreal, the Griffith family must have seemed the ideal of domestic bliss. "He (Clark Griffith) idolized her (Addie Griffith) and she idolized her husband," describes Calvin. "She was a woman of fun and very fair to me. She gave me hell every once in awhile for staying out too late or something. But she was a good second mother, no question about it."

Just as comfortable were their new living quarters, first at a rented home and, by 1925, at the Griffith's new palatial estate on Decatur and 16th N.W. on Washington's diplomatic row. Next door neighbors included notables such as South Korean dictator Syngman Rhee. Calvin's days of hardship had been suddenly replaced by a life amongst the rich and famous.

"That house was so damn beautiful it was unbelievable," says Calvin, describing special woodwork and carvings by Italian artisans. Brickwork in the house was all shaped like diamonds, he recalls. "Then they had lightposts all around the place that were round, looking like baseballs."

Other attractions included a nearby zoo, with all sorts of animals and strange creatures, and even some of the newest man-made devices. "I remember we had one of the first crystal sets that came into Washington," says Calvin. "We'd take turns putting that thing up to our ears. That was really great."

Later the Griffiths would own one of the first television sets in the city. "There were only 370 in Washington at that time. I know that because the first TV contract we (Senators) had, we got $370. The next year there were 700, so we got $700.

Sharing the house with the Griffiths, Addie's sister Jean, and an elderly black couple who served as cook and gardener, the grateful Robertson children soon adapted to their new lives as Griffiths—though they would never be formally adopted. "We were what you would call damn perfect children," remembers Calvin with total sincerity. "We would cater to 'em. We never got into trouble. We never started asking for this or that."

It was an approach that perhaps sheds light on Calvin's later attitudes toward ballplayer demands. But the immediate results were a life of domestic bliss.

There were adjustments to be made, as Calvin found out when he first attended school in Washington. "I was backward," he admits. "I didn't have a good foundation so the Griffith family had me tutored so I learned my ABC's and things like that. It was quite a thing for me to go through."

But if the Griffiths expected their adopted children to study with a tutor or attend Sunday school before going out to play, Calvin didn't complain, at least openly. "I just

8

went along. Going to church was the only way I could go to theater on Sunday afternoon and get myself an ice cream soda or something like that . . . . They also had a basketball team at Calvary Methodist."

Calvin had quickly found another reason to be grateful for his new life in Washington. "I was just happy as hell where I could go out into the street and play baseball (stickball). Where we started living in Washington was down on Sixteenth Street and all we had to do was go across the streetcar tracks and play baseball on the fields over there."

It was also Calvin's first opportunity to take control of a sports situation. "I played all the time 'cause I was the one that got the baseballs," he remembers with a laugh. "If I don't play, you don't play with my balls, that's all there is to it."

Other sports opportunities included a local boys club where Calvin took up boxing for a time. "I'm glad I didn't go into that longer or I'd be more cauliflowered," he says straight-facedly. "But it did me a world of good at the time."

Even the previously unbearable had a silver lining in Washington. "School was close enough to walk to, not more than two or three blocks away and they had all kinds of sports," remembers Calvin, again revealing the priorities of his new life. "It was the greatest thing in the world we ever did for ourselves to go there (Washington)."

The Griffiths' generosity soon extended to the rest of the Robertson family. With James Robertson's death in 1923 at age 42, Clark Griffith bought Jane and the rest of the Robertson children a home in then suburban Washington, near Walter Reed Hospital, and but a ten minute drive from Calvin and Thelma. "The twins had ponies," recalls Calvin. "It was nothing but farm country back then."

Bruce Robertson would die in 1926 at age 11 of rheumatic fever complications, but the others would also know a life far better than they had experienced in Montreal. "They all had a living, had food on the table and clothes on their back, and went to school," concludes Calvin. "That was it."

Thelma recalls that the Griffiths always encouraged closeness among the brothers and sisters. "While we've been a family that was reared in two different households, we've stayed very, very close and that makes it nice. They treated us all alike and we all got together for the holidays and everything. We saw our brothers and sisters almost every day. We had a wonderful life."

Calvin doesn't recall such everyday contact, but agrees with Thelma's conclusions on family unity, at least during that time period. "We have always been a very close family even without associating day in and day out. We had a feeling towards each other, that's the biggest thing."

It was perhaps baseball that provided the permanent family link. "We was always together at the ballpark, year-round," recalls Jimmy Robertson. "I remember the first Christmas morning I was old enough to drive, Unc' say's let's go for a ride. So we go down Decatur to Illinois Avenue, Illinois Avenue to Georgia Avenue and he (Clark Griffith) says, 'Well let's stop in at the ballpark and see how things are going' Christmas morning. That's how we stayed together."

By a technicality of law, Calvin and Thelma would never be formally adopted by the Griffiths. "Unfortunately when the time came and we went down to court we found out I was 17 days too old," remembers Calvin. "Uncle wouldn't adopt her (Thelma) unless I was adopted, too."

But the teenagers did have their names legally changed. "We went down to the District Building and did it," recalls Calvin. "Of course my real name was Calvin Griffith Robertson, so we just reversed it to Calvin Robertson Griffith."

It was a symbol of their gratitude toward the Griffiths that would last a lifetime. "I've thought of this same thing so damn many times," said Calvin in 1983. "If Clark Griffith hadn't come along and taken me out of Montreal, what would Calvin Griffith . . . . What would Calvin Robertson be doing today? What in hell would have really happened to me? I talk to Uncle Clark and say, 'Thank you, I hope I've fulfilled all your wishes'."

Chapter 3

CLARK GRIFFITH

CALVIN'S HORATIO ALGER

"He was an individual that was impossible to copy.
He was a saint. Next to God, Clark Griffith was it.
Course I shouldn't say that with all the atheists around."

There is no mistaking who the central figure in the Griffith family has always been. In life and in death, Clark Griffith's presence has remained a dominating influence on his family. His photographs and memorabilia still dominated Twins offices until the 1984 sale of the team. Their removal hasn't eliminated his presence.

"As far as I'm concerned this is still Unc's team," Billy Robertson said to a reporter even in 1987, over thirty years after Clark Griffith's death.

A battle-toughened, even stern man on occasion, Griffith nevertheless had a heart of gold, say his family members, who haven't forgotten his lessons in generosity. "He tried to teach us all to be kind and considerate, caring for each other," remembers Billy Robertson, softly describing Griffith's frequent free rentals of Griffith Stadium to religious and civic groups. "I used to say, 'Unc', let's at least charge enough for the cost of cleanup.' But he wouldn't even let me do that."

Washington newspaper columnist Shirley Povich described how Griffith once was so moved by the photograph of a widow and her homeless family that he picked up a six-month tab for their housing and found the woman a job. "Then, remembering I was a newspaperman," wrote Povich, "He looked at me sternly and said, 'If a word of this shows up in the paper I'll take you out to the woodshed and give you what you deserve!'"

Calvin Griffith obviously experienced his foster father's unquestioned generosity. "He was just one of the greatest persons in the world—kindhearted. He never took credit for it. But he always taught us to share," says Calvin, with reverence almost dripping from each word.

Yet Calvin also found that Clark Griffith had a tougher side. "He was stern as hell. When he got mad at you, you knew he was mad because his eyebrows stood straight up and his eyes would pierce you. Thank God that Thelma or I never did anything to displease him."

11

Billy Robertson defends any sternness that Clark Griffith may have exhibited to family or employees as part of his paternal role. "When you're in that business you have to be stern. There wasn't ever anybody who played for him that didn't love him. When you're stern with people it's usually for their own good."

Clark Griffith liked to regularly quiz even the youngest members of the family on their baseball knowledge. "We used to sit around this big table with Cokes and he'd ask about this or that," remembers Jimmy Robertson with a smile. "You had to really know your baseball inside out."

Certainly the "Old Fox," as he already came to be known by the age of 25, had learned every aspect of the sport. As pitcher, player-manager, co-organizer of the American League, and finally an owner of a Major League franchise, the colorful Griffith would eventually work his way into baseball's Hall of Fame.

Griffith's father died in a hunting accident shortly after Clark's birth in 1869. As a mere youth, the son helped his mother work the family farm on the post-Civil War Missouri frontier at a time when outlaws such as Jesse James were regular acquaintances.

"I remember his telling how he watered Jesse James' horse. He met him," says Calvin Griffith. "Jesse James wasn't such a bad guy 'til the sheriff bombed the house and blew off the arm of his (James') mother," is how Calvin remembers being told the history of the Missouri outlaw.

Another favorite Clark Griffith story was of the hanging tree conveniently adjacent to the Vernon County ballfield. Primarily serving as the final stop for ex-Civil War marauders and guerrilla raiders, Calvin learned from his uncle of how one night in 1876 it served to teach of honesty in baseball and life.

"Clark Griffith used to tell of how all the people pitched in five or ten cents to get a new Spaulding ball instead of a homemade one," remembers Calvin. "They got up a dollar and a quarter or so. That was a lot of money back then. Finally one of the guys volunteered to go into town to get it. And he rode off and came back with a new ball.

"But on the first pitch," Clark Griffith said, "the batter hit a hard line drive and when they picked up the ball it was all flattened on one side—and that guy that bought it was nowhere to be found! He'd pocketed the money."

It was to be a costly heist however, as the baseball charlatan made the mistake of coming back to Vernon County several years later. After hearing dogs barking throughout the night, Clark Griffith went down to the ballfield in the morning and sure enough there was the thief hanging from the tree. "That's how he learned 'bout honesty," says Calvin of his adopted father.

Clark Griffith was learning other baseball lessons as well. After contracting malaria and moving to Illinois in 1883 for health reasons, he not only recovered but at age 17 discovered his future—earning $10 for pitching the local Hoopeston team to victory in a semi-pro game. By 1888 he would star for a Milwaukee team in the organized minor leagues, earning salaries in excess of $20 a game.

While physically slight and only 5′ 8′′ in height, Clark Griffith learned to use every possible pitching trick and strategy to get hitters out, even claiming to have discovered the screwball, despite similar claims by others. It was one of several altered pitches he would master, although ironically he would later become a strong advocate for abolition of the spitball in 1920.

By 1891 Clark Griffith had made his way to the major leagues, helping Boston win the pennant of the later defunct American Association. His 15-year career earned him 240 wins and a reputation as one of baseball's most feisty competitors.

But times were different then even for the most popular ballplayers, as Griffith found out the next year when a financially troubled Oakland franchise balked at paying his agreed-upon salary. Baseball of that era had only minimal organization and even less financial stability for its players, who were regarded as something akin to migrant workers.

"During the wintertime he had to work on the Barbary Coast (San Francisco)," recalls Calvin of his uncle's later tales. "He worked in a saloon playing a bass fiddle in the orchestra. He used to tell us how these god-danged guys would get drunk and get shang-haied out to sea. They'd take 'em to a backroom and put 'em down a slide. When they'd wake up, they'd be out on an ocean."

While Clark Griffith avoided that fate, he told his future heir of other hardships suffered by turn-of-the-century ballplayers. "They weren't welcomed into too many hotels because they all chewed tobacco," Calvin Griffith recounts his uncle's description. "They were considered thugs back in those days—people they didn't want around."

It was a lesson Clark Griffith would remember years later in his pioneering efforts to make baseball more socially respectable—including the gift of free season passes to Washington's clergy. As Calvin remembers it was a mutually beneficial arrangement. "We gave passes to the preachers for the simple reason that Sunday baseball was never legalized in Washington. Mr. Griffith had the foresight to do it and also to sit down with the different denominations and work out the hours so they wouldn't interfere with their services. Then we had a chance."

But first, Clark Griffith would continue making his mark as one of baseball's premier pitchers, helping Cap Anson's Chicago Nationals win a National League championship in 1895 and personally winning more than 20 games a year for six straight seasons.

Then in 1901, the man who would later teach his descendants to revile players' associations and free agentry was one of the first stars to jump to the recently formed American League. "The maximum salary in the National League in those days was $1600 a year," explains Calvin without any obvious embarrassment. "These new fellows were talking about paying a player $2400 a year, so my uncle was more than willing to listen to them."

In fact, as vice-president of the Ballplayers' Protective Association, a quasi-union organization, Clark Griffith helped lure other National League players to the new league. "He got 19 out of 20 he tried for," said Calvin Griffith. "The only one he didn't get was (Pittsburgh Pirate shortstop and Hall of Famer) Honus Wagner."

Made playing manager of the Chicago team by his old friend Charles Comiskey, Clark Griffith led the White Sox to an American League pennant in the league's first year. It was not to be his last pennant, though his playing days were limited.

In 1903 Griffith was selected to manage and operate the newly established New York franchise, the Highlanders (later to be known as the Yankees). New York was then the stronghold of the mighty New York Giants, managed by Griffith's old personal rival John

McGraw. Though facing a hostile press and a Tammany Hall-organized boycott in the beginning, Griffith almost brought a pennant to the Highlanders in their first season. He did firmly entrench the American League in New York before, ironically, jumping back to the National League as manager of the Cincinnati Reds in 1911.

But at the end of the 1911 season, Clark Griffith received the opportunity he had really been waiting for. A purchase of ten percent in the struggling Washington Senators, then called the Nationals, put him in the influential position of being the largest single stockholder. Later, with the help of a friend, Griffith would purchase greater control of the club.

"He sold the ranch in Montana and borrowed some money," recalls Calvin Griffith. "The funny thing about it is that I was told if Uncle wanted to borrow more he could have bought the whole ballclub for around maybe $50-70,000. Course in 1912, hell, that was a lot of money and Unc' never did like to borrow money."

Clark Griffith made the most of his limited investment however, making himself manager of the Senators and leading the team to second place in his first season. It was also in 1912 that he helped create the informal ceremony that annually certifies baseball's place as the national sport, by persuading President William Howard Taft to throw out the first ball at the opening game of Washington's season.

"In 1912 he knew Taft was at the Opening Day game in a box on the first base line," Calvin would later hear the story told. "Unc' strolled over to the President just before the game was to begin, shook his hand and pulled out a baseball. 'Why don't you throw this to Walter Johnson, Mr. President?' 'As long as he doesn't throw it back'," Taft reportedly quipped in reply.

A total of eight presidents would participate in the symbolic ball-tossing and would call themselves Clark Griffith's friend during his lifetime. Griffith used to joke that no man had ever been elected president who did not first have his picture taken at a ballgame with the Senators owner.

The "Old Fox's" combination of patriotism and pragmatism was further evidenced during World War I when he founded the Bat and Ball Fund, which supplied hundreds of thousands of dollars worth of baseball equipment to American soldiers despite the torpedoing of a ship carrying the first load to France. It was a popular move which helped keep baseball alive despite calls for postponement during the "Great War" and would serve as a model for baseball's political reaction to World War II.

By the end of World War I Clark Griffith had recognized the need for more stability in his own Washington organization. With the backing of Philadelphia grain trader William Richardson he was able to gain control of the majority of Senators' stock for less than $100,000. Griffith was made club president and given full authority over matters of club policy. "He (Richardson) never interfered with Clark Griffith running the ballclub," remembers Calvin with perhaps a bit of envy of the relationship that lasted nearly 30 years.

By 1924 Clark Griffith's shrewd trading assembled what some called the cheapest championship team in the history of the game. "He had to do it that way," describes

Calvin. "The only way he made it was through wrasslin' matches, fight (boxing) in the park, things like that. But when he wanted a key player, he'd go after them."

Of course Clark Griffith did have some advantages modern-day general managers don't enjoy, remembers Jimmy Robertson. "In the old days, Unc' would call up Connie Mack and say, 'I need a second baseman and you need a pitcher. Let's make a trade.' If it wasn't equal they'd make it up in the next one. It isn't like that now. Everybody always wants to screw the other guy."

With 28-year-old second baseman Bucky Harris appointed as field manager and with stars such as Goose Goslin, Joe Judge, Ossie Bluege, Sam Rice, and the incomparable pitching ace Walter Johnson, the Senators clinched their first American League pennant that year and went on to defeat John McGraw's Giants in a sensational seven-game World Series.

While the Senators lost a heartbreaking World Series the next year and their winning combination would soon break up, Clark Griffith had reached baseball's pinnacle. "How many people in this game of baseball can start out as a player and end up as an owner?" his heir, Calvin Griffith, would ask rhetorically years later.

Often referring to those who came about their team ownership by means of wealth accumulated outside of baseball as "bushwackers," the Senators owner also believed in working your way up from the bottom. His baseball success exemplified the American dream and the work ethic to his descendants.

On his desk Clark Griffith had a sign that Calvin remembers well. "Long life. Sleep plenty, eat moderately and keep your conscience clean." Every night he would keep his regular routine of lighting up a Robert Burns cigar, drinking an ounce of Old Grand Dad bourbon and taking a nap before returning to talk or study baseball.

Clark Griffith's influence on Calvin and the other young family members went further than his baseball success however. "He was quite a person. He was a self-made man," says Calvin. As an example he notes how, even during the off-season in Chicago, Clark worked to better himself by studying law at Northwestern University.

Apparently he also made some contacts on the other side of the law, including a friend named Al Capone who Calvin recalls Clark Griffith visiting at the Atlanta Penitentiary in 1933. "He just thought of him as a businessman," says Calvin.

But more a model of Clark Griffith's self-definition was the star of a radio show to which he used to listen daily. The Lone Ranger, whose photograph hung on the wall of the Senators owner's office for years, fit both his Western background and his values. "He has been my guiding star and the sort of man I wanted to be," said Clark Griffith in his later days.

There was never any question about who served as a role model to Calvin, both as a youth and throughout his life. "You had to give Clark Griffith a lot of credit, coming from a god damn prairie and ending up as he did. Next to the President of the United States he was the biggest man in Washington, that's all there was to it."

Povich agrees that Clark Griffith's lessons couldn't help but be remembered by his descendants. "Everybody looked up to him. He was a man to be admired in many ways," says Povich. "He taught Calvin well—among other things the work ethic. He expected

Calvin to work and Calvin did work. In the same manner he did so by his brothers. While they were privileged there was always the sense that there was work to do. Nobody had a free ride."

Physically small, Clark Griffith would forever ride tall in the saddle of his heir's mind even after his death in 1955 at the age of 85. "He was only 5′ 6′′ or 5′ 7′′, but he had the—what's the word?—statue of a giant," Calvin would later say. "He was an individual that was impossible to copy. He was a saint. Next to God, Clark Griffith was it.

"'Course I shouldn't say that with all the atheists around."

Chapter 4

LEARNING TO PLAY THE GAME

"Listening to smart people was a great advantage.
No matter how dumb you are
you're gonna learn something by listening to smart people."

Calvin Griffith's strongest memory of the 1924 World Series is one of youthful terror. Then 12 years old, one of Calvin's jobs as batboy-mascot was to retrieve all bats and balls at game's end.

But when Earl McNeely's famous bottom of the 12th inning grounder hit a pebble and bounded over the head of the Giants unlucky third baseman Fred Lindstrom to bring home Calvin's favorite player, Muddy Ruel, and give the Senators a seventh game victory and their only World Championship, pandemonium broke out. Frenzied, souvenir-seeking fans stormed the field.

"After it quieted down, I went out to get the balls," recalls Calvin, whose own boyish excitement must have been considerable. "They were all in a cage in the ground (behind home plate) then, and all the balls were gone. I thought, 'Oh, my God, am I gonna catch hell for this!'"

But needless to say, Calvin had little to seriously fear on this occasion. Indeed, the adopted son of Clark Griffith had also been adopted into an almost perfect boyhood world. "I never had to polish shoes or pick up jockstraps like they do here now," remembers Calvin, whose pictures of the era never fail to show a smiling face. "I was Clark Griffith's boy and I was the batboy."

Calvin's responsibilities began with the basics that first summer of 1922. "When the game started I used to pick up the bats and bring them outside," he says. "I'd have the bats ready for the first hitter each inning. Most of the time ballplayers had two bats they'd swing around and I'd get rid of the second when they went up to bat."

Later in his youth he graduated to taking fielding practice, shagging outfield fly balls and even throwing batting practice. "It was really a great thrill, especially when you travelled around with them to the other cities. I travelled with them in '24 and '25 all over."

17

Calvin fondly remembers the postgame entertainment as well. "We played all afternoon ballgames back then. So you had to think of something to do in the evening," he points out. "Most of the ballplayers were kids themselves, and we'd all go to amusement parks and play games, ride the roller coaster. We used to have it where this guy would sit on a plank and we'd throw balls and put him in the water all the time. Some of those carnivals, we'd go home with so many dolls and things they'd have to give away that we'd almost break them."

Tricks of survival on the road stuck with the young batboy. "Back in those days we didn't have any air-conditioning and I remember ballplayers used to, in St. Louis especially, have a big ice bucket full of cabbage leaves. And they used to put the cabbage leaves under their caps when they went out to play the inning and that would keep them cool. At night, they taught me to soak the sheets."

On the evening before the Senators clinched the 1924 pennant in Boston, young Calvin tried another unusual way of sleeping. "In the middle of the night, the trainer who was staying in the room with me couldn't find me anywhere," Calvin remembers, laughing. "The windows weren't open, the door was locked. Boy was he worried! Finally he found me under the bed. I told him I was too excited to sleep in that soft bed—I had to get on the floor."

His excitement must have been almost as great at all the post-World Series celebrations. Included was a ticker-tape parade and a trip to the White House for the first time to meet President Coolidge. But the youngster didn't share in the Senators' handsome victory shares of $300 per man.

Calvin's memories were not quite all positive, however. "It was wonderful training for a kid overall," he says, recalling the thrill of catching future Hall of Famer Walter Johnson during warmups. "But I remember one time in Cleveland during batting practice there was a fly ball and I looked up. It was a high sky and I missed that ball, so I covered my face and that damn ball hit me on the back of the head."

Nevertheless, the association with Senators stars such as Johnson, Harris, Goslin and indeed all the great ballplayers of the era was more than enough to make up for any such misfortunes. "Hell, they all knew who the hell I was. Lou Gehrig, Babe Ruth, Ty Cobb, Tris Speaker, Rogers Hornsby, George Sisler, Eddie Collins, Connie Mack way back in those days, Miller Huggins.

"Clark Griffith was thought of so highly, every manager who came to the ballpark would come up to see him," Calvin remembers with a smile. "I don't know how come I used to accidentally be in his office too when they showed up, but I used to listen to the conversations. Yeah, I met 'em all, I met 'em all."

Particular heroes would still bring emotion to his voice years later. "Ty Cobb was just outstanding," he says of the controversial Detroit Tiger star that even teammates described as ill-tempered and vicious. "He put on a show for the people. Off the field he was peaches and cream. Least that's the way I thought he was anyhow. I never had dinner with him. If somebody gave him a bad dinner or something I don't know what he'd say. But just being around him the little bit I was, was great."

Similarly, the Senators soft-spoken pitching ace Walter Johnson was a man who seemed larger than life to young Calvin. "He had that super-human body, you know. His arms went down below his knees. He'd be so goddamn great today it'd be unbelievable if he pitched under these lights. He pitched in daylight all the time. He could hit the ball in the upper deck here. That's how far he could hit the ball when he pinch-hit. He was a hitter."

The young Senators batboy would also directly experience the thrill of victory, such as the Senators dramatic 1924 championship, and the agony of defeat, as in their 1925 loss to the Pittsburgh Pirates after leading three games to one. "They shoulda called that game," says Calvin of the rainy, decisive seventh game. "Then Walter Johnson had Kiki Cuyler struck out in the ninth and everybody knew it but the ump. He (Cuyler) hits one foul down the line and the ump calls it fair—an American League ump, too! But that's sports. Sometimes you win, sometimes you lose."

Just as important to Calvin Griffith, the future baseball team owner, were the lessons he learned those first years watching Clark Griffith construct an American League power-house. "In the winter months he'd sit down in his chair with this great big legal pad and he would make out lineups. He'd get two or three out of Boston's ballclub and mix 'em with what we had, or whatever. We used to talk baseball. All we did was talk, talk, talk."

"On-the-field strategy was also an important topic," recalls Calvin. "When you start talking you talk about everything. When to hit and run. Certain players should never do it. When you're a catcher you have to watch what the batter and runner are doing. We'd talk strategy more than anything else. What to do at the right time, how to stop making a lot of headaches for yourself.

"It was just conversation. He'd talk about what managers should or shouldn't do. The biggest problem with managers he said was that they didn't know how to run a pitching staff. They would have pitchers warm up down there two or three times a ballgame. He'd say when you warm a guy up the third time either put him in the ball game or tell him to take his uniform off. Clark Griffith was one of the first to have specialty relief pitchers," Calvin remembers, referring to the key contributions of Fred Marberry in 1924.

During off-days, most of the family could be found on the golf course talking baseball while learning yet another sport from Clark Griffith. "He was a great golfer all the way to his final years," says Calvin, noting that Clark Griffith did not take up the game until in his fifties. "He used to be able to shoot lower than his age."

Everyone in the Griffith-Robertson families was expected to have summertime duties at the ballpark. Jimmy and Billy Robertson worked first as program vendors then as hot dog concessionaires. Sherrod and Mildred, and later Thelma, were found office roles in the Senator organization.

All of them found social roles too, as Thelma remembers with obvious fondness. "When I was young, the ballplayers didn't have enough money to get married early, so we always had a lot of young players in spring training camp. We did things as a group and I was probably the only girl with maybe eight or nine or ten of 'em some nights that we'd go to Harpers and drink Coke and dance to the jukebox."

Calvin primarily worked as batboy, but his responsibilities increased as his own athletic abilities grew. "I caught batting practice. I pitched batting practice for the Washington ballclub. I did whatever was needed," he remembers.

As Clark Griffith reassembled another pennant-winner in 1933 around 26-year-old shortstop/manager Joe Cronin, Calvin played his own minor role in the Senators rise and fall. "I pitched batting practice the whole summer," he recalls. "Then when the World Series came around they gave me the gate and signed up a fellow named Garland Braxton. He was a lefthanded screwball pitcher. They was worried about Carl Hubbell. What they should have done was forget about Carl Hubbell and thought about the righthanded pitchers. Cause, goddammit, Hubbell just shut 'em out two games and the righthanders beat 'em also. We only won one game of that series in '33. Four and one."

Although Calvin could not know it, 1933 was to be the Senators final pennant-winning year. Clark Griffith's organization was already struggling to compete with other, more cash-wealthy organizations. Yet the "Old Fox's" ability to find ways to field generally competitive teams would continue to impress his young heir.

Calvin remembers his uncle's unsuccessful involvement in an attempt to form a giant baseball corporation with each team as a member franchise. Essentially the proposal, only possible under baseball's antitrust exemption, would have created an equal sharing of revenues from radio, television, and stadium operations. It is a concept that has since been at least partially adopted by other major sports operations.

Hardly a socialist, Clark Griffith was already looking ahead toward his survival. "He was one of the only independent owners," says Calvin. "You had Rupert with his beer. You had Budweiser and Wrigley chewing gum, Tom Yawkey and his enterprises, his gold mines and timber. All he had was a baseball team."

While that grand scheme would fail, like all later proposals of shared revenues against the opposition of the larger ballclubs, Clark Griffith would still find other, more wily ways to survive. A living example was a talented, but journeyman pitcher named Bobo Newsom, who was part of the Senators organization five times in his career between 1929 and 1954.

"'Unc' used to say that Bobo kept him in business," Jimmy Robertson would tell a reporter of Clark Griffith's ability to sell the player to contending teams in late season. "Unc' would say, 'I used to get Bobo cheap and then sell him like he was caviar.'"

Calvin would especially remember hearing of Newsome's memorable Opening Day win in 1936 when he defeated the Yankees 1-0 after being hit directly in the head by a teammate's throw in the first inning. "He went out there and kept pitching. And after the game I think he passed out."

Watching and listening, Calvin was learning about ballplayers and the game. "Listening to smart people was a great advantage," says Calvin modestly. "No matter how dumb you are you're gonna learn something by listening to smart people. You learned that by observing and by talking to Clark Griffith. If there was something you didn't understand you went up to him and asked.

"I also had the opportunity to stay in the office when Joe McCarthy came in, Connie Mack came in," Calvin continues. "They'd come in and talk about baseball going back into the 1890s. You'd get the history. That's how I learned my business."

It was the beginning of a lifetime of learning baseball's history and its business. Like many an American youth, Calvin soaked up anything he could about the game and its players. But unlike most youth, his role as batboy represented more than a temporary infatuation. The lessons Calvin learned at his uncle's knee were the beginning of a training that could only take him upon one course for a lifetime.

Calvin Griffith's apprenticeship under Clark Griffith would continue over 30 years. Yet Calvin would vehemently insist years later that he was never guaranteed a future as a major league owner. "There wasn't no assurity he was gonna leave the club to Thelma or I," he said, noting competition from two other nephews, Earl and Shirley. "They were always in my mind. If I didn't show enough, Unc' could turn the ballclub over to them."

Thelma Haynes recalls an earlier cousin, also named Clark Griffith, as the initial front-runner for heirship to the ballclub. "Had he lived I think he might have been the one that came into it since they (Griffiths) weren't able to have kids. They were crazy about this nephew but he went in for a simple tonsillectomy and they gave him an overdose of anesthesia and he died. He was 21, I think. We never knew him, never met him."

Calvin remembers with some obvious glee getting the better of Earl's team in an amateur game while he played for a highly successful team called the Corinthians. "Clark Griffith came out and I just happened to have a really good game. I got three hits and I played shortstop and made some really good plays. It was just one of those days when everything in the world went right for you."

But Calvin proudly maintains he was unaffected by the prospect of family competition. "No, I just went along with it as best I could. I wasn't worried about it," says Calvin. "If you start worrying about things like that you're gonna do things you didn't wanna do, you know. You're gonna, what the hell's the word for it? You're gonna cater to him to a degree where it may be, uh, hostile to him. He'll know you're trying to put on a show for him. I was just as natural as could be. I just didn't put on the air or anything like that."

Calvin's main worries in life were generally more superficial. "Thank the Lord I didn't have to mow the lawn or anything like that," he said later. "'Cause I know damn well I could never handle a lawnmower on that house's hill. So they always had some person coming over cutting the hill for 'em. I was not too appreciative of flowers either, so she (Addie Griffith's sister, Jeanne Robertson) took care of them and that relieved me of any duties."

Off-season duties were certainly introduced to Calvin's life by the time he entered Staunton Military Academy in 1928 at age 17, however. "That was quite a different life," he understatedly describes his five years there. "The only time you came back was at Christmas and summertime. I was pretty nervous at first."

One of his first cadet experiences must have increased his anxiety even as it also increased his understanding of political connections. "I despised guard duty, and the first night on duty I'm walking the post over in the south barracks and who the hell was the officer of the day but Barry Goldwater. Boy, was he a military man! It was a good thing I knew all the right answers!"

Giving wrong answers at Staunton could be costly to a cadet's social life, as Calvin found out. "You used to get demerits and you couldn't go downtown to the theater on Friday nights. It was the only thing you could do unless you had dates. I never had any dates then anyway."

Even worse was the often degrading and brutal treatment that a beginning cadet could face at the hands of older cadets. "I was a 'rat'," remembers Calvin. "I had to clean my superior's gun and make sure there were no specks on it for Saturday morning inspection. 'Cause if he got penalized he'd get me in a room and paddle me. Sometimes they'd even hit you with a damn sword. I didn't like that. It'd hurt you for two or three days."

Yet amazingly, Calvin looks back at Staunton with great fondness. "I really enjoyed it. The professors were great. The food was good. And I always got the upper bunk. I figured it was safer."

Interestingly, Calvin was reunited with his sister after a few months when Thelma entered a girls' school, Stewart Hall, in Staunton. "After that I think we very rarely went out on a date that we didn't do together," says Thelma with a laugh. "We had a very close relationship."

Once again sports played a key role in Calvin's adjustment to a new situation. "That really helped open me up to things there," he remembers. Having Hall of Fame catcher Mickey Cochrane's brother as a roommate was certainly a big assist, as well as providing Calvin with a ready supply of catcher's mitts.

Highlights of Calvin Griffith's own athletic career at Staunton included two years as captain of both the Virginia state champion basketball and baseball teams. At his uncle's instruction, he stayed away from football. Photos show a relatively tall (about six foot) and surprisingly slender Calvin in both his basketball and "honors" squad roles.

A fellow Staunton cadet described to a local reporter how the young Griffith made his own athletic mark even before his family connections were known. "Calvin was spotted as a basketball prospect when first enrolled at Staunton. Being a quiet sort of a boy, he just went after a job and landed it. The same held good for baseball. Having not the slightest inkling who he was or what his connections were, several more experienced boys put up a whale of a scrap for his job, but Griff beat 'em all out."

Primarily a catcher and sometimes a pitcher, Calvin most proudly remembers his hitting success. "I was a free swinger. I used to strike out. But in my almanac, er, yearbook I had the distinction of reading where I hit the longest home run ever hit at VMI (Virginia Military Academy). I remember hitting one over this great big, high wall. Well, it wasn't a wall. It was just like a circle cut into the ground to make a ballpark. But when I hit it, it was just like a firecracker going off. I could hit the ball real hard."

Playing before his family in Griffith Stadium against the Washington city champs, he remembers the fear of wondering if the big hit would ever come. "My first three times up I struck out. And I made an error and I was really sick. But we came up into extra innings and I hit one off the left field wall for a three-base hit to win the game. In the clutch, I got the key hit and I was smiles from ear to ear."

Calvin admits his adjustment to military regimen also reflected at least some aware-ness of his family role. "I wasn't gonna do anything to get in trouble. I was always very,

very cautious about it because I didn't want to hurt the Clark Griffith name. I kept my name out of the paper as much as I possibly could not to belittle him."

But life in a uniform and military discipline didn't make a scholar of Calvin Griffith. "I flunked chemistry and I had to go back and take chemistry over so I could get my degree," he openly admits. "I started taking Cicero and I started taking calculus (sic) and I said to myself, 'Man, what am I doing taking Cicero and calculus (sic) and all that stuff. I'm not gonna need all that, I'm going into baseball. I gotta start figuring how to get the ballplayers out, you know. If I was gonna be a doctor or something like that it'd be a different story. I'd already decided I was gonna try to be a ballplayer."

By his senior year Calvin was already announcing his career goals to reporters. "I want to be a ballplayer and if I can make good at it that'll be my profession. I've been following the sport a long time and naturally like it better than anything else. If I can't be a big leaguer though, I guess I'll give it up. It's the top or nothing for me—otherwise I'll change my plans."

Calvin may have felt he was ready to tackle his dream of a professional playing and coaching career by the time he had graduated from Staunton in 1933, but Clark Griffith apparently had other ideas for his foster son, though he was diplomatic in expressing them to reporters. "I've always hoped that Calvin may some day take over the job I'm holding now. He's a bright boy and already is a thorough student of the game. Nothing would please me more than to have him take my place when I'm through. Whether he does or not though is entirely up to the boy himself."

With that message in mind, Calvin's choice was to continue on to George Washington University in Washington, D.C., where he could both continue playing baseball and study economics as a backup while living at home. "In college I never did flunk a course," Calvin says proudly. "But I dropped this public speaking class. I made a mistake. After getting into public life like I did, I know it would have been better to have a lot of expertise about what I was saying," he concludes.

"But that professor told me to make a speech on how the bees make honey," explains Calvin with a scowl. "I didn't even know they had to get pollen from trees back in those days. And I didn't know nothing about love."

But Calvin was learning some social skills in his days at George Washington. "It was an outstanding school," he says sincerely. "They had something going on all the time. I went to a dance on Friday night, a dance on Saturday night. I joined a fraternity. I've still got a picture of my prom date here. She was the granddaughter of Alexander Graham Bell."

But Calvin never forgot his self-discipline in approaching the number one priority of his life. Included among his mementos of that period are a handwritten list of personal rules for the start of spring training. In order, the list called for: "1. No more than two dates a week. 2. One movie a week. 3. Only one night a week out after midnight. 4. On nights before games he would be in bed by 10 p.m. 5. Get plenty of rest."

Whether it was training or family background, Calvin's baseball success certainly continued at George Washington. Again both catching and pitching, he won six straight games in his first two years of college, leading the Colonials to their most successful season ever in 1934. Pitching back-to-back wins in Griffith Stadium with two days rest earned Calvin the nickname of "Iron Man."

Calvin also earned a contract offer from an interested Cubs scout, which he wisely declined. "If I'd have taken that contract I coulda walked right out of the house forever," he says with a shake of his head, thinking of what Clark Griffith's reaction would have been.

After spending the summer as an assistant in the Senators front office and in Chattanooga, Tennessee, he was named captain of the team before his junior year in 1935. Yet Calvin had reached his limit with formal schooling and its delay of his chosen profession. Writing to Clark Griffith at spring training in Orlando, Florida, Calvin asked to join the Senators' organization fulltime.

"I said I could learn more of baseball by being in baseball," he describes his letter and outlook on life. "They teach you enough to broaden your mind in school and get you to do some thinking. But they don't teach baseball."

When Clark Griffith came back to Washington he had a mixed response for his foster son. "He came back from spring training and said, 'How'd you like to go to Chattanooga?'" recalls Calvin. "I said, 'I'm ready to go tomorrow.' And I went out and got my first car, a rumble-seat Ford for $468."

But while Clark Griffith was undoubtedly pleased at Calvin's enthusiasm for making baseball his life, he made clear that he foresaw a particular role for his foster son and heir as he gave him his first assignment. Rather than as a player, Calvin found himself joining the Chattanooga Lookouts, the Senators Southern Association farm team, as secretary-treasurer in 1935. Calvin's regular playing days were ended.

It was a fate that Calvin quickly accepted. "My uncle told me there was more security in the front office than on the bench or as a manager. And managers were made to be fired." Calvin remembers Clark Griffith's words. "He said, 'I'm not gonna fire you from the front office unless you get too stupid.' He kept me in the front office and I was in the front office from 1935 until '84."

That Clark had faith in the front-office potential of his adopted son was becoming apparent. Just as clear was the unabashed desire of Calvin to live up to his uncle's standards, as he told a reporter at the time. "Gee! You don't know how happy I'll be if I can make good down in Chattanooga. I've got to, that's all, else Uncle Clark will sure be disappointed and I hate to even think of that."

Chapter 5

CHATTANOOGA TO CHARLOTTE

A REAL LIFE BULL DURHAM

*"I think I may be the only man to have the distinction
of fining both his brother and his (future) brother-in-law.
Sherrod (Robertson) didn't slide on a close play and cost us the game.
And Joe Haynes broke curfew.
The funny thing is that he was running around with my sister at the time.
She's still trying to get the $25 back."*

In 1935, at the age of 23, Calvin Griffith again went south to enter a far different world. Seedy hotels, long bus trips, and characters who were throwbacks to more rough-and-tumble days of baseball, were normal parts of life in minor leagues of the era. Making $250 a month to cover all expenses including food, clothing, and travel, Calvin was there to learn the ropes.

His tutor in Chattanooga was a colorful baseball promoter named Joe Engle, who had bounced around the Senators organization as a scout until becoming president of the Chattanooga Lookouts in 1932. Before that, Calvin remembers Engel as a family friend around the Griffith household, charming Addie Griffith with his wit and practical jokes.

It was Engel who, at Chattanooga, would give Calvin his first, if not always favorable, experiences with marketing strategies. "He was the Barnum and Bailey of baseball. Bill Veeck got most of his ideas off Joe Engel," says Calvin, shaking his head. "Nobody was his equal in coming up with gimmicks."

Outside of the Negro Leagues, Clark Griffith was, ironically, one of the first to provide entertainment at baseball games. "He had two of the greatest performers in Al Schacht and Nick Altreck," remembers Calvin. "They would really put a show on. But our acts were before the game or after it, but not during. When that first pitch went out he (Clark Griffith) didn't want anything to disturb the game."

In contrast, Engel rarely ceased promoting. Arriving just in time for the season's first game and to oversee ticket sellers, Calvin quickly found that entertainment was the main event at Chattanooga. "He'd (Engel) have circuses and elephant hunts and tiger hunts, jackrabbits and every other damn thing on the field. It was really something to watch."

Engel also had his tasteless moments, including one Fourth of July festivity in which a greased pig was loosed in the infield to be captured by the all-black grounds crew while a largely white crowd howled in patriotic delight at their futility.

Calvin's major concern as treasurer however was trying to make sense of how the Lookouts could continue packing in fans to beautiful "Engel Field" while showing almost no profit. "He'd (Engel) give away a completely furnished home with a Lincoln car in the garage. He'd have money scattered around the infield and get somebody out of the stands and give them two minutes to get as much as they could. But how in the hell can you spend $2.01 and bring in $2.00?" Calvin asks rhetorically, with a look of disgust.

Calvin's suspicion of marketing operations was further fueled by incidents such as Engel's ill-fated attempt to advertise via loudspeaker truck. "We're out on the golf course one day and I just keep hearing it and I think, 'Boy that's loud.' And we keep going on the course and it just gets louder and louder. Then we finally get to the last hole and we see the truck sitting there with the guy asleep."

Apart from the financial concerns however, Calvin had few complaints about his Chattanooga assignment. "That was really life down there. You could really say you were a free man. I got a big old house up atop of Lookout Mountain. That house overlooked Georgia. That was something," he says, recalling the signal lights of moonshiners that were visible throughout the surrounding hills.

"Every Friday or Saturday we used to go to the square dance," continues Calvin, whose photographs from the period show a slender, handsome, young man. "I used to love to watch those mountain people dance. They'd park their squirrel guns by the door and really go. Those people only lived one way. They loved life."

Calvin's lessons in psychology as he assumed more roles with the Lookouts included contacts with some rather bizarre figures in baseball, including one down-on-his-luck ex-Senator that Clark Griffith had brought in to manage the Lookouts in 1935. "His name was Mule Shirley," remembers Calvin. "He got loaded one night and he wore a topper (hat), bow tie, shoes, cane, and nothing else. And he started walking downtown. The players had to go get him before the cops did. Talk about a character."

Calvin took over complete operation of the struggling Chattanooga franchise at the beginning of 1936, inheriting another colorful manager named "Rawmeat" Bill Rodgers. "He's the one that got me to stop eating red meat," explains Calvin of his nickname. "Goddamn, we went into a fancy restaurant in Birmingham, Alabama, and he ordered a damn steak and told the waitress just to put it on the griddle a couple of seconds on each side, just enough to get the frost out, and bring it on in to him. I had to get up from the table and leave. I couldn't take it."

By the end of July, with the team near last place, Clark Griffith had seen enough of Rawmeat Bill Rodgers also. At age 25, Calvin was made manager of the Lookouts.

He immediately ordered extra workouts emphasizing fundamentals for a team noticeably short on discipline. "You had to be firm," he remembers. "We practiced day in and day out on certain things. You couldn't kid around with them. You're the boss and you had to lay the law down. They were a wild bunch. Some days I used to go into my office in the morning and wives would be there waiting, 'Where's my husband?' they'd say."

Temptations of the road were understandable to Calvin though, especially when his teams visited New Orleans, then known as the South's answer to Sodom and Gomorrah. "I only used to just say (to the Chattanooga players) if you couldn't get it before midnight forget it."

Calvin had his own unforgettable experience in New Orleans on August 16, 1936 at the hands of what he remembers as a foul-mouthed, abusive umpire. Less than objective local newspaper accounts describe Polly Mclary as the victim of verbal assault by the Chattanooga manager.

Regardless, Calvin would definitely be the final assault victim. "I went in the clubhouse and told him to stop cussing the hell out of my ballplayers," he recalls. "He (the umpire) stood up and he was about 6' 3'', 220 pounds. I ran about 160 then. Without saying a word, he knocked me right out the door, loosened a couple of teeth. That's how dignified some of those minor league umps were."

The team's renewed discipline and morale paid off though, says Calvin. "The first day I managed we lost a doubleheader in Nashville. But we started turning around then and we won 12 out of 15 when we got back home and nearly made the play-offs."

Clark Griffith must have been impressed, promoting Calvin in 1938 to president, treasurer, and manager of the Charlotte Hornets in the Class B Piedmont League. It was an obvious career advancement. Yet the future major league team owner would find that his first chance at complete control of a team did not guarantee a glamorous lifestyle.

"Back in the minor leagues we used to play all night baseball," Calvin would recall. "We'd leave Charlotte, North Carolina after a ballgame and drive all the way to Richmond, Virginia, Portsmouth, Virginia, Norfolk, Virginia, places like that. That's a long ride. We used to get in about eight o'clock, ten o'clock the next morning, sleep all afternoon, and try to get up and play ball."

Even so, Calvin loved his new assignment, which included making daily written reports on ballplayers to Clark Griffith. "(But) the best part of baseball to me was managing," remembers Calvin. "You were close to players and yet you had to make quick decisions and you've got to have enough courage to face the second guess from yourself, the fans, and the experts. I thought I was a very good manager. What I really wanted to do was manage a major league team."

Calvin's Charlotte team nearly won the league championship in his first year, losing on the final day to the Yankees' talent-laden farmclub at Norfolk. "I had an exciting ballclub," he says, recalling that eleven team members, including future Hall-of-Famer Early Wynn, went on to spend considerable time in the majors.

"Minor league baseball in those days was so superior to anything today," judges Calvin. "'Cause they'd keep ballplayers down there longer and they had more experience. Today if you show anything they put you on the major league roster, which is a good thing for the ballplayers but a bad thing for a ballclub."

Nevertheless, Calvin's success required overcoming a number of unusual obstacles, including communication problems with the large number of non-English-speaking Cuban players on the team. As third-base coach on the team, he resorted to blowing a whistle to halt baserunners. "That didn't do much good," he recalls. "So I got me a red flag till the umpires took it away."

It is perhaps little wonder that the previously teetotalling Calvin took up a little drinking during this period. "I never smoked or drank 'til I started managing," he claims. "I never even had a bottle of beer. Then when I started managing your nerves get the best of you and you did this to relax. And it helped, no doubt about it. But I didn't go overboard."

Calvin once literally went overboard on a fishing outing, with nearly disastrous consequences. "Calvin jumped out and was swimming around till he decided to go down and touch bottom and there wasn't any," recalls his younger brother Billy Robertson, who with Jimmy Robertson was visiting at the time. "It scared the hell out of him. It was a good thing Phil (Howser, a college friend of Calvin) was there. He did a lot to keep Calvin afloat and get him back in the boat. But I never saw Calvin in the water again."

Equally important to the financially-strapped Senators organization as their on-the-field success was how well the Charlotte franchise performed at the gates. "We drew over 110,000 to Warner Field," remembers Calvin. "That was the first time in the history of our farm system that anybody made money--$11,000. That was a lot of money back then."

One key to Calvin's financial success may well have been his liberal fining policy. "Of 18 ballplayers on my team I think I fined 15 during the season," he recalls, admitting that the $25 fine came from salaries averaging barely $150 a month. "I used to always fine on free gas promotion night," Calvin laughs. "That way I always got paid in free gas all summer."

In a later season, Calvin would claim another unusual managerial prize. "I think I may be the only man to have the distinction of fining both his brother and his (future) brother-in-law," he says with a laugh. "Sherrod (Robertson) didn't slide on a close play and cost us the game. And Joe Haynes broke curfew. The funny thing is that he was running around with my sister at the time. She's still trying to get the $25 back."

But it was hardly a bed of roses for Calvin either, who operated for most of four years at Charlotte as a combination front office executive, manager, coach, batting practice pitcher, and in other assorted roles. Included was his return to active play as catcher for a hard-throwing Cuban pitcher named Roberto Ortiz.

"We had two catchers, both of them got their hands broken up," remembers Calvin of the unusual circumstances. "I went to General Crowder, manager of the Winston-Salem club and I said, 'How 'bout me catchin' it, or we're gonna have to forfeit and you're gonna have to give the money back to the fans.'"

With Crowder's agreement, Griffith took his place at catcher for the fastballing Cuban. "I went out there and I said 'Give me a chance to see the damn ball. We're gonna start with some curves or something so I can see the spin on the ball."

"First goddamn pitch is a fastball over my head," recalls Calvin. "It went over my head and hit the screen. I said, 'Uh, ain't this gonna be good.' It was a goddamn double-header. The next day I was so stiff all I could do was lay in epsom salts for a couple of hours. God, I'll never forget that one."

Even pitching batting practice could be dangerous to your health in those pre-protective-screen days, as Calvin found out when struck by a line drive one day in 1938. "That ended that," he remembers.

Calvin's competitive fires weren't entirely quenched however, as evidenced by his arrest during a baseball brawl at Durham, N.C. The future major league owner was carried bodily from the field by police after a near-riot broke out in which Calvin claims he was merely protecting his players from a violent crowd.

"There were fans all over the field and I saw somebody grab my catcher around the throat," he says. "It wasn't 'til after I hit him that I found out it was the Durham safety director. I was charged with assault. But fortunately the charges weren't pressed because I bought the man a new $35 pair of shoes to replace his spiked ones."

Calvin also learned several lessons in dealing with the media during his minor league days. At Chattanooga he was caught red-handed trying to conceal his fraternal relationship to the team's struggling shortstop, Sherrod Robertson. "I learned not to try to deceive newspapermen," says Calvin, pointing out that Sherrod's hitting slump soon turned around and he became a local favorite.

In Charlotte, Calvin learned another lesson after he cancelled the pressbox credentials of a critical columnist. "His name was E.T. Bales and he started a column from the bleachers after that. Boy, he took us over and never let up. Never again. I figured it's better to have them in the pressbox."

Perhaps Calvin was ready for more stability by the 1939 season when he finally met an attractive local girl who, with her successful dairy-farming father, used to watch nearly every Charlotte game from a box seat above the home dugout. "Some of the ballplayers finally took me out to her house to meet her," Calvin remembers of his first meeting with Natalie Norris. "We talked about baseball. But I don't remember hitting it off too well. She was a college girl."

Nevertheless, the courtship continued over a year, including highlights such as visits to the hayloft of a nearby farmer named Billy Graham. "I still have a gold Bible I got from him in exchange for a baseball," Calvin would recall years later.

Graham did not preside over the couple's Methodist wedding in February, 1940. But Clark and Addie Griffith, along with several hundred guests, came to the gala affair, featured in a front-page photo by the Charlotte newspaper.

"I said I wasn't gonna get married 'til I was 30," remembers Calvin. "But I just got tired of running around with every Tom, Dick, and Harry. I didn't get too many quiet evenings. I was ready to settle down."

By the end of Charlotte's 1941 season, Calvin had apparently learned the minor league ropes to the satisfaction of Clark Griffith. A death in the Senators organization opened a position as head of concessions. The impending birth of Calvin and Natalie's first child, Clark Griffith II, may have been another factor in convincing the "Old Fox" that his adopted son's odyssey should end.

Thelma claims to have also helped prepare the way at both ends. "I think Calvin was happy at coming back, though his wife didn't think much of it," she recalls. "But I said to him you better come back because the only time we have an opening around here is when somebody dies and you don't know when that's gonna happen again."

Despite Natalie's reluctance to leave Charlotte, Calvin doesn't recall any hesitation when the chance to return to Washington for the 1942 season arose. "When he asked me to come work in the Senators' office, I said, 'Yes, sir,' no questions asked," remembers Calvin. "I was always wanting to get back in town."

Having left as an inexperienced young man eager to learn the ways of the (baseball) world, Calvin Griffith was now returning as an executive, albeit a minor one, ready to assume more power in the organization he was clearly being groomed to run.

Chapter 6

CALVIN JOINS THE SENATORS

"I was always wanting to get back in town, but not to run concessions.
During the war you had rationing points on practically everything . . . .
I was over talking to the people at the OPA (Office of Price Administration)
more than I was talking to myself."

It was a different Washington D.C. and Senators ballclub than the one he had left in 1935.

The Depression was drawing to a close, although war preparations abounded in the nation's capital in 1941 even before the Japanese attack on Pearl Harbor. A military draft had already begun, and there was even talk of suspending baseball in time of war.

Calvin quickly found that his new Senators job was not the cushy position he had expected. After U.S. entry into World War II, being a concessionaire meant dealing with a nightmare of bureaucracy and material restrictions. Calvin had to make weekly pickups and deliveries of sugar to the local Coca-Cola plant so that they might prepare Griffith Stadium's allotted amount of the soft drink.

"I was always wanting to get back in town, but not to run concessions," admits Calvin. "During the war you had rationing points on practically everything. You had to get points for your hot dogs, your Coca-Colas, and every other damn thing. I was over talking to the people at the OPA (Office of Price Administration) more than I was talking to myself."

Night baseball had also been introduced to the Major Leagues in 1938, a practice which increased dramatically during the war years. One of its strongest backers was Clark Griffith, who ironically had been an outspoken critic of the "unnatural" lighting for years.

But by 1941 he had begun to recognize that the Senators shrinking economic fortunes left few options to the popular practice. "He had to, or get out of the game," says Calvin in defense of Clark Griffith's installation of $230,000 worth of lighting at Griffith Stadium. Survival would always come ahead of purity to the Griffiths.

Another explanation for the installation of lights came in the form of a $125,000 interest-free loan from the American League. "If they wanted him to play baseball they had to," Calvin explains of his adopted father's influence. "Clark Griffith was so liked by all the other clubs that they wouldn't turn him down on anything big. He and Connie Mack could do no wrong."

Night games were bad news for a still young man's social life however. "I went up there hoping to get nights off. Then I get up there and the American League had lights," remembers Calvin, while nevertheless again defending his foster father's flip-flop. "But it was a government city and you wanted your games when the workers got off. That's why Unc' had to go for it."

There had been changes in the Griffith organization also. Joe Cronin, manager and star shortstop of Senators teams in the mid-30s, as well as future Hall of Famer and American League president, had been sold to Boston for $350,000 in 1935 despite, or because of, his recent marriage to Calvin's older sister Mildred.

It was one of the oddities of the family-oriented Griffith organization that Clark Griffith felt having ballplayers as in-laws subjected all parties to excessive public and media criticism. "My father always said if you married a ballplayer he had to leave," remembers Thelma Haynes. "My sister married Joe Cronin, I always say she married the rich ballplayer. So he went to Boston for, at that time, a lot of money."

Thelma then stepped into Mildred's job as Clark Griffith's personal secretary. It was a role she clearly enjoyed, not realizing how soon history would repeat itself. "In the summertime, when the ballclub was on the road, Mr. Griffith and I would go down to Virginia Beach and we would scout the Portsmouth club and the Charlotte club. I knew boys on all the clubs," remembers Thelma, whose photographs of the period show an attractive, young blonde. "So when they came up to the big leagues we've always had a very close relationship with them."

That relationship became particularly close with a handsome young pitcher named Joe Haynes, who played under Calvin at Charlotte. "He came into the office and I wrote on the little index card, 'Very good looking prospect,' and underlined it in red ink, never thinking that I'd end up marrying him," remembers Thelma.

"Then Joe and I were gonna get married and he (Clark Griffith) said wait one year and let him get started (with the Senators)," she recalls, knowing the eventual outcome. "He traded him to the Chicago White Sox (in 1941), where Muddy Ruel was pitching coach, so I knew him and felt good about that. We went there and I came back and forth to see my family."

The family shakeups further cleared the way for Calvin's rise in the Senators administration. In 1942, he was officially made a vice-president and entitled to go to American League meetings.

"It was something," recalls Calvin of his first opportunity to regularly rub shoulders with major league management, though not yet as a fully equal participant. "Back in those days it seemed like the only people who said anything were the eight club presidents. They were a closed club, that's all there was to it. They had their differences but they knew the facts and stayed that way."

Whether because of awe, or later perhaps contempt, Calvin concedes that he was never one of the most vocal participants in baseball meetings. "I didn't talk too much unless there was something really very important. I gave the lawyers hell more than anything," he says. "When I thought I had to say something, I stood up. But I don't know why in the hell we had to have repetition. I'd been through everything year-in and year-out and all these new owners had to get their names in the record books when the minutes came out. I used to laugh about it."

Owners used to be more directly involved in the game, Calvin recalls. "People back in the olden days really enjoyed baseball," he says. "They really loved it. It wasn't a toy. Now for some of them, meetings are just to talk about TV revenues and such, if they come at all."

Active on a committee level throughout his ownership, Calvin learned baseball's ropes alongside power brokers such as Del Webb, Gussie Busch, and Tom Yawkey. But his strongest memory is of Walter O'Malley, the Dodgers owner and one of the few lawyers whose logic he could stomach. "O'Malley was a master. He had a lot of finesse with him," recalls Calvin. "He'd give you a little tomb with a lot of big words that were sinking into your head. He'd get up on the floor and what he wanted, he would get, no question about it. Things that he wanted done, he got eighty or ninety percent of the time."

Calvin also has strong memories of legendary Commissioner Kenesaw (Mountain) Landis' iron hand going awry in one dealing with Clark Griffith. "My uncle didn't feel well and didn't want to go to Chicago," remembers Calvin. "But Landis demanded he come, and Clark Griffith went to Chicago and had his appendix burst on him. He was in the hospital over two weeks and you talk about a man apologizing. Landis was all over himself apologizing."

There was no lasting ill-will towards Landis, however. "He was great," praises Calvin. "He was for the game of baseball and the American public. He came in after the Black Sox scandal (1919) and saved baseball. He was the dictator. What he said went, no question about it."

Included was Landis' suspension for life of Shoeless Joe Jackson with seven other Chicago White Sox suspected of throwing the 1919 World Series. "Uncle always said he (Joe Jackson) didn't throw any games though," remembers Calvin.

The Senators lack of success on the field since 1933 had not yet approached scandalous proportions. But the lack of an effective farm system had begun to take its toll. Only once in the next eight years would the Washington club finish in the American League's first division.

Things got so desperate that Bucky Harris would be rehired as manager in 1935. Harris would actually manage the Senators on three different occasions. "He was Clark Griffith's Billy Martin," Calvin would later say with a laugh.

Yet somehow Clark Griffith kept the family operation afloat and even turned slight profits for 17 straight years despite the Senators faltering attendance. Once again, on-the-field entertainers and rentals of Griffith Stadium helped. In 1934 he signed Allen Benson, a bearded pitcher from the House of David team, so that he could claim the only bearded baseball player in the Major Leagues.

Another major change to the Senators organization, and to the major leagues, came from Clark Griffith's association with a chunky, disheveled, ex-minor leaguer and journeyman scout named Joe Cambria. The Italian-born Cambria would become invaluable to the Senators organization, delivering Latin American talent to North American rosters.

"I used to catch for Cambria's semipro team in Baltimore on Saturdays and Sundays. I got gasoline money for going over there," Calvin Griffith explains how the connection developed. "Clark Griffith became acquainted with Cambria when he used to go over to see the semipro games. Cambria then became a real good friend for many years. At one time, he and Joe Engel were practically the only scouting system that the Senators had."

Cambria would bring Cuban players to the United States throughout the 1940s and 50s. They would begin with a brief stopover at a military base in Key West before typically embarking on a barnstorming tour of the South. "They were just happy as hell to play ball. They were coming right out of the sugar fields of Cuba," recalls Calvin of the attraction to the United States. "Everybody had a town team back in those days, and Cambria had a bus that would take them everywhere. We'd give Cambria money to feed 'em and we'd get them to stay in a hotel every once in a while."

But Clark Griffith's instincts for survival reached their peak after the Japanese attack on Pearl Harbor drew the U.S. directly into World War II and threatened the very continuance of baseball during those years. The "Old Fox" used every trick in his collection to convince federal officials of the national pastime's importance to the country's morale and war effort.

Griffith's Washington connections made him the perfect unofficial lobbyist for baseball's interests in the capital. Especially handy was the Senators owner's friendly relationship with President Franklin Roosevelt, begun in 1917 when as assistant secretary of the Navy, Roosevelt had joined Senators players carrying bats on their shoulders to simulate rifles in marching to the flagpole at Griffith Stadium on Opening Day.

Recognizing that such substitution for military service by ballplayers would never be accepted in World War II, Clark Griffith nevertheless made repeated visits to the White House on behalf of baseball's continuation. "Especially during World War II, he used to go down and see Roosevelt all the time," remembers Calvin Griffith.

"He had to do it quietly. He couldn't do too much talking about it," says Calvin of his adopted father's keen understanding of politics. "But Clark Griffith had such prestige he could call up anybody and talk."

Finally, on the eve of the 1942 season, the Old Fox's arguments won out. "Roosevelt gave baseball the green light," remembers Calvin proudly. "That was because of Clark Griffith, he convinced Roosevelt. He was the man. He was the man to get the green light."

Roosevelt's background as a baseball fan, cultivated by Griffith's habit of providing season passes to political leaders, didn't hurt, of course. "I think he was (a fan)," says Calvin. "He used to enjoy himself and at least stay to the end of the game."

Wartime restrictions on travel and resources did cause changes in the game however. The Senators temporarily abandoned their spring training camp at Orlando, Florida, established in 1935, and practiced in often frigid conditions at the nearby University of Maryland. "That's when you couldn't go south of the Potomac River," remembers Calvin of baseball commissioner Kenesaw Landis' directive.

"Hell, we still had great trainings for chrissake," says Calvin nostalgically. "We'd go to Norfolk to play the service team down there—the navy base outside Washington

(Quantico). They had all the great players—Dom Dimaggio, Albie Fletcher, Phil Rizzuto, Bob Feller. They used to beat us pretty good."

Ironically, the Senators fortunes took a brief upswing in American League play during World War II, with second-place finishes in 1943 and 1945. Like the other have-nots, the St. Louis Browns, Washington was aided by the natural equalization of teams by the military draft. Clark Griffith's skill at making the most of limited resources kept the Senators near the top until the final week in both years.

"We had some decent teams in those years. We got beat out of the pennant in the final days one of those years," Calvin remembers. "In 1945 Hank Greenberg (of the Detroit Tigers) got back just in time to beat us with a home run."

Griffith's strategy of signing Cuban and Latin players who were, for a time, ineligible for the military draft also gained some advantage. His regular lunches with the head of the Selective Service didn't hurt either, as the Senators received short-term deferments for several players.

Despite being 34 years old with two children, Calvin had his own near-miss with the draft in the war's final days. "Yeah, I was drafted—general duty," he recalls. "I went over to this place right outside of Washington and I was in the latrine and I hear these officers talking that the war's over. So I call up the ballpark and I say, 'See if you can get me a 30 day extension or something.' I got it, and then I got a notice not to report, that I was too old."

Calvin had another reason to welcome the war's end. The safe return home of his twin brothers Billy and Jimmy from service in the South Pacific brought both personal and professional joy. "The happiest day in my life was when my brothers got out of the service," remembers Calvin of the war's end. "I said you can take over. You're the concessionaires from now on out."

Calvin was now able to be reunited with his family year-round, despite severe post-war housing shortages. Natalie, Clark, now aged four, and newborn Corinne came from Charlotte where Calvin had only been able to visit during the off-season and occasional summer trips. Another child, Claire, would be born shortly after the family built a home in Washington.

Yet Calvin admits he still was often not able to spend much time with his family during this period. "The thing is, in Washington we used to have wrestling matches, Negro League baseball and all these things. Someone had to stay to supervise all these things going on, and I was the low one on the totem pole. I had to stay around and make sure everything was taken care of.

"And of course that affected my home life," he remembers somewhat defensively. "A lot of times I didn't get home 'til late and the kids would be in bed. The wife would be in bed and all that other stuff. But if I didn't do it, I don't know where I would be today. Clark Griffith could say, 'Well, he's not even interested in the ballclub. Why should I leave it to him?'"

A certain level of insecurity may have affected the entire underfunded and under-manned Senators organization at the war's end. With the ending of World War II also came a return of pre-war stars such as Bob Feller, Ted Williams, and Joe Dimaggio to other American League teams. The Senators had no such returning stars.

"I tell you this," Calvin would say years later, "We lost (in World War II) the man who would have been the centerfielder of all centerfielders. Name was Elmer Gideon and he was a Big Ten hurdle champ. You know Willie Wilson, he's fast, but Elmer Gideon could have run circles around him. And we had a pitcher named Forest Brewer who was killed and a pitcher named Joe Beck who lost an arm in service."

One of Washington's returnees was a one-legged pitcher named Bert Shepherd. Shepherd didn't last despite a valiant effort. Even his public relations value to the Senators was offset by a lawsuit by another veteran, Bruce Campbell, who won a settlement from Clark Griffith on his claim that he was discriminated against in his efforts to remake the Washington roster.

Calvin's sense of discrimination would be offended more by Ted Williams' recall to military duty just a few years later in the Korean War. "The Selective Service said they needed someone of his statue (sic) to help talk to the young ones for the country," remembers Calvin with a shake of his head. "But I think that they just did the guy wrong, that's all. He flew his missions. He woulda made baseball records that would been pretty hard to be broken."

Like his uncle, Calvin rests on the argument that baseball has served its civic duty both in wartime and peace. "It was for the morale," he says of the Green Light decision. "Baseball never asked for any favors. We never asked for any favors."

Whether accurate or not, that understanding of history fits Calvin's inherited understanding of baseball's central place in American life. Wars and politics may come and go like fashions, but baseball will always remain. Even when the Griffith name would no longer be a part of the game, family members would be able to remember their part in keeping alive America's national pastime.

But the Senators second place finish of 1945 was to be Washington's last taste of baseball success. Even a brief name change, to the Washington Nationals, couldn't help. The Nats, as they soon became known, could only manage a fifth place finish in 1952-53, during Bucky Harris' last stint as manager.

As other American League clubs reorganized in the postwar years, the Griffith family's lack of resources became increasingly apparent, although the Senators would post their all-time attendance high of over one million in 1946. The turnstiles would soon slow however: attendance didn't break even half a million until 1959.

Military demobilization and Washington's wind-down in the postwar period didn't help. "The problem was Washington was just a one union town," explains Calvin. "That was the federal industry and when that wasn't going good we didn't have anything. The federal government doesn't advertise, and we just didn't have the natives going to games.

"In Washington we just didn't have the population," Calvin continues. "What we had left were all foreigners. We had people who just came out to see New York or Detroit or Cleveland. We'd only sell 50 season tickets a year. And we had very limited advanced sales, maybe five or ten groups a year 'cause we didn't have boxed seats or many areas for advances. That's unbelievable."

Longtime Washington Post sports editor Shirley Povich finds fault with the Griffith organization however, for failing to adapt to change. "They were trying to be a corner grocery store in a supermarket world," Povich says, making a common comparison. "They got behind the times in minor league development and in payrolls . . . . Mr. (Clark) Griffith used to be a gambler. But in later times when the pot got too big, he shied off. Maybe he didn't think he had the resources."

There was no question about Clark Griffith's favorite son status in Washington during those years however. The "Old Fox" would be honored by induction into Baseball's Hall of Fame in Cooperstown, New York. A special ceremony at Griffith Stadium in 1948 would draw distinguished admirers that included President Harry S. Truman. With Connie Mack's retirement in 1950, Clark Griffith was the American League's most respected elder figure.

Yet in late 1949, Clark Griffith's control of the Senators organization was challenged by an outside investor, John J. Jachym of Jamestown, N.Y., who bought up 40 percent of the club's stock from the estate of the recently deceased William Richardson—despite Calvin's frantic but somewhat naive efforts to outbid Jachym.

"I even on my own offered them (Richardson's estate) $2 a share more," he remembers. "But that was verbally and that doesn't matter anywhere. If I'd have sent a telegram, they'd have had to accept. But what the hell did I know about business like that?"

Jachym's obviously larger designs came to a standstill one afternoon in Washington, however. "That's the only time I ever seen Mr. (Clark) Griffith get really mad," remembers Calvin. "Jachym came in there to Washington and went up to the office after buying the stock, and Mr. Griffith knew he'd try to buy Woody (Eugene) Young's stock too, and that would have given him control of the ballclub. So Mr. Griffith came in and he (Jachym) was sitting at Mr. Griffith's desk and he (Griffith) says, 'Get the hell out of my chair. You'll never sit there.'"

"I was in there, I'll never forget it," says Calvin. "He (Jachym) started apologizing. But Mr. Griffith knew damn well what he was doing and that he (Jachym) wasn't ever going to sit in that chair."

Griffith did maintain control of the presidency, and the team, while working out an agreement with another investor, H. Gabriel Murphy, who eventually bought out Jachym's interest. Griffith was able to gain 52 percent ownership of the team in exchange for Murphy's first purchase option on Griffith's stock. It was an agreement that would later result in its own conflict and considerable misunderstanding.

"Nobody knows why he did it," says Calvin years later. "But Murphy thought the agreement was that if Mr. Griffith died he'd be given so many shares. But there were some loopholes, if we could pay the inheritance taxes, and fortunately we didn't ever have to sell to Murphy."

Calvin was learning his lessons in baseball management under the tutelage of his adopted father during this period. "You used to talk baseball every time. I used to pick him up in the morning, drive him to the ballpark, drive him home afterwards, and at nighttime we'd sit down and go over the ballgame play by play, and he'd tell you what was bad and what was good."

Concessions, public relations, farm director, and travelling secretary were all roles that Calvin filled at least briefly in the post-World War II period. "I gave up the travelling secretary duties because I figured it out at the end of the year and I had lost $700," he would later tell a reporter. "I went to my uncle and told him how much it had cost me out of my pocket. He said, 'Where are your receipts?' I didn't have any, so I was out the do-re-mi."

In his role as press secretary, Calvin argued for improving press box and lunchroom facilities. It was a form of promotion in which the Griffith organization would never again be considered cheap.

Also among Calvin's responsibilities at Griffith Stadium was supervising a young, unimpressive scoreboard operator by the name of Bowie Kuhn, who would later become Commissioner of Baseball. "He was a tall, skinny kid," remembers Calvin. "But he always showed up on time. He wanted to see the games."

Calvin's many roles in the organization still included a great deal of travel. "I used to scout quite a bit. I liked to go out and see our young ballplayers and come back and say we've got so and so at Chattanooga. I was very, very lucky in my predictions of who would make it for how many years," he says in retrospect, although perhaps forgetting that he once publicly predicted that Yankee great Mickey Mantle would never wear the shoes of Senators' outfielder Jim Busby.

But most of Calvin's predictions turned out better. "It's instinct," he says, without any attempt at false modesty. "It's something you get acquainted with out of association with Clark Griffith. He could tell if you walked out on the field whether you were gonna make it as a ballplayer or not. That's how great a judge he was."

Life on the road as a scout or travelling secretary was beginning to lose its thrill, however. "It got monotonous, year-in and year-out," says Calvin, who insists he sought more time to spend with his family. "But unfortunately Clark Griffith got so he didn't like to travel at all and he wanted somebody he trusted. He needed help and somebody to run errands and things like that. He was the boss."

In later years when travel became less necessary, Calvin would be preoccupied with other responsibilities of running the organization. "There was always something more important," bitterly concludes Clark Griffith II, who was then entering his teens. "He never had time for his children."

Calvin defends himself, noting that he was always willing to foot the bill for his children's private schools even when times were tough. "Back in Washington we didn't have any money. What was I making—eight or ten thousand dollars a year? That wasn't much money, raising a family. But I sent them all to schools where they wanted to go. I bought very, very few clothes myself. I used to buy clothes on Washington's Birthday cause you get them fifty percent off."

His was a traditional sense of fathering that centered more on providing financial security to his family than emotional support. "If it wasn't for me, I don't know where our family would be today if I didn't take the responsibility from Clark Griffith," Calvin says simply. "He needed help and I gave him the help he wanted."

Calvin still seemingly harbored an orphan's insecurity about his future despite his years of service. "I tried to protect if there was any interest for me in the future of the ballclub that I was gonna get it. Clark Griffith's brother (Earl) still had a couple of sons he could've passed it on to. And we were just adopted kids."

More realistic threats were the changes in baseball that began to catch up with the Senators in the late 1940s as wealthier organizations broadened their minor leagues. "Mr. Branch Rickey started working agreements with all these teams," recalls Calvin of the process that totally changed the way talent flowed to the major leagues. "At one time he had ballplayers on 22 ballclubs.

"Clark Griffith used to have some really big arguments (with Rickey)," remembers Calvin. "He'd say, 'Well, here's the brains of baseball. Sonofabitch you're gonna ruin the game of baseball. You're trying to drive everybody out of business.' He (Clark Griffith) said you could only play nine players at a time anyway."

But Rickey's approach soon became the accepted model, with recalcitrant organizations paying a price. A fifth-place finish in 1952 and again in 1953 was the best that the Senators could give Washington fans however. "We didn't have much of a farm system," admits Calvin. "Mr. Griffith had 'friends' all through the Triple A. We were used to buying players from all the clubs."

Yet despite the Old Fox's cunning and friendships, Washington could no longer effectively compete while using a farm system that totally depended on ownership of only three franchises—Charlotte, Chattanooga, and Orlando, Florida. "We didn't have to work out agreements, we owned 'em (ballplayers)," remembers Calvin. "But we may have had to rush a few ballplayers."

Almost like an expansion team, Washington increasingly depended on the leftovers from other major league teams. "We had to draft from other ballclubs," admits Calvin of the Senators. "We always drafted three, four, or five ballplayers every year to fill up our club with."

Problems with television and radio revenue began to mount also. An old-fashioned approach to business hurt the Senators, says Calvin without any sense of irony. "Clark Griffith was so honest. He had a broadcasting deal with Chesterfield for, I think for $150,000. And they came in and they didn't want to continue the contract. They said it was only worth $100,000. So he refunded the difference. That's the way he was. He didn't want to skin anybody."

Calvin's increasing assertiveness quickly changed that situation. "I heard that and said to myself, 'Hell we can't do that and survive.' So I came in and said we could get contracts for a helluva lot more than that. I went out to Baltimore and got the brewery over there, National Bohemian. And they gave us, I think $250,000. Of course, when Baltimore came in that killed that too. But that's how I got started negotiating radio and TV contracts."

Calvin seized the opportunity to jump into another major role with his 1952 trade of then-star Irv Noren to the Yankees for Jackie Jensen and Frank Shea. "Uncle exploded when I told him," Calvin would later recall to a reporter. "But Jensen made me look good

39

and when Shea also produced, Uncle looked more kindly upon me. It gave me the confidence I needed in the baseball trading business."

The young Griffith was even instrumental in the hiring of Charlie Dressen as manager in 1955, "Uncle wanted to promote a player. I listed Phil Rizzuto of the Yankees, Cal Ermer, our manager at Chattanooga, and Dressen, who was at Oakland," remembers Calvin. "Dressen was my number one choice, but Uncle frowned on National Leaguers. I finally won out."

But other problems were developing that Calvin could only temporarily hold off. Acting as voting representative at American League meetings, Calvin claims he was able to delay the return of Major League baseball into nearby Baltimore for nearly two years, despite Clark Griffith's public statement of support for the move.

"Clark Griffith didn't go to the meetings anymore," explains Calvin. "So I had the people voting my way. I didn't make any promises. I said 'Hell, it's gonna kill me and the Griffiths if Baltimore moves in. Which it did.

"But I think my uncle Clark Griffith got smart, wise to why they weren't all voting for Baltimore," says Calvin. "So he went to the next League meeting and got them in. He kept his word, and we paid for it."

The 1954 shift of the St. Louis Browns to Baltimore, where they were renamed the Orioles, cut out a sizeable share of the Senators already troubled market. "When Baltimore moved in, that knocked us out of a lot of money," says Calvin. "We used to have Arrow Beer over there in Baltimore. They used to give us $3000 a game. We used to put in 30 games a season. That's 90,000 bucks."

As acting Senators representative at league meetings, Calvin was on the losing end of another franchise shift dispute in 1955. The Philadelphia Athletics, still officially owned by Connie Mack, were in the midst of an economic and family crisis greater than the Griffith's as they contemplated a sale to several Kansas City-based bidders, including one named Charles O. Finley.

"Connie Mack was at that time senile," says Calvin matter-of-factly. "One son wanted to move and one wanted to stay. The mother stepped in and she ruled the roost. She talked to Connie and had prepared a speech by her. Everybody, including Clark Griffith respected Connie so much that they finally let them out of Philadelphia, which turned out to be one of the worst things in baseball, because Philadelphia was an American League town. The A.L. regretted that they ever let them leave town."

The franchise was also sold to Kansas City businessman Arnold O. Johnson despite violation of procedural rules, claims Calvin. "Charlie Finley was the only one with a certified check for $250,000 to prove he wanted to do it. Johnson came in late and as it turned out he was a close friend of Dan Topping and that's what got Johnson the franchise. It came out that he and Topping were partners in Continental Concessions that had the rights to concessions."

Calvin's efforts must have been appreciated by Clark Griffith however. With his health beginning to fail, the truly "Old Fox" realized the need to make plans for the future. In mid-1954, he made his 42-year-old adopted son executive vice-president of the club, "with expanded authority." Shortly thereafter, Clark Griffith also quietly made adjustments to his will.

A little over a year later, on October 28, 1955, Clark Griffith would die at age 84. "We didn't expect him to die when he did," remembers Calvin. "But he came up with a bad back and that took a lot of strength from him, a lot of strength. He died from losing his strength. I don't know what was wrong with his back, whether he had arthritis or what. But he was in agony."

Several hundred people including most major league baseball owners and officials, as well as representatives from the five living United States presidents, attended the funeral. The Old Fox's death, which came just a few months after Connie Mack's, was widely felt by more than just the Griffith family.

But Clark Griffith's death at least ended Calvin's agony over his own future role with the Senators. "Yeah, we were certainly worrying about what was in store for all of us," he recalls. "'Cause he didn't tell me what was what. But he left a letter saying that if anything happened to him, Calvin would be in charge of the ballclub, which I was grateful to have after a certain incident occurred. That was one damn letter I really relished. It made Calvin the man in charge, and that was it."

Actually, the will made Calvin and Thelma the trustee co-owners of 52 percent of Senators stock, while other relatives received minor shares. Neither of the adopted children could sell their half of the stock without the other's permission.

Thelma, who had returned to Washington in 1949 with her husband and new Senators vice-president Joe Haynes, would quickly accept her relatively backstage role in working with her brother despite some apparent discussion in the organization of Haynes' succession to the team presidency. There would be no contesting Clark Griffith's decision.

"We were well trained along that line," says Thelma. "The Connie Mack family had a lot of trouble along that line, and that was always quoted to us, not to be fussing over stuff," she remembers. "We talked about all the big decisions, but he (Calvin) was president of the club and I didn't interfere with the ballclub operations."

Thus the day-to-day job of maintaining the family enterprise fell to 43-year-old Calvin Griffith. With only a reported $25,000 in the bank at Clark Griffith's death, the Senators organization already had buzzards flying overhead. There was also the matter of inheritance taxes and Murphy's claim to the team.

His uncle's death brought him a certain amount of power, but also brought immense responsibility and the burdens of gaining acceptance. "Clark Griffith was a fellow that depended on his friends more than anything else. He was not guaranteed or assured or anything like that," remembers Calvin. "But he was in a class where the other clubs had to help him somewhere down the line—maybe let him buy a ballplayer for $5000 instead of $10,000, something like that.

"People got a little more cutthroat after he (Clark Griffith) died," concludes Calvin. "They said if you're gonna stay in the majors, really get your feet wet."

Chapter 7

CALVIN INHERITS THE HELM OF A SINKING SHIP

"This is my home. I intend that it shall remain my home for the rest of my life. As long as I have any say in the matter and I expect that I shall for a long, long time, the Washington Senators will stay here too. Next year. The year after. Forever."

Calvin Griffith would not wait long to establish his mark on the Senators organization. Within a week of his uncle's funeral, he had pulled off a nine player trade with the Boston Red Sox, now under general manager Joe Cronin. Included from the Senators side were popular stars Mickey Vernon, a two-time batting champion, and Bob Porterfield, the club's last 20-game winner—who had publicly voiced his salary complaints.

"It would have taken us years to develop the players we got from the Red Sox," Calvin explained to newspapermen at the time. "We hated giving up Vernon and Porterfield. But that's the only way we could make the deal."

His first "youth movement" wouldn't turn out as successfully as later ones, but Calvin had no regrets years later. "Well, we needed ballplayers and that's the only way we could get them was to trade for players who could develop," he explains. "We didn't have much of a farm system or scouting staff back then."

One product of the Senators scouts and a tip from an Idaho "Senator" had already caught Calvin's eye however. Harmon Killebrew was hard to miss even without U.S. Senator Harmon Welker regularly sitting along the third base line, where he could remind Washington managers to put his prized constituent and rough-edged third baseman in the game.

"First time I saw him was in batting practice," says Calvin, remembering his awe. "He hit the ball out of the ballpark up into the bleachers. And anytime you hit a ball out there it showed you had power. 'Course his hands were like concrete. But he was just a kid. We just wondered how long it was gonna take him to mature."

Another of Calvin's housecleaning projects would help pave the way for the powerful young Senators sluggers. Within the next week he made a dramatic change in the features of Griffith Stadium, moving the fences in nearly 30 feet all the way around the outfield. "It was still one of the toughest (parks to hit in)," he says without apology. "The left

43

field wall was, I think, still 408 feet. Center field was 438 feet and the right field wall was 380 some feet with a 31 foot wall."

But in addition to adding offensive fireworks to Griffith Stadium's attractions, the shortening of the fences allowed for another controversial innovation that Clark Griffith had always avoided. Despite being more than willing to receive regular advertisements for alcohol, the Old Fox had stuck to antiquated moral standards that prohibited its sale in the ballpark. Lost Senators' revenues were the only obvious result.

Perhaps not as influenced as his uncle by the numbers of free clergy in the stands, Calvin Griffith would open a beer garden in left field during the 1957 season. "We did it for revenue. We wanted to sell beer out there to stay in baseball," he again says without apology. "We had to do something different."

Yet Calvin insists that it was not a reversal of Clark Griffith's policy. "He told me that if the time ever comes that selling beer will keep you in baseball, then go ahead. So we finally put up a beer garden in left field."

One thing that didn't change was the assignment of relatives and close friends to key positions on the club. Jimmy Robertson stayed officially in charge of concessions, Billy Robertson moved from travelling secretary to stadium operations. Sherry became farm director upon the conclusion of his major league career in 1952. Former Senators third baseman Ossie Bluege became comptroller-treasurer, and Howard Fox, who had joined the Griffith organization in the late 1930s, became Calvin's replacement as travelling secretary. All would be with the organization for over thirty years.

Charges of nepotism that had never seemed to plague Clark Griffith would harass young Calvin. But the new Senators president would shrug off the criticism as he did in a bylined Washington Post article of January 13, 1958. "I do not aim to apologize that Sherry and some of my other relatives draw salaries in this organization as long as they are qualified and earn their pay. Key posts in some of the biggest corporations in America are held down by qualified relatives of the boss. This is true in the newspaper world too."

Calvin saw the baseball abilities of his family members as almost a continuation of Clark Griffith's spirit. "Sherry was another one that could tell you whether you were gonna make it as a ballplayer or not. And my two brothers right now, Jimmy and Billy, they don't get fooled. I think Jimmy could tell you more about hitting than any goddamn batting coach."

But many observers and media critics did not see the situation that way, questioning Calvin's leadership and his background to lead a major league club. "The papers they crucified me," he mimics. "'Griff's little boy. What the hell's he know about this? What's he know about that? He hasn't had the experience to do this, to do that.'"

Povich suggests that it was only renowned tax attorney and board member Leo D'Orsay's benign influence that helped Calvin survive this difficult period. "Calvin came to lean on him for almost all of his business decisions. If Calvin were uncertain what direction to take outside of basic baseball decisions he'd depend on D'Orsay, particularly in squabbles with Murphy," says Povich.

A quick-witted and quick-tongued Irishman, Murphy continued to challenge Calvin's leadership throughout the organization's remaining years in Washington. "(But) D'Orsay gave Calvin the confidence, the backbone he had to have. He was an innocent in the business world."

Even a more experienced executive would have been hard-pressed by the organization's capital-short financial situation and Murphy's troublesome opposition. "I'd say that was the toughest time of Calvin's life," Billy Robertson concludes. "All the criticism, the unfair comparisons to Clark Griffith, and the strategy of Murphy to force a sale were hard on him."

But if Calvin felt pressure, he doesn't admit it now. "What the hell! I'd managed in the minor leagues and had pretty good luck," he says. "I sent a lot of players to the major leagues. I felt confident."

If Calvin's self-confidence wasn't enough, he could also rely on an almost psychic recollection of Clark Griffith's teachings. "I used to shut my eyes and say 'I have a pretty good idea what you're thinking,'" remembers Calvin, reenacting the communication. "The guy is so similar to so-and-so ballplayer and you gave your blessing to keeping him, or at least thought he had a chance. We were in a situation where we needed the near-ball-players."

Calvin did sometimes make trades for other reasons, but found they often backfired. "I traded (Pete) Runnels to the Red Sox (1957) for the simple reason that I felt sorry for the fellow," he says. "He (Runnels) was a lefthanded hitter and our field in Washington was 408 feet and he'd hit them up against the wall. So I said 'No use us keeping him, he's not gonna help us.'

"I traded him to my brother-in-law, Joe Cronin, and he led the American League in hitting that year and in 1960 too," says Calvin with a grunt. "I don't remember who we got even, to tell you the truth."

With the assistance of D'Orsay, Calvin used some bookkeeping ingenuity to hold both the inheritance tax collectors and Murphy at the door. "What we did on that was that we got an extension and another extension and another. I think we got it extended at least two or three years 'til we eventually got the cash," he remembers. "We finally got around to selling the stadium (Griffith) to Howard University for about one and a half million dollars. That money my sister and I got we finally paid the inheritance tax, our share of it. It was $900,000, almost up to a million dollars by that time. That saved us."

But Calvin's successful juggling of tax problems couldn't offset the Senators immediate economic problems. As Washington fans continued to stay away from Griffith Stadium in droves, the organization could not depend solely on baseball revenue. Like his uncle, Calvin decided he had to find outside income or other solutions to avoid the worst of all fates—a visit to the banker."

"When I took the club over in 1955 I think we had $25,000 in the treasury," remembers Calvin. "What saved us was the Redskins playing in our ballpark seven or eight games a year. Rent and concessions, that's the only things that saved us. We didn't want to borrow money, cause if you borrow money in Washington, you're gonna owe so much you'll never make it."

Such concepts of business were already being called outdated by the media, and Murphy, who would be rebuffed in his 1958 outright bid to buy the team as well as in many more lawsuits, called for a more "daring" business philosophy. "I would like to see the Washington club strive more determinedly for better results for the money we are spending," he told a reporter.

With less than well-disguised personal motives and few detailed solutions, Murphy threw out a virtual declaration of war that was continued for nearly ten years. "I would like to dedicate myself to giving to Washington a more representative ball team. That is very important for the nation's capital, more important, let us say, than for Kansas City."

Calvin claims he had no particular concerns within the Senators organization, however. "Gabe Murphy used to say some things," he remembers with a laugh. "That's why we let him on the board, so he couldn't say he didn't know what was going on. But practically everybody else on the board, except Gabe and a lawyer, were in the family. It was four to three on the board, so the family couldn't get overruled."

As the public continued to vote with their feet against his club, Calvin had little choice but to be good-natured in response to jokes at the Senators ineptitude. When "Damn Yankees" opened on Broadway, the Washington owner was there to see the play about a man who sells his soul to bring a pennant to the Senators. "Douglas Wallop (author) and I were good friends," he says. "We went backstage and everything."

Calvin didn't quite share his uncle's well-known animosity toward the New York Yankees, although he disapproved of their dominance in the 1950s. "It wasn't good for baseball. But you couldn't ask anybody to slow down."

In fact, Calvin's admiration for the Yankees led to enough trades between the two teams that critics would often suggest that a farm team relationship existed with Washington serving as a Triple A franchise. "I liked to trade with a winner. I think it rubs off," explains Calvin. "George Weiss (Yankee president) was a tough one to deal with. He was a tough SOB. But he was a good executive."

American League executives all noted the continually disappointing attendance of the Senators when their teams came to Washington. "We had complaints from all the other visiting teams," remembers Calvin. "They couldn't even pay their hotel bills, for chrissakes. We had some awful crowds, in the hundreds sometimes."

Fans did come out for the 1956 All-Star game, with an overflow crowd drawn to Griffith Stadium. "It was quite an undertaking," remembers Calvin of his role as host. "In Washington you've got all the Senators, Congressmen, and, of course, all the baseball people. Back in those days you had all the baseball people at the All-Star game and World Series. It wasn't like today when all the people making money off baseball don't even show up at the big events. That's what really hurts. Not like it used to be."

While over 28,000 watched the National League claim a 7-3 win that night, only 241,000 had come to see the Senators in Calvin's first half-season of ownership. Of course, the Senators inept play did not help, with a disastrous May heading the team toward an eventual seventh place finish.

1957 was even worse as Washington lost 16 of its first 20 games, as well as its manager. "I went out to Detroit to keep Charlie Dressen upbeat and give him encouragement. And the Washington Post ran a story saying I was gonna fire him" remembers Calvin with seeming sincerity. "I told him, 'Charlie, I don't want to fire you, I can't afford to pay a second manager's salary.' But he got all upset and quit, so I hired (Cookie) Lavaget-to."

Paying his managers and players would require some creativity. While he would decry marketing techniques throughout his life, Calvin was not above a few of his own gimmicks such as the "Lucky Charm Night" of June 27, 1957 held to help Chuck Stobbs break a personal 16-game losing streak. Stobbs won the game after 3,200 charms including rabbits' feet and horseshoes were passed out.

Sometimes though, a frustrated Calvin launched verbal attacks through the media, questioning the loyalty of Washington fans. "What do our Washington fans want?" he asked in 1959, failing to understand why only 615,000 fans came out to see a Senators team finish last despite showing signs of becoming a future powerhouse with stars such as Killebrew, Bob Allison, Roy Sievers, and Jim Lemon.

"Calvin was thin-skinned and thick-skinned both," summarized Povich of the Senators owner's response to criticism. "It was one thing his uncle hadn't been exposed to, he was so well liked. Calvin lacked the polish to deal with it often. So he was not a very popular figure in Washington, often."

Despite pledges of civic support and season ticket drives, there were few Washington relief efforts besides the elimination of a $12,000 annual fee for police protection at Griffith Stadium in 1957. Media and public reaction were largely unsympathetic to Calvin's claims of financial hardship. Interestingly, though he was being accused of cheapness even during those lean financial years, Calvin would turn down Cincinnati's half million dollar offers apiece for Killebrew and Pascual.

Offers and visitors from cities such as Los Angeles, San Francisco, Minneapolis and Louisville began to interest Calvin. As early as October of 1956, a representative of Kentucky governor and former American League president A.B. (Happy) Chandler attended a Senators board of directors meeting to pitch Louisville's proposal for a 50,000 seat stadium and a guaranteed attendance of one million a year for three years. The Senators board's response was noncommittal, but obviously interested.

Clearly the Griffith family was arriving at a crossroads, even if they kept their discussions very private. A seven-hour battle behind closed doors at the Senators October, 1956 meeting resulted in enough embarrassing leaks about the franchise leaving Washington to prevent any action before 1957.

"It was something you couldn't discuss," says Calvin of his uncharacteristic close-mouthedness. "I was even afraid to bring it up to the board because they might object and then it would get out publicly. You couldn't afford to do what Chicago's doing (White Sox in 1987-88) because we were drawing so little and if they'd (fans) have boycotted us we'd have had to go to the bank and borrow, borrow, borrow and pay the interest. Then you're in bad shape."

Once again, Calvin says he relied upon his memory of conversations with Clark Griffith for guidance. "I talked to him about whether we were gonna move. He told me what to do and what not to do. He told me, 'You're not gonna make it here in Washington 'cause there's not enough money for radio and TV.'"

Clark Griffith even offered another piece of advice that, if followed, might have changed baseball history. "He told me if you really want to make it big go to Toronto," remembers Calvin. "Go to Toronto cause it's a great baseball area up there. And that was way back. We gave Toronto a lot of consideration. But then we found out to be the boss you had to be Canadian. We couldn't control it. So we gave that up in a hurry."

Calvin initially denied interest in another northern city that was beginning to put out feelers for a major league franchise. He admitted to Washington reporters that he had received a telephone call from Minneapolis lobbyist Gerald L. Moore on August 21, 1957, but downplayed the contact. "He said his city was getting up a brochure pointing out what it had to offer a major league team. I told him it was a fine idea but we planned no future meeting," said Calvin.

"What happens in the future I can't predict," he added, cagily. "But I'd definitely discount the Minneapolis story."

Calvin's attention at that point was more directed toward another frontier, he now claims. In what would have preceded the Dodgers and Giants historic moves to the West Coast, the Senators were seriously considering a move to Los Angeles in 1957. "Norman Chandler (publisher of the L.A. Times) guaranteed me that if we moved out there they would build a stadium for us equal to none. We were sure thinking about it."

Only one hitch prevented the move, says Calvin, perhaps unaware of Los Angeles mayor Norris Poulson's low regard for the Senators since his days in Washington as a Congressman. "Jerry Hoffberger, chairman of National Brewing Company, had one more year on our (advertising) contract. He wouldn't let us out of it. He said he would, but then I met with him and he said his board wouldn't approve. I said, 'Come on, you are the board, Jerry.' But he said he couldn't do it and that was that. If it hadn't been for that, I would have gone to Los Angeles."

Calvin's California dreaming wasn't quite over however. Spurred on by an important legal counselor, the Senators owner was assured there would be no trouble with moving his franchise, even against the opposition of other American League owners. Not only that, but Supreme Court Chief Justice Earl Warren was even willing to help provide connections.

"I used to go up there (Supreme Court) and talk to him in his chambers," remembers Calvin with obvious pride. "He was telling me I should go to California—either Los Angeles or the San Jose area. He said, 'Just let me know and I'll get those politicians together for you.'"

Calvin was seriously considering the move for 1958, he maintains. "But the first thing I know, California was taken up by the Dodgers and Giants."

Unwilling to take on those two established organizations, Calvin's interest in a franchise move was quieted most of the next year. In fact, in a bylined article in the Washington Post of January 15, 1957, he pledged, in words not to be forgotten in Washington, not to leave the nation's capitol.

"This is my home. I intend that it shall remain my home for the rest of my life," wrote Calvin. "As long as I have any say in the matter and I expect that I shall for a long, long time, the Washington Senators will stay here too. Next year. The year after. Forever."

It was a pledge that the Senators and future Twins president would often be reminded of—and still denies having made. "That was our PR man, Herb Heft, made that announcement," Calvin protests, referring to Heft's regular ghostwriting role for the Senators owner. "I said 'Where'd you get that idea?' He said, 'I assumed that from your uncle.' I said, 'I'm not my uncle.' But that caused a lot of concern. I got called a liar and every damn thing. But everybody's got a right to change their mind."

While Heft is no longer living to help clarify that emotional, contradiction-filled period of history, Calvin's ambivalence at leaving the nation's capitol now seems apparent. "Being in Washington opened up so many opportunities for you," he remembers. "We used to have all kinds of (U.S.) Senators come out to the ballpark. I remember Huey Long used to be out there all the time. They used to ring this bell when they had to be back for a vote or something.

"Senator George of Georgia, Senator (Lyndon) Johnson of Texas. He used to come out and eat hot dogs. I used to go out and sit with 'em and tell 'em about all these new ballplayers and who was coming in." continues Calvin. "Course that's when he (Johnson) was minority leader. When he became majority leader he had to change his style of living. But I was their official connoisseur of baseball."

Griffith Stadium's history and decaying charm also had an obvious place in Calvin's heart. "It was a great old stadium," he says nostalgically. "The streetcars used to stop right at the ballpark and everybody'd empty out. You think back to the '24 Series and you're a batboy. You think of the Presidents behind you, all the diplomatic people, parties and every damn thing . . . . I used to go to Nixon's place when he was vice-president and talk baseball with him."

Yet with only 200 parking places adjacent to the aging ballpark, Griffith Stadium's future was falling victim to not only the Senators futility on the field, but also to the tides of suburban growth and racial segregation. White flight led to the abandonment of inner-city ballparks along with other urban institutions not immediately accessible to the automobile.

"The problem that we had run into in Washington was that our ballpark was in a very black district, and people were afraid of getting their tires cut up all the time and things like that, not that whites don't do the same thing I don't mean that," says Thelma Haynes, expressing a common attitude of the times that critics such as Povich suggest only served as a convenient alibi for the Griffith organization. "But it was hard to control and we didn't have parking facilities like here (Minnesota)."

When Congress first considered a $6 million new stadium proposal for Washington, Calvin publicly expressed approval for the idea, while disagreeing with the chosen site—across from the National Guard Armory in northeast Washington and in a largely black neighborhood. It was also distant from the most rapidly growing southern and western suburbs.

But as Congress failed to act on the measure, and Washington continued its last-place ways both on the field and in attendance, public discussion of a possible Senators move heated up once again in 1958. Calvin received additional ammunition in the form of new

American League president Ford Frick's May 20 attack on the condition of Griffith Stadium and the lack of Congressional action on a new stadium.

"From the standpoint of baseball it is not good to be leaving the nation's capital," warned Frick. "But you have to think of the poor devil who is holding the franchise."

By the July 7 American League owners' meeting, Calvin was openly saying that there was a "strong possibility" that he would request permission to move the franchise to one of four cities—Houston, Dallas, Minneapolis, or Toronto. His attitude was described as upbeat and confident.

Yet after the two-hour session in which the subject did not come up, at least officially, an obviously defensive and shaken Senators owner responded heatedly to reporters' questions. "I never said that I was gonna make any such request," said Calvin. "All we talked about was possible realignment. Further than that, I have absolutely no comment." Several unnamed American League officials reported that Calvin simply had not had the support of the necessary six team owners. At least one owner said the Washington owner had taken a verbal tongue-lashing for the timing of his public statements.

One reason for the skittishness of American League owners was perhaps made apparent nine days later when Calvin made an appearance before a Senate subcommittee considering legislation that would affect baseball's exemption from anti-trust action. It was not a friendly audience. Responding very respectfully to the sharp questioning, Calvin said that he "wanted to stay in Washington" and that he would seek no offers in the future to move elsewhere.

In November, Calvin was still claiming that he "never sought out any city." But the team owner also pushed through a reversal of a club resolution against discussion of shifting the franchise, and continuing talks with cities such as Minneapolis and Indianapolis. "I just don't think any organization should have that hanging over its head," he argues. Two members of the Senators board had already quit in apparent opposition to Calvin's plans.

Yet once again he would run into trouble from his fellow American League owners, in particular the New York Yankees, the Boston Red Sox, and presumably the Cleveland Indians—who were themselves looking at many of the same relocation sites as Calvin. Despite steady complaints over their lack of revenue from their Washington visits, the other owners weren't ready for nearly two years to even seriously consider letting the Senators leave the nation's capital.

"A lot of these owners are in such big business that they didn't want Congress messing around with baseball 'cause it might affect their other businesses too," interprets Calvin.

The 1958 meetings did discuss possible financial concessions to the struggling Griffith organization, an idea to which Calvin reacted with injured pride and a contradictory response. "I don't want to become an object of charity," he said to reporters. "I will weigh the many factors in our situation and I will return to the American League with a bill of particulars."

Regardless, little significant help came from those quarters. Calvin's leverage in American League meetings was somewhat limited, he admits. "They have cliques. Everybody has cliques in the League. I wasn't in any clique cause I was too damn independent. I didn't have any money to be in a clique. I couldn't agree to be in on this or that. I had to be with the regular group and wait and see what was what."

Yet Calvin's sense of urgency was growing as he developed another serious concern about staying in Washington. "I am not worried about the seasons of 1959 and 1960," he said, referring to renewed plans for a new publicly-owned Washington stadium (later to be known as RFK Stadium) to include both the Senators and the football Redskins as tenants. "What bothers me is what I might face after two years with expiration of our contract with the Redskins. The revenues we get from football and the concessions are important to us."

It was an argument that would be echoed years later in Calvin's mixed response to yet another stadium proposal. Then he would be in a slightly stronger position to argue for a share of concessions and other stadium revenues. But for now, and through 1960, the Senators did not have the option of leaving either Griffith Stadium or Washington.

Chapter 8

FROM D.C. FOLLIES
TO FROSTBITE FALLS

"When I was trying to make a decision whether to come to Minnesota out of Washington
I used to shut my eyes and say, 'Well, Unc', the time has come.
Something has to give. We want to stay in baseball
but we can't make it as it is right here.'
I think he'd have agreed we were very, very fortunate
to have Minnesota to come to."

Slowly but surely, Minnesota had worked its way into Calvin Griffith's heart, even if only by working through his wallet. "They were promised so many times that they were gonna have a ballclub. They got slapped in the face so many times. Like Gerry Moore and a fellow named Chet Roan (former Metropolitan Stadium manager).

"(Minneapolis sportswriter) Charley Johnson used to come down and see Clark Griffith way back in the early 50s, maybe even the 40s," continues Calvin, sympathetically. "I used to say, 'what the hell is he doing out here? Nobody's gonna move out there to Minnesota. It's too cold.'"

Calvin laughs as he remembers a mid-1950s winter meeting in Minneapolis that confirmed his fears of Minnesota weather. "Ossie Bluege and I were up at the Nicollet Hotel where the baseball meetings were. We stayed up there until two or three in the morning—nothing but smoke-filled rooms, geez it was terrible.

"We got outta there and decided we were gonna walk from the Nicollet to the Radisson (the hotel where they were staying). And every street you went by, whew, it was cold," continues Calvin. "Then we get to the Radisson and they had this heater thing, around ten feet of space on the ground you walk over. And goddamn it almost blew my lungs out, my lungs were so cold and then to come up against that. And I turned to him and said, 'You know Ossie, you gotta be a goddamn fool to live up here.' And here we are!"

But Minnesota's summer beauty, complete with over 10,000 lakes all suitable for an avid fisherman like Calvin, would eventually offer a nearly equalling attraction. A two-year weather chart that he began from that point would also allay most of his fears about any negative weather effects on the baseball season in Minnesota.

Calvin even became convinced there might be a positive side to Minnesota's cool spring and fall weather. "We always felt that playing in Washington took a lot of life out of our ballplayers," he remembers, making a comparison to the often-noted, late-season fatigue of Texas Rangers players. "We wanted to go to a place where the ballplayer could get rejuvenated. That's one reason why we liked Los Angeles and Minnesota. They were cool in the evenings."

But more importantly, the persistence of the Minneapolis delegation paid off. Gerald Moore made numerous visits, some unexpected, to Washington's Griffith Stadium under an assumed name. "He'd come walking in and I'd say, 'Now if I introduce you to anybody it's as Jerry White or Jerry Brown, but no Jerry Moore,'" admits Calvin. "I didn't want it getting out and everybody getting all excited."

Calvin was now even facing opposition in his immediate family. "I went out to his house and met the family," remembers Moore. "His wife at the time wanted to stay in Washington. She was into society and all that. So it was pretty touchy . . . . And the press in Washington was really against it. So he had a lot of pressure."

Yet Calvin was clearly growing excited at the financial incentives being thrown in his direction. "Hamm's Brewing Company offered us a three-year contract for $750,000 a year," he describes perhaps the clinching offer. "Back in Washington we were (only) taking in $150,000 or $200,000, or $250,000 for our radio and TV. I never dreamt of anything like that."

Washington sportswriter Shirley Povich describes Calvin as almost starry-eyed in reaction to the offers being thrown his direction from Minneapolis. "They seduced him. He saw it as almost a new sex life out there," says Povich with a touch of sarcasm. "The rosy picture they painted—and they made good on almost everything . . . . Nobody was more persuasive than Minneapolis."

Press reports in 1959 indicated further Minneapolis guarantees to Senators attorney Leo D'Orsay of a minimum attendance of 750,000 and minimum net profits for the Griffith franchise of $430,000 a year for five years, although that offer was apparently later dropped.

Calvin was already impressed by the profits reaped from a quickly arranged exhibition game on July 21, 1958. The Senators made the trip for a sold-out contest with the Philadelphia Phillies at then shiny, new, state-of-the-art Metropolitan Stadium, which had been awaiting a major league tenant since its opening in 1956.

"Chet Roan (Met Stadium manager) practically bribed me with $10,000 for that game," Calvin remembers with a smile. "That's when we were getting maybe in the hundreds for playing exhibitions most places, even in Chicago and New York. They really wanted to get us up here to show us around."

But Minneapolis' wine and dine strategy almost backfired at a luncheon in a restaurant overlooking a busy highway in Bloomington. "Every car that went by had a boat on the back," Calvin remembers. "That wasn't too good a information. But still we only played 12 Sundays over a year so I decided not to worry about it."

But Calvin was not about to be pressured into a hasty decision, having learned from his previous, unsuccessful approaches to the other American League owners. At a Chicago hotel room meeting prior to the American League's 1959 fall meetings, the Minneapolis delegation got an introduction to the Washington owner's independent nature, even in the highest business dealings.

"They asked me to come up to the room. They all thought I was gonna ask permission at that meeting," remembers Calvin with a grunt. "I had no intention of doing it. I said the time has to be right.

"Boy, I tell you. I never saw such a goddamn tongue-lashing as I took from those guys," he describes, before narrating his response. "I stood up and said, 'Who the hell are you all? Do you think you're gods? Nobody gave any indication that we were thinking of moving out of Washington at this time.' And I said 'If I get anything more like this you all can forget it.' All their heads sank down to their navels and that was it."

Calvin was determined to be more cautious after his embarrassment at the 1958 owner's meeting. There was good reason, with Senator Estes Kefauver heading up a major study of baseball's antitrust status and House Judiciary Committee chairman Emanuel Cellar also warning of more hearings should the Senators be moved from Washington.

"Young Griffith wants to go to Minneapolis because he thinks he can make more money there," the Brooklyn Congressman said, likely remembering how his Dodgers had so recently left for Los Angeles. "If baseball is a sport, then what Griffith is thinking of doing is not likely to happen. But if it's really a business, as it seems to me, then it is only natural for Griffith to move where he can get the most shekels for his team."

Calvin, who might have privately agreed with the latter analysis, had his own perspective on governmental "protections" of the sport. "When they were talking about building the new ballpark in Washington they wanted a section set aside for the House of Representatives and their aides and the Senate and their aides," says Calvin with disgust. "And I said there ain't no way they were gonna have any free load on me. I pay my taxes and everything else."

Nevertheless, Calvin knew he had to back down again on any more plans in November, 1959 when New York and at least two other American League organizations opposed the Senators move. "The Yankees do not wish to stand in Calvin Griffith's way," New York owners Del Webb and Dan Topping said in a joint statement. "However, they are opposed to leaving the nation's capital and would vote 'no' on the proposition to transfer the franchise unless there were an immediate replacement in the American League circuit, in Washington."

Calvin realized he could not challenge the powerful Yankees lobby despite having gained the informal support of A.L. owners just weeks before at the 1959 World Series. But this time he had at least a somewhat better grasp on the political realities behind the turnaround. "It was because of Del Webb and all his casinos in Las Vegas and his construction business," says Calvin. "That's the reason why that was. He needed all the political help he could get at the time."

Calvin's temporary acquiescence to political realities didn't mean he had forgotten his personal priorities. "Some people (owners) were always saying remember about the politicians in Washington," he remembers. "I said, 'I can't worry about Washington. I've gotta make a living. Politicians don't pay for X number of seats in the ballpark.'"

If Calvin was feeling increasingly desperate in Washington, he at least was holding his main nemesis at bay. Another of Gabe Murphy's nine lawsuits was rejected, this one prohibiting the sale of any team assets such as Griffith Stadium, was dismissed the day before the 1960 American League fall meeting.

"Murphy would have liked to keep the team here so he could be a hero. The lawsuits were frivolous. Murphy's idea of keeping Calvin in Washington was mostly meanness," says Povich, who himself supported an unsuccessful effort by attorney Edward Bennett Williams to bring a stockholder action against the Griffiths.

Just as the courts legally cleared the way for a Senators move, baseball's winds of change finally started to sweep in Griffith's direction. In particular, Branch Rickey's widely publicized promotion in 1958 of a third baseball league, the Continental League, to serve growing cities like Minneapolis drew the attention of the existing major leagues—though the plans never came to fruition.

The Washington Senators owner accidentally got an early earful of information on the Continental League one night in a Miami hotel room. "I was lying in bed and I hear all this noise and I said, 'That sounds like Rickey,'" describes Calvin. "He was in the next room talking about the Charge of the Light Brigade or some battle like that. 'We gotta be like them and lead the charge,' he said. Boy, he could use those words! But we were never really worried."

But Minneapolis businessman, and later Twins board member, Wheelock Whitney maintains that major league baseball owners were worried by the progressing strategy of Continental League advocates to force major league expansion. "We decided we would go after the major leagues in the place where they were weakest, which was in the reserve clause," remembers Whitney. "You could get legislation through Congress that would abolish that reserve clause if you could get enough support from Congress by convincing them it was that reserve clause that was keeping baseball tied up so there was no mobility of players, making it impossible to have expansion.

"This is what we did, and it resulted in the long run in expansion, which is what we wanted," insists the gravelly-voiced Whitney, citing an oral agreement worked out with major league expansion committee heads Walter O'Malley and Del Webb in August, 1960. "We never wanted a third major league."

Calvin's interpretation of history attaches more importance to the National League's establishment of a foothold on the lucrative West Coast. The Brooklyn Dodgers successful move to Los Angeles and the New York Giants similar surprise relocation to San Francisco in 1958 proved that transportation and scheduling problems were well worthwhile. Now word crept out that they were considering another expansion, further embarrassing and infuriating baseball's junior circuit.

Regardless, by their October 26, 1960 meeting, American League owners were ready to take action. In fact, the speed of the process struck even some insiders as surprising. "It happened so goddamn quick it was unbelievable. We went up to New York for a meeting and no one, no one ever thought about expansion," says Calvin, though press clippings from the period suggest otherwise.

"And all of a sudden, first thing I know Bill Veeck (Chicago White Sox owner) started talking about putting a team in Los Angeles," Calvin continues, reenacting his shock. "Then first thing I know they awarded Hank Greenberg (actually Gene Autrey) an expansion club in Los Angeles.

"I told Minneapolis (supporters) before the meeting there's no way there's gonna be any expansion," he remembers. "It wasn't on the agenda. Then I sat there (at the meeting) like a damn fool wondering what the hell was going on."

Calvin and the Minneapolis delegation were not totally unprepared however, having met the evening before to hammer out their own final agreement. "At 5:15 on Tuesday evening the Minneapolis people brought to my hotel a proposal I felt I could not turn down," he told reporters after the next day's League meeting. "It guaranteed me nearly a million admissions for three years. It gave us full concession rights and a low stadium rental. It changed my thinking and I decided to ask permission to move."

Charley Johnson would later write in the Minneapolis Tribune of an even more dramatic midnight meeting at the Savoy Hilton in which Calvin gave a list of demands to be met by 8:45 the next morning. Included was $250,000 worth of indemnity payments to the Boston Red Sox and the Dodgers for removal of their minor league teams from the Twin Cities, in addition to other admissions and concession demands that the Minneapolis delegation quickly accepted.

Minnesota interests had not been the only ones involved in secretive dealing even before the doors of the Williamsburg Suite closed behind the American League owners that Wednesday morning, however. Longtime maverick owner Veeck would later describe in his 1962 autobiography the aura of intrigue and political in-fighting that dominated those 1960 American League meetings. Included, said Veeck, was his expectation of receiving Calvin's help in placing a friend at the head of a Washington expansion franchise in return for supporting the Senators move to Minnesota.

Calvin vehemently denies Veeck's version of history. But certainly he at least saw in the expansion issue a leverage opportunity that he could not pass up. "So I made up my mind and I said, 'Mr. President, before we get too far gone in this expansion thing I want to make a motion to move the present Washington team to Minnesota. And that really hit the fan."

Despite the recent pigeonholing of the Kefauver bill revoking baseball's antitrust exemption, many owners were still adamant about keeping a team in the nation's capital. "They said Calvin can't go out there unless somebody goes into Washington," remembers Calvin. "I said 'I know one person who wants in there and he's married into Pulitzer money.' So they got in touch with Quesada and he said 'yes.'"

General Pete Quesada, head of the Federal Aviation Administration, was not actually confirmed as holder of the new Washington franchise until several weeks later. His confirmation came after surviving a power struggle with a Yankee-sponsored candidate, and Veeck's choice—first Jerry Hoffberger, then Edward Bennett Williams. It was reportedly Calvin's vote that eventually carried the day for Quesada and earned Veeck's charge of a doublecross.

Interestingly, Povich recalls that Washington interests had also been working behind the scenes to promote Quesada's candidacy. "We had a lot of discussions with Del Webb. He had interests in Washington," says Povich. "Phil Graham (Washington Post publisher) and I knew every move. We decided Quesada should be the owner of any new team," backing Calvin's argument that he was only thinking of Washington's best interests in his vote.

"There was something going on," Calvin would say with a puzzled look, years later. "They were trying to get together a clique to control the league. I've been accused of double-crossing people like Bill Veeck. But I never agreed to do anything . . . . I talked to them all, everybody, about moving my team and some of them changed their minds when it came to a vote."

If Calvin had been part of a larger plan in his effort to gain permission to move, the immediate voting results didn't show any benefits for the current Senators owner. "They voted and I got voted down," says Calvin, remembering his chagrin. "So I said to myself, 'Calvin old boy, you have attended your last meeting in baseball. When you get back to Washington they're (fans and media) gonna ride the hell out of us 'til we have to sell.'"

But there were several more twists and turns in store for Calvin, who now appears to have been totally perplexed by the meeting's events. "Then we recessed for lunch and Dan Topping came over and he said, 'Calvin, are you really serious about moving to Minnesota?'"

"And I said, 'Dan, the only way the Griffith name can stay in baseball is if we're allowed to move out of town,'" says Calvin of the brief conversation that changed his life.

"So he said, 'If that's the case, don't worry about it.'"

For whatever reason, Calvin's cause was now taken up by the powerful Yankee organization, whose influence would be key, especially in convincing Baltimore owner Joseph Iglehart to at least temporarily change his vote. "They brought it up again after lunch and voted on it again and I was allowed to move to Minnesota," says Calvin matter-of-factly.

"Then a half hour or 45 minutes later Iglehart stops the meeting and said, 'Hey, I just realized what I did. I wanna rescind my vote," recalls Calvin with a laugh.

But family connections came in handy for the Griffiths at that point. "(League president, Joe) Cronin slapped the table (with a gavel) and said, 'Too late, Calvin's in Minnesota.'

"That was it," says Calvin. "We won it by one vote. Thank you, Joe. It paid to have a brother-in-law at that time."

At long last the Senators were leaving Washington, as the sports world would soon learn to its general surprise. Included among the surprised were even the Robertson brothers, who had spent the afternoon at a Silver Springs country club practicing the second-most important pastime they had learned from Clark Griffith. "We came off the golf course that day with Willie Wolk, a doctor, a good friend of ours," remembers Jimmy Robertson. "And we come in off the golf course and a guy comes up and says, 'Nice going, you sonofabitch.' Another guy comes up and he's cussing out me and Billy and Sher. And these was good friends! So we said, 'Willie, go in the clubhouse and find out what's going on.'

"When he came back he was white," remembers Robertson. "He said, 'You sonofabitches moved to Minnesota.' That was our first inkling of it."

As co-owner of the team, Thelma Haynes was kept in better contact with the New York activities of her brother. "I told Calvin it (Minnesota) sounds like Antarctica to me," she remembers with a chuckle. "But if that's what you've got to do to survive it's all right with me."

Less convinced, at least initially, was Calvin's wife. "I was there (at the New York owner's meeting) trying to comfort Natalie that Minnesota wasn't as cold or as bad a place as everybody said," remembers Whitney. "Having lived in Washington all their lives they were pretty scared about it. She was particularly concerned about moving. Natalie wasn't all that excited about leaving Washington."

Minnesotans were, of course, elated at news of the decision. Banner headlines and reactions from public officials and local fans dominated newspapers, nudging out the Kennedy-Nixon presidential race for one day. Minneapolis newspaper columnist Dick Cullum profiled Calvin as part of "real baseball people . . . . It's his life and he has a deeper understanding of it than these quick-profit, capital gains operators who can read bookkeeping but couldn't read a baseball sign if it were flashed to them in neon."

Calvin's own brief greeting to the Twin Cities was to assure them that he had never forgotten Minnesota since his first visit there three years before. Despite delays, "I never got Minneapolis and St. Paul out of my mind," he said, expressing his regret at delays in the move.

Popular reaction was of course very negative in Washington, although a minority of fans welcomed the chance for a new franchise that would be more appreciative of the city. Nearly 750,000 fans had come out in 1960 to see the Senators finish in fifth place.

"It isn't quite true that they weren't drawing," still argues Povich, who nevertheless expresses continued personal fondness for Calvin. "Relative to the teams they had, they were drawing very well. And he took the team out just at the time it was maturing and blossoming."

But Calvin's conscience was apparently clear. "It was difficult to uproot our fan tradition in Washington," he told reporters. "But I would like to emphasize that it was my own stipulation that Washington fans would not be without a major league team."

Years later, Calvin would simply shrug off the criticism. "We had all kinds of people fussing at us. I don't remember what I said, to tell you the truth. But we did it to stay in baseball."

Nevertheless, as one Washington Post correspondent said, Griffith's 'dirty trick' would long be remembered in the nation's capital. "We put up with the bad teams all those years." he said. "Now when they're getting good, they leave. I'd like to see Veeck come in here. The old gentleman (Clark Griffith) will turn over in his grave."

Of course the letter-writer couldn't have known that Calvin had indeed gotten his approval from Clark Griffith. "When I was trying to make a decision whether to come to Minnesota out of Washington I used to shut my eyes and say, 'Well, Unc', the time has come. Something has to give. We want to stay in baseball but we can't make it as it is right here.' I think he'd have agreed we were very, very fortunate to have Minnesota to come to."

Chapter 9

THE EARLY YEARS
IN MINNESOTA

"Those first few years at the Met were like paradise.
We got big crowds all the time. Everybody was so goldarn happy . . . .
I got a license plate that said 'TWINS' on my car,
and people would drive by me, honking their horns and smiling and waving.
Not like later on, when they'd give me the finger."

The Washington Senators were now the Minnesota Twins. "A lot of the people in Washington thought we'd named the club after me and Jimmy," remembers Billy Robertson with a laugh that causes him to take off his glasses to while wiping his eyes. The team name, of course, really referred to the Twin Cities—with a seeming multitude of people (including Calvin) claiming credit for the idea.

After 50 years in the nation's capital, the Griffith family finally had taken their business northwest-ward to baseball's frontier. "It was hard," says Thelma Haynes, still retaining some of her Southern accent even in the late 1980s. "When you've been brought up in Washington and made friends there for 20 or 25 years, it's hard to take up roots and go somewhere else."

If Calvin shared that feeling he has continued to hide it well. "We said to ourselves, 'We're in baseball and it don't matter where we go. We're gonna make more friends, especially going to an area where they really want you." For a singularly possessed baseball man like Calvin, roots existed anywhere that four bases were thrown down in a diamond shape.

Indeed, he lists the thrill of going to the White House to give out presidential season passes as his sole personal loss in leaving Washington. "That was the biggest thing. Just the idea of going in and sitting down with the President and talking," he remembers. "Eisenhower and Nixon were really good fans. Richard Nixon was a real good baseball fan. I used to go up to his house for parties. But Uncle always told me to stay out of politics."

Yet Calvin would keep his display of presidential photos and other Washington memorabilia on prominent display at his new Metropolitan Stadium office. Included were numerous pictures of Clark Griffith, a small statue of Babe Ruth, scores of autographed baseballs, and a giant marlin fish mounting, which hung for years over his desk would all bring the past along on his trip to the future.

Yet physically moving the franchise in time for a season less than six months away was no easy task. "We brought practically the whole organization with us," says Calvin, with only slight exaggeration. "We had to put them up in a hotel and pay their meals for a month 'til they got established. We had to have people we knew were honest. You can get a lot of kickbacks and bribery in concessions and buying stuff."

Again it was primarily family members upon whom Calvin would most count. But there would be others, including Howard Fox, George Brophy, Ossie Bluege, Charlie Daniels, Tom Mee, Don Cassidy, Dave Moore, Jack Alexander, Gil Lansdale, and Angelo Giuliani who would either come with the team or soon join the organization in Minnesota as longterm, trusted employees.

Past friendships in the baseball world also helped the cash-short Griffiths make the transition. Owners Tom Yawkey of the Red Sox, with brother-in-law Joe Cronin again helping to pave the way, and Walter O'Malley of the Dodgers gave lenient terms of the $450,000 owed for their minor league territorial rights in the Twin Cities. "They were nice to me," remembers Calvin. "They didn't make me pay them the money I owed 'til July. They were good to me or else I would've had to borrow $200,000 more to pay them off."

Calvin would later complain that the promises of Minneapolis' businessmen to reimburse him for his expenses were often forgotten. "I spent nearly $790,000 coming from Washington out here," he complains. "I was told I was gonna get $500,000 back and I got $250,000 in receipts on stock in the ballclub. So a lot of things didn't come around the way it should have been."

Nevertheless, there was a love affair in effect that fall and winter of 1960-61 as Minnesota welcomed its first major league baseball team, and its owners. Calvin's first visit on November 4, after the decision to move the team, rated a front-page photo on both Minneapolis and St. Paul daily newspapers as well as an airport greeting from both the mayor of Minneapolis and the Minnesota governor.

"I think it was the happiest time of Calvin's life," says Billy Robertson. "Hell, everybody was happy. We knew everybody from bartenders up to vice-presidents."

Calvin was even named state chairman of the Christmas Seal campaign and given honorary keys to the Twin Cities. He and his wife Natalie were profiled by newspapers when they bought a house on Lake Minnetonka.

"Calvin was a hero. People loved him and overlooked his shortcomings," remembers Twins media relations director Tom Mee. "The guys in the early years around the (baseball) beat respected him. They were all knowledgeable about the game, and they recognized that he was. Even though he didn't speak well, they respected him."

Always outspoken, Calvin still stopped short of explicit promises but gave fuel to hopes that the new Twins might improve upon the 73-81 record of the 1960 Washington Senators. "We've got a sound, young club with a farm system that is starting to produce," he said to reporters. "I wasn't surprised at our fifth place finish last season and expect to move higher."

It was true that the gradually expanded Griffith farm system had begun to reap benefits, with names like Bob Allison and Harmon Killebrew already beginning by 1959 to strike fear in the hearts of opposing pitchers. A young Cuban pitcher named Camilo Pascual had already earned respect as the American League's top curveballer as well as an example of the club's continued Latin American connection.

Master scout Joe Cambria still scoured Cuba even into the Cold War 1960s. "When nobody could go into Cuba, he could go in anytime he wanted. Everybody in Havana knew him and knew he was strictly baseball and wasn't reporting anything," says Calvin. Latin connections would even get Calvin an autographed baseball from Cuban leader Fidel Castro, who must have by then forgiven Cambria's rejection of his pitching potential in the early 1950s.

Calvin had first-hand experience with Cuban baseball of that era. "Howard (Fox) and I used to go down there in the wintertime. We'd send ballplayers down there to develop and we'd go down there to watch them," he remembers of the mid-1950s. "In fact, we (Washington Senators) used to play exhibition games in Havana."

There was no question about the caliber of the opposition in Calvin's mind. "They had some Cuban ballplayers that were as great as any ever born in the United States," Calvin says. "We had so many pitchers from there. Some of them won 20 games for the Washington ballclub. They was something to look at."

There is also no question about Calvin's other fond memories of Havana attractions. "Cuba, to me, was one of the greatest cities that anybody'd ever want to visit. Absolutely fantastic. They had the greatest nightclubs in the world, gambling casinos, music all night long, anything you want down there. I really enjoyed it down there. No bugs. Boy!"

But the Twins Cuban connection would be brought to an end by the U.S. government embargo in 1961, though not before smuggling out a young outfielder by the name of Pedro (Tony) Oliva. "Politics is politics," says Calvin with a shrug. "There wasn't nothin' we could do about it." Another young Cuban for whom Calvin made a special trip to see at Geneva, N.Y. (Class A) in 1958, 19-year-old shortstop Zoilo Versalles was already being singled out as a star of the future. "Versalles can make our club an American League contender if we can settle him mentally," Calvin was predicting during the winter before the Twins first season. "He has the physical equipment."

Certainly Calvin had every reason to be optimistic both on and off the field before the 1961 season. Advance ticket sales were topping many complete season attendance figures in Washington, improvements in Metropolitan Stadium were on schedule—enlarging the seating capacity of the former minor league ballpark to 30,000 seats, and lone holdout Harmon Killebrew was signed early in spring training for the then-princely sum of $22,500.

Calvin was at his peak, being hosted at luncheons and favorably portrayed in nearly every media description. "It has made a new man of my husband," Natalie Griffith said of the move. "He looks ten years younger and acts 20 years younger."

Mrs. Griffith went on to add that she was, herself, necessarily an ardent baseball fan. "I think it's good that I am, or I might not see much of my husband. We talk baseball at home but only when it's going well."

Things were certainly going well early that first spring. On April 12, 1961, the same day as the Russians launched the first cosmonaut into space, Minnesota newspaper headlines screamed of the Twins season-opening 6-0 win over the New York Yankees behind Pedro Ramos' three-hitter. "It's important to get a good start when you move into a new community," Calvin said to reporters. "And it couldn't have been better."

Calvin still remembers the heady feeling of that first Twins victory. "We went to dinner at Toots Shors (restaurant in New York) and everybody was congratulating us. We were on cloud nine, no doubt about it."

The Twins owner's outlook continued to be rosy, despite reversed results in the Minnesota team's home opener, a 5-3 loss that ironically came at the hands of the new, expansion Washington Senators. Over 24,000 fans came out despite the cool April weather, and the still muddy, unpaved Met Stadium parking lots.

Calvin complained at the time, but afterwards remembered the day fondly. "I sat downstairs in the dugout throughout the game and had a good feeling," he recalls. "Getting off that opening day was really a big thing."

The Twins gave the appearance of being pennant contenders that first month, winning nine of their first twelve and vaulting into first place. But it was a short-lived glory as they soon fell into a slide that not only cost them any pennant chances, but also their first manager.

Cookie Lavagetto, who Calvin had borne with despite three straight eighth place finishes in Washington, wasn't to be so lucky in Minnesota. On June 6, he was given a "vacation" during a 13-game losing streak that included an Allison-Pascual dugout fight. Calvin at first insisted to reporters that he had no intention of firing Lavagetto.

But when Lavagetto returned on June 13 and things didn't improve, the axe finally fell. Citing a lack of leadership and discipline, measurable by a lack of fines and the team's 29-45 record, Calvin sent Cookie packing—into a scouting position. "Lavagetto was just getting downhearted," remembers Calvin. "And when you're downhearted, you're no good for your club."

One of the few players speaking up for Lavagetto was a veteran second baseman in his final playing year named Billy Martin. "They fired the wrong guy," said Martin, without giving further explanation.

Into the breach was thrown relatively inexperienced third-base coach Sam Mele. The already white-haired Mele couldn't offset the Twins abominable fielding and leadfooted baserunning. Moreover, the Minnesota pitching staff set club records for walks, hit batsmen, and team ERA. It was a combination that headed the team toward a final 70-90 record and seventh place finish.

But Calvin saw enough signs of progress to decide he had found the Twins manager for the indefinite future. "Mele turned out to be a goddamn good manager, one of the best managers I ever had, no doubt about it," praises Calvin. "He knew how to handle pitchers. If you can handle a pitching staff, you have a good chance to win."

The offensive potential was clearly there, with the powerful Killebrew hitting 46 homers and driving 122 runs, and Allison chipping in with 29 homers and 105 RBI. A young catcher named Earl Battey, whom Calvin had acquired from the White Sox with Don Mincher just before the season for Roy Sievers, hit .302 with 17 homers and 55 RBI.

But the real numbers Calvin loved to see were those at the turnstiles, as 1,256,723 fans streamed into the Met. Revenues were so good, along with a $1.5 million return from the sale of Griffith Stadium in Washington, that salary increases went to all family members. Calvin's own salary went from $40,000 to $75,000, he admitted in response to a shareholder suit filed and lost by the persistent H. Gabriel Murphy.

"What a year it was. The best my associates and I ever had," Calvin would bubble to reporters. "Sure the terrific support the Twins received at the gate during 1961 was enjoyable. But the success was so much greater than I had anticipated. It has been like starting over again. It was a year I'll never forget."

Later, Calvin would be even more ebullient. "Those first few years at the Met were like paradise. We got big crowds all the time. Everybody was so goldarn happy. . . I got a license plate that said 'TWINS' on my car, and people would drive by me, honking their horns and smiling and waving. Not like later on, when they'd give me the finger."

In contrast to later comments on Griffith finances, media treatment at this time was quite lenient. "It is not fair to say that Griffith and his stockholders are just piling up the dollars for their own personal gain," wrote Minneapolis sportswriter Charley Johnson, citing the organization's nearly half million dollar investment in minor league programs—then a considerable sum.

Again in some contrast to some later media analyses, Johnson also lauded Calvin for being "receptive to constructive criticism" in complaints about seating prices and concession operations.

In fact, the Twins owner contributed over $400,000 in improvements in Metropolitan Stadium before 1962, including an elevator, ticket booths, better lighting, a plush, carpeted Stadium Club, and improved concessions facilities. Jimmy Robertson promised better food products including a "German Heidelberg hot dog that sells for 30 cents."

Calvin lived up to some of his own promises to improve the team when, a week before the 1962 season began, he traded veteran pitcher and spring training holdout Pedro Ramos to Cleveland for first baseman Vic Power and pitcher Dick Stigman. "I'm sure we'll play .500 ball." he said to a reporter. "We have more depth, better pitching, and the best all-around ballclub we've had for a long time."

Calvin's prediction couldn't have been more accurate as the Twins, including a pair of young infielders named Rich Rollings and Bernie Allen, began to jell. Killebrew and Allison's bats continued to blaze and Pascual, along with a young lefty named Jim Kaat, formed the basis of a solid pitching rotation.

On August 26, Minnesota's Jack Kralick pitched the first no-hitter in Twins history while defeating Kansas City 1-0. Calvin, who had not missed a game in two seasons, had unfortunately chosen that day to make a trip to Charlotte and Orlando to check on minor league improvements and his old friend, Charlotte general manager Phil Howser. "I was just glad he (Kralick) won," remembers Calvin. "I saw Early Wynn pitch one and lose in the minors on an error and a couple of wild pitches."

But the Twins owner shared the rest of the season's highlights as his team amazed most of the American League with its battle with the powerful New York Yankees for first place. "We're so close to the World Championship," said Calvin in mid-August. "We're maybe two or three players away. . . After paying all the taxes we did last year we won't let money keep us from getting anybody we want."

Calvin did his best to come through, purchasing former National League star Ruben Gomez from Cleveland to aid Ray Moore's nearly one-man bullpen efforts. It wasn't enough however, as the Twins continued fielding problems and lack of experience paid their toll in the season's final weeks.

Yet the Twins second place finish and 91-71 record was the franchise's best since 1945. Attendance had again boomed, with an American League high of 1,433,116 fans crowding into the Met in 1962. "Now I'm convinced we will hit 2,000,000 some year if we ever get a permanent stand set up in left field comparable to what we have in right field," Calvin said to a reporter.

The improvements would never be made and Calvin's prediction would be forgotten years later when the Twins 1988 attendance of 3,000,000 was considered miraculous. "We proved that the Twin Cities are a good baseball area. They're not proving it now," he maintains. "They're not gonna get rained out or have forty-five degree weather. They have every advantage in the world.

"But back then we were the kingpin there's no question about it," Calvin says with pride. "We didn't have to take a backseat to nobody in terms of accommodations and what we have done."

Calvin's own contribution to Met Stadium improvements that year included a $19,000 hitting backdrop, as requested by Allison and Killebrew. "If it wins one more game for us, it will have been worth it," Calvin said, even while grudgingly giving a $4500 pay increase to Pascual, who had won 20 games in 1962.

But the Twins slow start in 1963 soon squelched most pennant dreams as the team fell to last by the middle of May. Poor weather and a series of rainouts had a similar effect on dreams of attendance records, though Calvin was trying to take the setback philosophically.

"The rain is good for the crops," he told reporters. "It will make the farmers more prosperous and we'll get more of them into our games (later)."

Perhaps his logic had some truth, for when the clouds lifted on the second half of the Twins season they finally began to surge toward the top again, both at the ticket window and on the field. Rookie centerfielder Jimmy Hall clubbed 33 homers and along with mainstays Killebrew, Allison, and Battey gave Minnesota the second highest home run total in major league history (225). Only a Camilo Pascual shoulder injury may have prevented the team from overtaking the Yankees, as the Twins finished third with a 91-70 mark. An attendance over 1.4 million again proved that the Minnesota move had been a wise financial decision by the Griffiths.

"We did beyond our expectations, to tell you the truth," admits Calvin. "After Washington, my God, it was a miracle. And it gave us a chance to extend our farm system a little and pay the players more, 'cause we never wanted to cheat them."

Yet Calvin again would not give in to Pascual's demand for a contract renegotiation that would increase his salary to the then-princely sum of $49,000. "If I did that I'd lose face with all the rest of the players on my team who've already signed," he explained to reporters, adding that if necessary he'd be willing to get along without the Twins pitching ace.

Years later, Calvin explains his annual contract battles with Pascual in almost jovial terms. "He was such a competitor. He had to win," says Calvin. "You can't blame a player for trying to get more money. I told him to try for all you can get. But once you sign that contract that's it unless you do something that really exceeds my imagination."

In contrast, during the off-season Calvin helped lead a successful fight to change the contractual distribution of revenues from national television broadcasts. "I understand the Yankees get something like $600,000 for their appearances on national television during the season," he had complained. "In Washington we used to be paid $50,000 for a few games. Here we don't get anything. One team can't put on the show. It takes two and we want to get paid."

With national attention now on them, the Twins seemed on the verge of even greater things. Calvin expressed that sense of optimism in 1964 spring training, lauding what he termed, "the best pitching staff I can recall," and the team's confidence. "They think they can win and so do I," he concluded.

But that optimism, as well as Calvin's estimation of his team, were to take a real setback when the season began, as the old problems of pitching and fielding continued. Old mainstay Pascual struggled through a 15-12 season, while Dick Stigman finished 6-15. 1963 relief ace Bill Dailey hurt his arm in spring training and was virtually useless during 1964.

There were bright spots however, including the emergence of another brilliant rookie outfielder, Oliva, who led the American League in hitting, and a June trade with Cleveland that brought Jim "Mudcat" Grant to the Twins pitching rotation. Calvin would also astutely pick up a pair of veteran relief pitchers, Al Worthington and Johnny Klippstein, who would anchor the bullpen. "That's what really improved us," he would point to years later. "Getting those guys who can come in and save the game really makes your team."

But in 1964 with a defense that committed 145 errors, the Twins fell out of the race by the end of June after losing 14 of 22 games. By September, Calvin's frustration at the "stupid, shabby baseball" was reaching the boiling point as his team was finishing in a sixth-place tie with a 79-83 record.

Sounding at times like a later New York Yankees owner, Griffith launched unusually harsh public attacks on his manager and team. "Mele has not rested players to my satisfaction," he said to reporters, while refusing to name his manager for 1965. "Whoever manages the Twins next year will sit down with me in the spring and discuss a general policy for resting players. There must be cooperation between the front office and the manager."

Calvin also suggested that it would not be an opportune off-season for players to ask for pay raises. "I'm going to have Howard Fox go through the season game by game," he said. "I want him to analyze just who left the runners on base, who gave up the walks and hits at crucial moments, and who made the errors that lost games. I will say that after a club falls from third place to second division, I wouldn't expect many of them to ask for salary increases."

Mele would be rehired as manager, though with a pay cut, and with fiery Billy Martin as a new coach, at Calvin's direction. Other enforced coaching additions would include Johnny Sain as pitching coach, and Jim Lemon as a base coach. "We are going to put a bomb under everyone," the Twins owner promised in the off-season. "We were too lackadaisical at times last year."

Calvin's threats of a housecleaning after building such a powerful nucleus of a team, in retrospect, seem almost ludicrous even to him. "1964 was the year we really felt we had put together a team with a chance to win," he recalls of his trades and Oliva's addition. "We had a nucleus. But they had to have the experience of trying to win. And we finally started winning."

But as Twins attendance fell by 200,000 in 1964, perhaps it was memories of a not-so-distant and generally dismal past that provoked Calvin's uncharacteristic interference in clubhouse matters. Or perhaps it was his newfound economic security that allowed the Twins owner to become more concerned with success on the field than mere financial survival.

Whatever the source, Calvin's call for very different results in the 1965 season would be answered.

Chapter 10

THE ECSTASY, AND THE AGONY

"That to me, made me a baseball man.
Nobody expected anything coming out of Washington.
Last in the American League, first in war, something like that.
Winning the pennant and going to the World Series . . . .
I thought we were really going to have a dynasty for awhile, which we didn't."

If it had been known in advance that Twins stars such as Harmon Killebrew, Camilo Pascual, Tony Oliva, and Earl Battey would suffer injuries in 1965, there would have been few takers on Minnesota's chances to equal, let alone improve on, its disastrous 1964 season.

Local sportswriters picked the Twins to finish fifth. Noting an attendance decline of nearly 200,000 the previous year, Minneapolis scribe Charley Johnson was calling it a "crucial year" for the Griffith family. Spring training highlights included Mele's fining of Zoilo Versalles for "lackadaisical effort," and the Minnesota manager's chastisement of pitcher Jim Grant for comments concerning Allison and Killebrew to the media.

Bad blood even appeared to carry over to the team's owner, as Calvin was forced to check into the Mayo Clinic for tests on what appeared to be a blood clot in a leg. It turned out to be a relatively minor problem, but the 1965 opener was to be the first the head of the Griffith family would miss since Clark had bought the Senators in 1922.

Nevertheless, in retrospect, Calvin maintains he was always confident that with Mele's renewed enforcement of discipline, the team would rebound in 1965. "We had the ball-players," he says. "I didn't have any worries that year. I was sitting on top of the world."

Certainly the Twins 5-4 opening day win over New York on recently acquired Cesar Tovar's 11th inning single set a pattern for a team that had in the past struggled for clutch play and consistent pitching. With an 18-7 start that included unblemished pitching records by Jim Grant and a rookie named Dave Boswell, Minnesota made it known that its bullpen weaknesses had been answered.

Calvin modestly gave credit to pitching coach Johnny Sain, whom he admitted had been his second choice after the unavailable Sal Maglie. "Sain told me what salary he had to have and we met it," said Calvin. "It was a lucky break when we were able to hire this man."

Calvin's trade for Grant turned out to be more than a lucky break, however. "We just knew that every time Mudcat stepped on the mound (for Cleveland) he used to beat us," explains Calvin. "I just said, 'That SOB can pitch.' And he was a good hitter and he must be a good person to have on the ballclub 'cause he was a dancer and a musical-minded person, you know."

For whatever reason that baseball teams suddenly develop a chemistry, the 1965 Twins had achieved the proper mix of elements. "They just all matured and started playing good ball and defense," says Calvin, simply. "They got hits when we needed and everybody helped, everybody."

Leading the way was Versalles, whose performance brought back memories of Bucky Harris' play in 1924 for Clark Griffith. "Zoilo just carried the team that year with his speed and his defensive play at shortstop. And when they needed the big, big hit he would be the one to do it," remembers Calvin. "Just like that year in Washington when we won the pennant, it was Harris, Harris, Harris."

The team owner also gave credit to the oft-criticized Mele as the team surged into first place. "In the past Mele tried to protect the ballplayer, regardless of what happened," said Calvin to reporters. "But this season Sam has taken over as the undisputed boss. The players now know that Mele means business."

Certainly the Twins meant business, with Harmon Killebrew's dramatic ninth-inning homer on July 11 giving Minnesota a five-game lead at the All-Star break and virtually knocking the defending champion Yankees out of the race. "Those things you don't forget. It was just a great thrill," recalls Calvin, again drawing comparisons to past Senators glories. "It was like in 1924. We went into Yankee Stadium two-and-a-half games behind 'em and we beat 'em three straight and they never caught us."

That year's All-Star game would also be a memorable experience for Minnesota fans, who were responding to their team's play with a season-record attendance of 1,463,258. Metropolitan Stadium was packed to see the National League pull out a 6-5 win despite another home run from Killebrew. In only its fourth year, the Twins franchise was surely justifying Calvin Griffith's hopes when he moved from Washington.

Midsummer night dreams continued throughout 1965. With Versalles winning the American League MVP award, and Jim Grant's 21-7 season heading up a consistently solid pitching staff, the Twins would never surrender their lead, clinching the pennant behind Jim Kaat's 18th victory in a win over the Senators on September 26.

Ironically, Calvin would not be in Washington to share in the celebration. On the advice of attorney Peter Dorsey, he avoided Washington to avert being served a subpoena in yet another H. Gabriel Murphy lawsuit. "I told him, make him come to Minnesota to sue you," explains Dorsey. "I guarantee you we'll win every lawsuit he brings against you in Minnesota. But the price you (and Thelma) have to pay is that you have to physically stay out of the District of Columbia. You can't expose yourself to a process server."

As a result, Calvin spent that afternoon watching the game on television in his private box at Metropolitan Stadium during a football game. "I am very disappointed that I couldn't be there," he told reporters. "I had to stay here and watch the Vikings instead, and keep track of the baseball game on television. Something like this might only happen once in a lifetime. The last time for us was in 1933 at Washington. I regret not being there. It is something everyone in baseball dreams about. It is a wonderful moment and I would have liked to have shared it with the players. They made it happen."

But the 1965 Twins were also a team shaped and designed by Calvin Griffith. Every key player had come through the once feeble farm system or had been picked up by an astute trade. Now the organization which had been laughed at only a few years earlier was headed to a World Series meeting with the National League champion Los Angeles Dodgers and their future Hall of Fame pitchers Sandy Koufax and Don Drysdale.

"That to me, made me a baseball man," Calvin says, remembering with pride the national attention now focused on Minnesota. "Nobody expected anything moving out of Washington. Last in the American League, first in war, something like that. Winning the pennant and going to the World Series, seven games, against a team that was supposed to be so superior to anything in baseball. It was a great World Series too."

With a sellout home crowd behind them, Minnesota lived up to their owner's optimism in Game One, defeating Drysdale and the Dodgers, 8-2. "I guess we showed them something, eh?," said a beaming Griffith to reporters afterward. "What a day, what a day. The biggest crowd (47,797), a beautiful day and a victory. I couldn't ask for more."

When the Twins followed with a 5-1 win over Koufax the following day, Calvin called it the second biggest thrill in his baseball life—coming only after the approval to move to Minnesota from Washington. His confidence, and that of Minnesota fans, was at a peak.

But disaster struck the Twins on their visit to Los Angeles' Chavez Ravine. Three straight losses to the Dodgers dropped Minnesota into a hole. "I should have remembered we didn't win a game in California (Chavez Ravine, where the Angels also played in 1965) that whole year," now concludes Calvin, who could only express shock at the time.

Calvin wasn't giving up the ship however. "With a little bit of luck we'll win it in seven," he predicted. "I'm just glad to get our club home. I can't believe that Claude Osteen (Dodger's pitcher) can shut us out for a second straight time—especially in the Met, where we have hit so well. I'm still confident we will win the World Series."

The Twins returned home to Metropolitan Stadium as though determined to prove their owner right. Knocking Osteen out early, they coasted to a 5-1 win to tie the Series.

50,596 fans jammed into the Met on October 14, with most of them sharing Calvin's hopes for a seventh game win and World Championship for the new American League franchise. It was not to be however, as Sandy Koufax again proved why he has been called the greatest lefthanded pitcher in baseball history. His shutout pitching on only two days rest and the Dodger's 2-0 win ended dreams of the first Griffith championship since 1924.

"That ball gets by (third baseman Jim) Gilliam (in the ninth with a runner on), then Versalles gets his hit and we may have won, or at least tied," Calvin says, remembering the Twins only semblance of a rally. "It was disappointing. But your ballclub played a good game and we just didn't get the breaks, that's all there was to it. You can't cry over certain things."

Calvin certainly wasn't crying over the monetary returns of owning a pennant-winning team and hosting four World Series games. Minnesota had clearly proven to be a financial godsend to the Griffith family. "Back in Washington we used to worry about pennies and nickels," remembers Calvin. "Here we worried about thousands of dollars at a time."

There seemed to be every reason to expect that the good times would continue rolling both on and off the field. While still trying to deal for a more effective second baseman and a backup catcher to Earl Battey, Calvin was confidently calling the 1966 Twins squad, "the best baseball club I've ever been associated with."

Yet in almost the next breath he was warning to reporters, "I just hope the players can stay calm if they should get off to a bad start. There always is this possibility."

The Twins owner's words would prove prophetic, as age, injuries, and a vastly improved Baltimore team caught up with Minnesota in 1966. Allison was sidelined with an arm injury, Klippstein, Pascual, and Battey were clearly showing their age, and Versalles and Grant's play were mere shadows of their 1965 performances. By the Fourth of July, the defending American League champs had already fallen to seventh place, 19 games behind the Orioles.

A lack of concentration would be Calvin's explanation for Grant's baseball falloff. "He got too serious in his musical business. I remember we had a reservation at the Hudson (Wisconsin) House to go and see him and his Kittens (female accompanists). And we were over there around ten minutes late and they cancelled us out 'cause it was so crowded," says Calvin of the post-season celebrity status of his star pitcher.

"Of course it was our fault," he curiously adds of the Hudson House incident. "When you gotta go from one house to another to pick up women you're gonna have problems, that's all there is to it. They all have to look prettier than the other."

A more clear sign of internal problems occurred in mid-season. Billy Martin, who as coach and later as manager always objected to having organization guests, relatives and other non-team members on charter flights, got into an argument with travelling secretary Howard Fox. Ill-feelings continued on the team bus ride and into the hotel lobby where the two exchanged blows, with the slightly-built Fox apparently getting the worst of it.

Calvin chose not to take action when the two men shook hands and declared the incident over, at least publicly. But the effects would continue to be felt by the organization long beyond the incident, say Twins insiders. "Howard supposedly threw the keys to him or did something he (Martin) didn't like," says Calvin with obvious distaste for recollection of the incident. "I don't know what the problem was. But there was some animosity there."

Minnesota rebounded from the shock of their first half collapse behind the steady efforts of Killebrew, Oliva, and Kaat, who had his best season ever at 25-13, to finish a distant second. But it was still a tremendous disappointment to their fans and owner.

Calvin was remarkably restrained in his comments during the team's disastrous year. But in retrospect he sees a pattern that has plagued many winning teams. "I thought we were really going to have a dynasty for awhile, which we didn't," he admits. "What happened the next year (after 1965) was one of those things. The glory carries on and they forget the routine things."

Pitching was the first fundamental area to go, recalls Calvin. "After '65 we had to worry about the pitching. They had good years and bad ones. It was up and down."

Pitching coach Johnny Sain became the center of a controversy when manager Sam Mele asked that he and bullpen coach Hal Naragon not be rehired. It was clearly a dilemma for Griffith, who would do some housecleaning of his own in the off-season, sending Jimmie Hall and Don Mincher to California for pitcher Dean Chance and Bernie Allen and Camilo Pascual to Washington for relief hurler Ron Kline.

Kaat recalls that it was Martin who originally clashed with Sain, with Mele backing him up, and Calvin forced into a difficult choice. "I have to believe that being a baseball man, Calvin had to have respect for what John Sain brought to the organization," says Kaat. "But at the time it was a matter of firing the manager and there wasn't justification then to fire Sam."

Calvin would eventually accede to Mele's wishes and dismiss the two coaches. But his unquestioned confidence in the Twins manager was clearly beginning to wane, despite protestations to the contrary.

"I have to back up Mele if he is right," Calvin said of his decision. "But I've got my own image to think about too. If Mele is wrong, I don't have to back him up. Is he wrong this time? I don't know."

Calvin's increasing differences with his manager had earlier been evident in what some considered his interference in Mele's attempts to make Harmon Killebrew into a leftfielder instead of a first or third baseman. "I've never made out Mele's or any other manager's lineup card, I never will," Calvin answered reporters' inquiries. "It is the manager's decision about who plays and where they play. But that doesn't mean I can't express an opinion on it."

After the disappointment of 1966, it was almost an unwritten rule of baseball that Mele's job would be on the line in 1967. That tension formed a subplot to the drama behind what would be one of the most exciting pennant races in baseball history. Recovering from another poor start, the Twins would battle three other teams into the final week of the season for the pennant.

But Mele would not be there to see it. A .500 start, 25-25, to the season was not enough to save Minnesota's longest tenured manager. Like so many managers before and since, Mele would perhaps be an obvious scapegoat for the team's failures. With the Twins in sixth place on June 9, Cal Ermer was brought up from Triple A farmclub, Denver, to take over.

"Mele did a good job for the Twins over the years," admitted Calvin to reporters. "The firing of Sam was an accumulation of things over the years," he said vaguely, while adding a vow to never again give more than a one-year contract to a Minnesota manager or coach.

If Calvin appeared somewhat sheepish in his public comments, Mele managed to remain diplomatic, praising his former employer while privately blaming other members of the Twins organization. "Calvin didn't meddle too much," Mele told reporters after his firing. "Many times I went to him and asked him for any ideas he had. As president of the ballclub he had the right to suggest anything he wanted to."

73

Years later, Mele would continue to praise his former employer. "He's a great man. He was a great man to work for because he understood baseball," says Mele. "We're still very close. He's said to me several times that he considers it (the firing) one of the greatest mistakes of his life."

One of Calvin's strongest suggestions to Mele was already paying dividends for the Twins in 1967. A skinny, Panamanian-born youngster named Rod Carew, who Twins scout Herb Stein had discovered playing stickball in New York's Spanish Harlem, would gain Calvin's immediate attention in batting practice at Yankee stadium. "I said get him out of there before somebody else sees him," he recalls of Carew. "You could just tell he was a natural."

Calvin would override calls for further minor league seasoning after spring training and install Carew as a starter at second base, where he would win All-Star and Rookie of the Year distinction. Even Carew's occasional temper tantrums, which would include a brief walkout from the team in 1968, didn't shake the team owner's patience. "He had a tough family life," says Calvin knowingly. "We had a lot of fatherly conversations. I think I was really a big help."

Carew and Tovar at the top of the Twins order in 1967 would set the table for the power hitting of Oliva, Killebrew and Allison as Minnesota mounted its comeback under Ermer. Winning 12 of 15 immediately, the Twins took first place in mid-August with newly acquired ace Dean Chance pitching two no-hitters to lead the way. Holding a narrow edge over Boston and Detroit, Minnesota took a one-game lead into a final two game series in Fenway Park.

The results of that series are now famous, or infamous for Twins fans. The Red Sox and triple-crown-winning slugger Carl Yastremski completed a storybook season by knocking out Chance and Jim Kaat back-to-back, while a Detroit loss handed them the pennant. It was a dramatic ending that Calvin suggests may have saved the struggling Boston franchise. "If they hadn't won the pennant they'd have been a second-class ballclub," he suggests. "It turned the whole complexion around and made them a competitive ballclub from there on out."

But it was certainly harder on the Minnesota owner. "That was one of the worst climaxes I ever had in my life," says Calvin bitterly. "I was so sure going into Boston with Kaat and Dean Chance going in that we would win both games. And then they both got hurt . . . . 'Course I'm still trying to figure out why Ermer put in that knuckleballer (Kline) in relief that last game," he adds, now calling the Kline trade his worst ever.

In a more charitable moment, Calvin would point to an earlier freak injury to reliever Al Worthington as the real reason for the Twins collapse. "We shoulda gone into Boston ten games ahead," he asserts. "But we didn't do it. That's where sports always have a way of evening things out."

Calvin at least had the consolation of seeing attendance rebound to an all-time high of 1,483,587. Minnesota was now considered a model of how a major league operation should be run.

"It's hard to believe now, but in those days the Twins really had a superior operation," says Clark Griffith II. "They really had the best and the brightest. That was the peak, the late 60s. Sherrod had developed a superior set of scouts, he and Brophy, that continued on. Jimmy (Robertson) was running a pretty good concession operation based on the old model. And Billy (Robertson) did well with stadium operations. In broadcast we did well, not by today's standards, but we could always sell our rights to Hamm's Beer and later Midwest Federal. And our reach, my God, we had people coming from seven states."

Calvin's own commitment to a future at Metropolitan Stadium was expressed during the 1967 season in terms of a $2 million proposal, to be repaid in reduced rent, to build permanent left field stands that would include offices and locker rooms for the Vikings football team. "This would give us one of the finer stadiums in the country," he argued, though the offer was apparently never taken seriously by the Metropolitan Stadium Commission.

Within the family also, future growth appeared to be in order. With Clark Griffith II now returned from college and apparently ready to take a role in Twins management, Calvin would drop several remarks to reporters that suggested his son could soon be heading the organization.

"I know I will not be running the club when I am 85, which was the age of Uncle Clark when he died," he said. "I have not decided how much longer I will work. But it is the thought of both me and my sister Thelma to install Clark as president when the time comes."

But like the team that summer of 1967, dynasties are difficult to sustain, with cracks already appearing in the Griffith organization. Few anticipated the bitterness of the breakdown that would eventually destroy any hopes of succession in ownership. But Calvin and his son were already undergoing a parting of relations that ultimately may be understood only by the proud parties involved.

In Calvin's mind, the split began when Clark refused to follow his time-honored path of beginning as a minor league executive before moving up to head of the Griffith organization. "Clark Griffith Sr. had always wanted a namesake to run the ballclub. We had been thinking that he may have been the man to eventually take my place," says Calvin of his son. "But you start at the bottom. I'm not gonna give him a job as president. I was gonna send him to the minors, yes.

"I wanted him to go to Charlotte, North Carolina," says Calvin, continuing an account entirely denied by Clark. "And I'll be damned if he didn't go out the next week and buy a house. How in hell could you go out and buy a house and then go to Charlotte. I don't think he was even married back in those days. But he was gonna live on his own, get away from Daddy. He didn't want to go to the minor leagues. He wanted the big stuff."

Roots of the conflict no doubt also run deeper into family history and psychology, as Wheelock Whitney suggests from his years of observation. "I think Calvin always wanted his son to have the best education and then when he got it, Calvin kinda resented it. This smart guy from Dartmouth coming back and trying to tell him how to run the team.

"I think maybe Clark wasn't as skillful as he might have been in getting the point across and came across as a guy who knew it all," continues Whitney. "I think maybe that irritated Calvin and certainly it irritated Billy and Jimmy (Robertson). There were a lot of crosscurrents in there between the brothers and Calvin, and Clark and Howard (Fox)."

Turbulent waters lay ahead. Just as 1967 had ended in turbulence and disappointment on the field, the Griffith organization would never again be able to steer a course of sustained peace and security. The Twins would again know glory days and its ownership would also enjoy times of well-being. But never would there be the combination of stability with success that Calvin had envisioned after 1965.

Chapter 11

FROM BOSTON TO BILLY BRAWL

*"I was astonished. I couldn't really believe what went on
and I couldn't really get any information
until about five years after it happened . . . .
I found out somebody held up Boswell and let Martin beat on him."*

Finding or restoring the proper chemistry on a baseball team is a tricky affair, as the Minnesota Twins would painfully learn in the late 60s. Their attempt to recover from the blow dealt them in Boston would result in a chain reaction of events from which the organization would never completely recover.

On paper, the Twins had every reason to expect to be considered among the American League favorites in 1968 despite the heartbreaking ending of 1967. But psychologically there was an impact that was undeniable. "It hurt," recalls Calvin. "It had an impact on the ballplayers and the fans." In what was to be a season of ill-luck, Minnesota was not psychologically prepared for more bad news.

Calvin had attempted with some success to solve a pair of personnel problems in the off-season with a major trade that sent Zoilo Versalles and Jim Grant to the Los Angeles Dodgers in return for relievers Ron Perranoski and Bob Miller, and veteran catcher John Roseboro. The results were certainly an improvement in the bullpen and at catcher, where Earl Battey had ended his career in 1967.

Jackie Hernandez was slated to fill Versalles position at short and aces Dean Chance and Jim Kaat were counted on to again carry the pitching load. Neither plan worked. "After 1965 we always had to worry about the pitching," bemoans Calvin. "It was up and down."

Actually the Twins started out 1968 with a 5-0 mark and returned home to pound Washington 13-1 in their home opener. But fortunes quickly changed as the club lost 12 of their next 20 to drop to seventh, their eventual finishing spot.

To be sure, injuries were a major factor in the decline, with Jim Kaat not recovering from his shoulder injury in the last game of 1967 until mid-May of 1968. Tony Oliva would be knocked out with his own shoulder separation on August 31. And Harmon Killebrew would have his season virtually ended on July 9 before a national audience at the All-Star game, when he pulled his hamstring doing the "splits" on a stretch at first base.

It was a series of unfortunate blows that could have dimmed any team's pennant hopes. But Calvin's patience with his manager was once again growing short. Ermer's quiet, patient style of play and personality had resulted in success during past minor league assignments, but now displeased his boss.

"It has become quite apparent to me that Ermer has lost control over the club," Calvin told reporters late in the season. "I feel like Leo Durocher, who said nice guys finish last. Ermer is a fine individual, but I do not think he just could handle the situation."

Once again, Calvin would be accused by some of trying to manage the team from the front office, a charge he would not weaken by some of his public comments. "There are some things we can see better from where we are than the manager can see up close," he said at the time of Ermer's firing. "For instance, I felt that the outfield played too deep most of the time and didn't take into account the count on the hitter or the wind. I talked this over with Ermer and he didn't do much about it."

Years later Calvin would still praise his former manager even while offering yet an even more curious explanation for Ermer's eventual dismissal a day after the 1968 season. "Cal Ermer knew and knows as much about baseball as anybody today," he says. "But unfortunately, Gloria (his wife) started answering the questions for him and the newspapers started raising hell with me. They wanted to talk to the manager, not the manager's wife. I said 'Hell, the only way to stop that is to get rid of him.' That's the only reason. He was a good manager."

Calvin would even think enough of Ermer to ensure him a continuing job in the Twins minor league system. "He said, 'Don't worry, you've always got a job with me," remembers Ermer. "They (the Griffiths) were very loyal people. They didn't have a pension plan. But if you did the job, they stayed with you. You don't get that same loyalty with all these multimillion dollar operators."

The 1968 season's effect on his financial situation could hardly have pleased Calvin. Attendance fell by over 300,000 during the lackluster season, despite promotional efforts that included Cesar Tovar Day, when the versatile Twin played one inning at each of the nine positions.

Calvin soon suffered another blow to his hopes for financial security. "My goal had been to get $4 million in the till in case of a rainy day," he remembers. "But first Uncle Sam came around and said we were accumulating too much money and fined us $35,000. Then that year (1968) we lost $982,000. We got the fine back. But that was a tough year to take."

Calvin insists, with some good argument, that his savings were never at the expense of his players, however. "Hell, we were the highest paid baseball club in the league for around five years—I think from 1966-1970," he says, noting that Killebrew and Oliva were among the first players to be paid over $100,000 annually. "We were the kingpin of the league in those days. Everybody forgets that."

The Twins owner's image of unwillingness to pay for a competitive team was largely developed in later years. 1960s era players remember negotiations being distinctly tough, but not as hostile as they would become in later years. "Calvin had a tough set of standards," says Jim Kaat. "If you had a good year he'd say, 'Well, big deal, that's a fluke. Now have another one and show me it wasn't.'

"You look back on the negotiating process and it was just a game," continues Kaat. "Calvin would say to me, 'Can you go out here on Cedar Avenue and find a job that pays you the kind of money that I pay you to pitch?' And I'd say, 'Can you go out on Cedar Avenue and find an 18-game winner?' So we'd kinda spar back and forth like that."

Despite several highly publicized salary disagreements between the two of them, Harmon Killebrew now offers a similar, almost light-hearted description of negotiations with his former boss in the years before arbitration or free agency. "He was tough. But Calvin and I always managed to work things out. I have a lot of fond memories and feelings."

Yet Calvin's role as a general manager-owner was often necessarily detached from the players. "You try to be nice with 'em, but you gotta be careful. I might say something they don't like," says Calvin, who gave up playing golf with Allison and other athletes for that reason. "Just like I tried to avoid going into the clubhouse. They might say something I don't like and don't wanna hear."

Best understood as a benign dictatorship in those years, Calvin's control over negotiations didn't mean he felt he had the right to abuse players, he insists. "It was always understood by the owners that if they got extra money it would go to the players," he maintains. "Ballplayers don't believe that. But it was a stipulation of the owners in the old days."

As evidence, Calvin points to baseball's opposition to the idea of a salary cap when the idea was proposed in the 1950s. "It would have been a restraint on trade," says the man who would later vehemently oppose free agency. "It wouldn't have been fair to the ballplayer. The good ballplayer should be paid more."

Yet Calvin made it clear by the end of the 1968 season that there would not be many pay raises that year, telling reporters that Twins players should expect tough contract negotiations in the off-season. "We may have had the highest payroll in the American League this year," he said. "But next year's payroll will be a lot lower. You fellows may have a lot to write about next spring."

But there would be much written about the team, and Calvin, before then. The Minnesota Twins were about to enter the Billy Martin era.

It was a fateful merging of two strong personalities that was made almost inevitable by Martin's great popularity with both fans and local sportswriters such as Minneapolis' Sid Hartman. Since he had become a coach under Mele, speculation was rampant as to when the fiery, former second baseman would eventually become the Twins field manager. His 1967 assignment to learn the minor league ropes at Denver was an obvious preparatory move, though Martin at first reportedly opposed the idea.

Ermer's firing sped up the process, even though there is no indication Calvin planned it that way. Martin's availability and success at Denver had made him an obvious candidate. Reporters immediately began turning discussion in Martin's direction even before Ermer's dismissal was hours old.

In usual fashion, Calvin didn't duck the issue, though his initial reactions toward Martin were clearly mixed. "I'm looking for a take-charge type of manager," he noted.

"Billy did a heck of a job at Denver this year. (But) the big thing is his temperament. He got kicked out of eight games and you don't help your team by getting kicked out of the game. Of course, my uncle Clark was kicked out of 50 games one year."

Calvin's doubts about Billy the Kid would soon be overcome by his appreciation of Martin's instincts for hardnosed baseball and by the popular pressure the Twins owner was feeling. On October 11 he announced Martin's hiring noting, "You people in the news media certainly promoted the decision. I'd never seen such a campaign in all my life about one personality. I say personality because Billy is a personality."

Calvin would go on to add that as recently as two years before, he had doubted that Martin would ever be Twins manager. "But he proved at Denver that I was wrong," Calvin said. "I feel that Billy has a chance to be another Casey Stengel. Of course my brother Billy (Robertson) says that Billy's (Martin) either going to be the greatest manager in baseball or the worst."

That historical question, of course, still is being debated. But baseball and Calvin weren't waiting around for the answer that winter.

1969 brought four new teams, including two in the American League, with the Major Leagues' second expansion in a decade. A new franchise in Kansas City was added to replace the A's, who were moving to Oakland under their controversial owner, Charlie Finley. Another franchise would be granted to Seattle, though the Pilots would last only one season before moving to Milwaukee and becoming the Brewers.

Baseball was finally at the point of being forced to adopt changes in its traditional league arrangements. The American League was divided for the first time into two divisions, East and West, with six teams in each. While a traditionalist, Calvin was also proving himself enough of an opportunist to accept the nearly unanimous feeling that an added level of post-season playoffs would soon represent added financial rewards.

"It was a situation where after expansion we'd have too many losers (in one league)," explains Calvin. "So we decided to have two leagues with two divisions and go from there. It was something new. You had to play with it for a while. But it finally turned out where I thought it was something good. It made a lot of money for a lot of people. After six or seven years it was just like another World Series."

As a senior member of the league Calvin had the advantage of being able to choose which of the American League divisions to enter. "I could have made Milwaukee (Seattle) stay in the Western Division and I would go into the East," he claims. "But I thought it would be better for the Twins to be in the West. We had a better chance of winning. If you win you're gonna make money," he says. "You can play with the big shots and lose. It turned out pretty darn good for us."

Not so pleased however was the Chicago franchise. Geographically deserving to enter the East, because of the White Sox' management's lack of seniority it was forced into the West. "They wanted to go into the East because of the time zone changes and because all the big clubs were there," recalls Calvin, admitting his role in denying the move. "But I wanted them in the West because it was a bigger city and because there was more tradition due to Clark Griffith being the first manager there. We had a helluva argument over it."

Despite Calvin's successful maneuvering and the hiring of Martin, there were no assurances that the West would be won in 1969. An improving Oakland team had edged out the Twins the previous year and many of Minnesota's weaknesses remained, though Calvin moved to fill one obvious hole in the off-season by acquiring shortstop Leo Cardenas from Cincinnati at the cost of promising hurler Jim Merritt.

Pitching concerns weren't lessened by the spring holdouts of both Jim Kaat and Dean Chance, nor by Dave Boswell's freak hand injury. Referring mostly to the contract battles, Calvin called it "the worst spring in my 44 years in baseball," while claiming to have only cut payroll costs by $50,000. "I'm still upset with the players who reported late. They've hurt the chances of the ballclub to get off to a real good start."

A 0-4 start seemed to confirm Calvin's fears for 1969. But Martin's baseball genius as well as the flowering of many of Calvin's acquisitions and farm system products began to show results by May. A new aggressiveness saw the Twins steal 115 bases, including Rod Carew's seven thefts of home during the season.

Sluggers Harmon Killebrew and Tony Oliva regained their powerful form, while Carew topped the league with his .322 average. Reliever Ron Perranoski led the American League with 31 saves, while starters Jim Perry and Dave Boswell both won 20 games. Twins talent was such that Chance's late arrival and subsequent arm injury was barely noticeable. Taking the Western Division lead for good by August, Minnesota held off Oakland to win the division by nine games.

It was a success that was only marred by Martin's pattern of personal incidents that peaked at a Detroit bar the night of August 7 in one of baseball's stranger episodes of managerial-player relations. According to some publicized accounts at the time, Martin settled a fight between Boswell and outfielder Bob Allison with a quick knockout of Boswell.

Immediate repercussions of the 1969 fight were generally limited, as Calvin was stymied by a ballplayers' code of silence in his efforts to investigate the incident. "I was astonished. I couldn't believe what went on and I couldn't really get any information until about five years after it happened. I had a meeting with them and I found out nothing. They were the tightest-lipped people I ever saw. (Later) I found out somebody held up Boswell and let Martin beat on him!"

Others would later confirm that it was something less than a mano-a-mano confrontation settled by two baseball men. Instead, Boswell describes the injuries, for which he was briefly hospitalized, as the results of an all-out brawl that Martin only joined belatedly—on the side of bar patrons against Boswell.

Hardly an innocent himself, the flamboyant Boswell, who sometimes carried a gun with him on road trips, admits he had pursued pitching coach Art Fowler into the alley outside the Lindell A.C. bar to continue a verbal argument. When Allison interceded, a full-fledged fight broke out in which the Twins outfielder was knocked down. "Next thing I know the bar opens up. I was a raging animal. They were hitting bottles over my head. They had ahold of me. There was blood everywhere," recalls Boswell.

"I remember seeing Billy's face," he continues, suggesting he expected assistance from his manager. "(But) Billy got ahold of my chain (around his neck) and pulled my head against a wall and evidently knocked me out. Then he kept punching me and that's where he got all the stitches in his hand. Billy's no wimp, but he couldn't whip me with a ball peen hammer."

Kaat recalls Boswell's condition the next morning as obviously too severe to be solely Martin's doing. "You looked at him and common sense says 'here's a guy 6′ 2′ ′ , 210 pounds. One on one he's not gonna look like that.'"

The scars would continue to mark both men for years, almost like Old West gunfighters. "You wouldn't believe how many people want to try you on account of that," says Boswell, whose public record of fighting would still never equal that of Martin. As New York manager in 1978, Martin would gain more notoriety and be fired following his fight with a marshmallow salesman in a Minnesota bar. Again in 1988, Martin would be dismissed from the Yankees after a mysterious incident in a Dallas nightclub in which he was again accused of sucker-punching a patron.

"I had a guy come up and slap me in front of my wife and family while we're sitting in a shirt and tie restaurant," continues Boswell. " And I took him completely apart. 'Course I took myself apart in the meantime. People have no idea what the repercussions are over that bullshit."

At the time, Calvin had little choice but to reluctantly back up his manager's fine of Boswell, though he made his unhappiness known. "Martin will never get me to agree with him that he had any right to be in the same bar with the players," he told reporters. "Before he was hired to manage the club last fall I warned him about visiting the same places as the players frequented. I also didn't like the idea of Bob Allison being with Martin when all the trouble started. It proved I was right. There wasn't any excuse for the whole thing."

The wheels were perhaps already in motion for Martin's dismissal. "He (Calvin) was sort of sparring around with the veteran players trying to find a reason why maybe to fire Martin," remembers Kaat. "I didn't want to be a part of that, though it was pretty obvious to all of us that Martin was a sharp guy in the dugout but very volatile off the field."

But in 1969 Billy Martin was very much a popular hero as the Twins swept on toward the first-ever American League playoffs and a matchup with Eastern Division-winning Baltimore. It was to be a short, though dramatic, series. The powerful Orioles, who won 109 games that year, took two one-run games at Baltimore before crushing the Twins 11-2 in the last game, played at Minnesota.

"We were snakebit. We had some balls really hit, but right at people. I'll never forget Blair's bunt," Calvin grimly recollects Baltimore outfielder Paul Blair's 12th inning suicide squeeze bunt that gave the Orioles a 4-3 win. "It was a miracle. With two strikes it coulda gone foul. He just made a perfect bunt, a 100-1 shot."

It was a painful setback. But most Minnesota fans seemed ready to accept their disappointment and hopefully wait 'til the next season, especially after seeing Baltimore meet their own fate in a dramatic World Series loss to the 1969 Miracle Mets.

Yet Calvin, who had expressed his displeasure with Martin's decision to start journeyman Bob Miller instead of veteran Jim Kaat in the playoff's final game, was less resigned. The manager's card-playing and record-playing on the charter flight home after the Baltimore losses had reportedly also irritated the Twins owner. Sidestepping a reporter's question immediately after the playoffs about Martin's rehiring, Calvin was clearly unhappy.

The clash of personalities had really begun even before the end of spring training, with Martin calling a press conference to protest the decision of the Griffith organization to send to the minors a couple of young prospects, including future St. Paul sportswriter Charley Walters, who had looked good in camp. "Just who was running the show anyway?" Billy asked rhetorically.

Some have since suggested that the real answer wasn't either Martin or Calvin. "(Howard) Fox used to try to run the ballclub," charges Clark Griffith II, describing clashes with not only Martin but also with Sam Mele and later, Gene Mauch. "He used to try to tell every manager how to run his team and he'd preface it by saying, 'Well, I've talked to the boss and this is how he wants it done.' And, of course, Fox had never talked to Calvin."

Fox vehemently denies ever having spoken for the Twins owner, but agrees that he often offered Calvin advice on team matters. "As a traveling secretary you see the players every game. He used to ask my opinion. I think Calvin had a lot of confidence in me."

How strong Fox's influence was in undercutting Martin is subject to debate. "If I'd have listened to Fox, Martin never would have been hired this year," Calvin would say to reporters.

But Calvin was clearly growing less comfortable with his mercurial manager's impact on an otherwise stable organization. "I feel like I'm sitting on a keg of dynamite. It's just that Martin is, so, well, unpredictable," he said in mid-season, even before the Boswell incident.

Calvin was clearly looking to reassert his authority at the season's conclusion when he told reporters on October 9 that he planned several meetings with Martin before renewing the manager's contract. "There were some problems on the team all year," he explained. "Martin is the boss on the field. But I'm the boss off the field. There still are a lot of questions to be answered about the entire organization. We've got to sit down and talk some more."

But with popular sentiment and sportswriters behind him, Billy would not be an easy man to reach an understanding with. Almost flaunting his power, the Twins manager cited out-of-town commitments, including a fishing trip, to delay the discussion several days.

Calvin would himself be less than tolerant in their first scheduled meeting. "I told him to come into my office at 11 o'clock to talk about next year. He shows up at 10 o'clock and I said, 'Billy, I'm not ready to talk to you. Look at all this stuff, pros and cons, these reports. I had a credenza full of stuff."

Angry at the disruption of his normal contract negotiation process and at Martin's reportedly already-underway job search, Calvin broke off the meeting after only 25 minutes. "I heard he was in Seattle. I understand he went to see Marvin Milks (Pilots general manger) and asked him to let him manage the ballclub there next year," maintains Calvin. "What's all this here stuff? These are the things that I had to get straightened out in my mind before I rehired him. So I said, 'Go ahead and go fishing and I'll see you when I come back from the World Series.'"

But that later meeting would never come about, as Calvin tells it, because of Martin's continued pressure tactics—using a Minneapolis sportswriter. "So I go to the World Series and that night I get a telephone call from (Sid) Hartman, and he says, 'Billy Martin says he doesn't have a job.' And I said, 'If Billy feels that way, then he doesn't have a job.' That's how it all happened," insists Calvin. "Sid Hartman fired him. Or Billy fired himself."

Others recall a meeting the next morning of major Twins officials in Calvin's hotel suite that resulted in near-unanimous support for the move. Even several members of the Griffith family with close personal contacts to Martin reportedly accepted the decision, while the manager's critics downplayed the impact of his loss. "I don't think Calvin realized the charisma that guy (Martin) still had outside the people in that room," says Twins media director Tom Mee, suggesting the Twins owner was being deliberately shielded.

Clark Griffith II is more direct in placing blame. "I think the crowning blow was Martin's (1966) fight with Fox," he says, though noting that several Twins players had also let their unhappiness with Martin be known to Calvin. "I think it was more the senior players who had come out of the Mele era, more macho and less into the Martin cult of heroes," says Clark.

Billy Martin was gone, regardless of who his enemies were, beginning a pattern of hirings and firings that would follow him to Detroit, Texas, and New York—five times at last count. "I always thought he'd be a good manager," says Calvin with an obvious sadness. "He had a great year on the field for us. But off the field he had a bad year."

It was the Griffith organization, however, which would be at the center of a firestorm of controversy after its October 14 announcement that the popular Martin would not be returning. Seemingly not since MacArthur's sacking by Truman was so much popular sentiment expressed for a fired employee. Bumper stickers calling to "Bring Billy Back" appeared all over the state. Planes trailing banners buzzed University of Minnesota football games. A country and western song glorifying Martin's career was written and regularly played on airwaves across Minnesota.

"Billy had a hold on this area like you wouldn't believe," remembers Mee with awe. "I've never seen anything, except maybe Kennedy's assassination, that compared to the gut feeling of despair all around me. It was like Calvin dropped an A-bomb on the community."

The Twins owner apparently thought that most fans would understand his position. "I think the people of Minnesota are smart enough to know that business is business and policy is policy," Calvin told reporters at the time. "What did Henry Ford just do? He had a great year. Still he fired Ted Knudsen, his chief executive, because he did things contrary to policy."

Calvin's emphasis on the former manager's inability to accept working guidelines and procedures proved a less-than-successful public relations strategy however. "I think the lesson was that you can't dismiss a popular and successful manager for vague reasons," says Clark Griffith II. "You have to be very specific about why."

Even Calvin's media-conscious son doesn't yet totally understand the vehemence of attacks directed against the Twins organization, however. "It was a strange thing," says Clark. "Martin went on to Detroit and won a pennant and got fired. The press in Detroit had an agreement among themselves that they would not destroy a franchise over one person. No such thing in Minneapolis and St. Paul. It continued for years. Billy Martin was hired and fired in Texas. But that was never really discussed the way it was up here. I never really understood that."

Most Minnesota fans either didn't get the message through a media clearly sympathetic to Martin, or perhaps by the late 1960s they had rejected Calvin's traditional message of a hierarchy that extended from the dugout to the owner's box. In an era of rebellion, Martin may have represented baseball's version of a rebel without a cause.

"Billy represented the blue-collar guy who wanted to tell the boss to 'kiss my ass,'" says Billy Robertson now. "And it wasn't just the blue-collar guy. Billy had a charisma that affected everyone. In my opinion it was the worst thing that ever happened to us. We'd probably still be running the ballclub if that hadn't happened. I wouldn't doubt it cost us millions of fans over five years."

Martin's firing was to haunt Calvin and the Griffith organization for years. "I never realized he (Martin) was so popular," Calvin now admits, with his own peculiar explanation. "I found out later that when he was working for Schmidt Brewery (during off-seasons and coaching years in early 1960s) every place he went he'd set people up for a beer. That's gonna make you popular."

The reasons for Martin's popularity were no doubt more significant than that, and so was the public relations damage done by his firing. Symbolically, it was perhaps the beginning of a downward spiral from which the Griffith organization never escaped.

THE BEGINNING OF THE END

"We just gave away baseball to the people that played the game
but have no responsibility of paying the debts.
We (owners) have to worry about the debts if it ain't making a go."

It was a long off-season for the Griffith organization. On top of the continuing public relations fallout from the Billy Martin firing, personal tragedy would soon strike in the form of a somewhat mysterious auto accident that took the life of Sherrod Robertson. Despite recently complaining of ill health, Robertson had decided to go pheasant hunting in South Dakota, where he was fatally injured when his car went into a ditch.

"You never expected anything like it," says Calvin of his reaction to the death of his popular younger brother. "I remember talking to him in Baltimore and I said, 'Sherry, why don't you go home and have an (doctor's) exam before you go hunting.' If he had done it they might have found something and he might still be alive."

Sherry Robertson's death followed on the heels of Joe Haynes' heart attack in 1969 and left a void that would be greatly noticed in the Griffith family and organization. Tom Mee recalls that the farm director was also sort of an informal social activities leader. "Sherry was the party guy of the ballclub. Life was one long party for Sherry," he says. "And yet he worked all day, he was a good farm director. We had a good farm system and he pushed a lot of good players onto this ballclub over the years.

"But as soon as five o'clock came, the gin game started in the office, the bottle was taken out of the drawer, and four or five guys were playing a tourney every night," continues Mee. "But everybody was included. With Sherry nobody was excluded. They'd go out and tie one on somewhere. He was just a great guy."

Sherry and Joe Haynes' losses were also felt in Twins operations, Billy Robertson remembers. "They had good judgement. Calvin worked more closely with them than anyone else. Jimmy (Robertson) had concessions and I had stadium operations, so he depended on them."

Clark Griffith II suggests the deaths of Sherry Robertson and Joe Haynes shifted the whole direction of the franchise. "Those were the people who could really talk baseball with Calvin and he would listen to," he notes. "But everything changed and the internal competition really began (after their deaths)."

In particular, Calvin relied more heavily on the advice of new farm director George Brophy and especially traveling secretary Howard Fox, say insiders. "I heard advice, yes," Calvin bristles. "Sometimes I took it, sometimes I didn't. I did what I thought was best for the organization 'cause I was the one who took the heat."

Yet Fox would seemingly be at Calvin's side in every situation, including sitting with his boss at all home games, driving to work together, and even briefly sharing the same roof after Calvin's 1973 separation from his wife, and offering his input on organizational decisions. The bespectacled Fox increasingly became Calvin's eyes and ears on the world. Whether friendship or manipulation, it was a relationship that most family, and other observers, came to see as central to the organization.

"Over the years there was some jealousies. Sometimes members of the family thought I was too close to Calvin. I sensed it," agrees Fox, who denies ever having any designs on leadership of the Twins organization, "as long as it belonged to the Griffiths."

Fox admits that he gradually increased his duties in the Griffith organization far beyond those of a normal traveling secretary. "We didn't have a lot of employees and the jobs had to be done," he argues. "So I guess you could say that I did a lot of things other than what the traveling secretary's duties were. Calvin was busy doing a lot of jobs and I was very close to Calvin. He confided in me."

Calvin later grudgingly recognized how adept Fox had become at assuming responsibilities. "I think he was an eager beaver, yes. He wanted to enhance himself. He wanted to do more. He wanted to stop traveling. It was one of those things."

One of the first organizational needs in 1970 was to stem the hemorrhaging from Martin's firing. After pausing long enough to give a reporter one of his most memorable if unfortunate quotes, "I can't tell you exactly what I intend to do, but I can tell you one thing, it won't be anything rational," Calvin moved quickly to find a managerial replacement for Martin.

The goal was to find someone who could offer the same type of popular attraction as well as on-the-field managing ability. It was a hopeless task.

But Calvin nevertheless came up with Bill Rigney, a survivor of nine years in southern California where he led the generally talent-poor expansion Angels to several high finishes in the standings. More importantly, his personality and reputation seemingly fit the Twins needs.

"Rigney was supposed to be popular. That's the reason why he got the job," explains Calvin, who also had overcome Rigney's initial doubts. "He had a good team too (in Minnesota). I told him, 'Bill, don't worry about it. You're gonna win with ease.'"

Calvin would make several off-season trades designed to ensure his prediction, but which would only add fuel to the flames of criticisms already being fanned against him. In particular, a trade to Cleveland that sent outfielder Ted Uhlaender, Dean Chance, reliever Bob Miller, and rookie Graig Nettles in exchange for veteran pitchers Stan Williams and Luis Tiant would draw criticism from fans and some sportswriters like Sid Hartman, who attacked the deal as a "Brinks robbery."

In fact, Uhlaender, Chance, and Miller soon disappeared from the major leagues while Williams went on to finish 10-1 with 15 saves and a 1.99 ERA for the Twins in 1970. Yet the loss of future All-Star Nettles, and the later waiving of Tiant (who would recover completely from what looked to be a career-ending injury) created the images carried away by many Twins watchers.

"We had a chance to give them (Cleveland) Jim (Nettles) or Graig Nettles," admits Calvin. "My scouting department said to keep Jim because Graig couldn't run. And it was told to me by two managers, I think it was Martin and Rigney, that Nettles wouldn't ever be a defensive player."

Regardless, Minnesota would not need Nettles or Tiant in 1970, although El Tiante would win seven games early in the year before breaking his right arm. The club's quick start carried them through most of May, and by June 1 they had taken a hold on first place that they would never relinquish—despite Rod Carew's knee injury and late-season threats from Oakland and California.

With hitting paced by Oliva's .325 average and Harmon Killebrew's MVP numbers of 41 homers and 113 RBI, and pitching paced by Cy Young winner Jim Perry, 20-12, 3.03 ERA, and Ron Perranoski's club record 34 saves, Minnesota would actually top its 1969 mark, finishing at 98-74.

But still there was somehow a sense of disinterest or distrust among many Minnesota fans and media, who had not yet forgiven the firing of Martin. Despite the Twins continued successes, there was still a sense of looking back to a lost romance. Indeed, Billy's rehiring by Detroit dominated Twin Cities newspaper headlines on October 3, even as Minnesota hosted Baltimore in the playoffs opener.

The results of the three-game affair did little to reverse the trend, as the Twins were quickly wiped out by a combined score of 27-10, including the final game loss suffered by a 19-year-old rookie pitcher named Bert Blyleven. "Unfortunately every time we faced the Orioles they'd be in the middle of a 12, 15 game winning streak or something like that," remembers Calvin. "And I don't know what happened to us."

What had happened, though few could have realized it then, was that the sun had set on the glory years of the Twins under Calvin Griffith. Despite generally competitive teams, not until 1984 would Minnesota again finish as high as second.

But Calvin remained outwardly optimistic despite the disappointing 1970 playoffs. "If I was a betting man, I'd bet on the Twins again next year even if we don't make any changes in our team," he told reporters immediately after. Unable or unwilling to admit the team's growing age and pitching problems, he certainly did not foresee a collapse to fifth place in 1971.

Financially, the two quick playoff losses were certainly an immediately recognizable disappointment, with the Twins losing an estimated $4 million in playoff and World Series ticket purchases and concessions. It was a capital loss that might well have sustained the organization in coming leaner times.

A harbinger of the changes that would soon be dominating baseball was that fall's brief umpire strike, the first in the history of the major leagues. "It was a disgrace to humanity," says Calvin with disgust, remembering the use of poorly trained replacement umpires in the national pastime. "But to me, some of those scabs were better than some of them umpiring in the summertime," he adds, explaining his ultimate support for management's position. "With unions you can't fire them."

Calvin's opposition to unions' growing role in baseball would soon get even fuller venting. Yet he insists he is not against organized labor, noting his uncle's own leadership role in early ballplayer associations. "Unions when they first started out were great," he agrees. "They helped the working man, no doubt about it. But then they just got too political and into too much."

That vaguely defined perception was undoubtedly substantiated in Calvin's mind by another, and much more serious threat to baseball management than the umpire's strike. Curt Flood's shocking challenge to the reserve clause, launched in January, 1970 when he refused to accept a trade to the Washington Senators, was proceeding through the federal judicial system with implications for many more than just the St. Louis Cardinal star.

"It was a big thing for the owners," agrees Calvin, recalling ownership's frenzied discussions of the case's potentially destructive effect on the contractual system holding their players in place. "We were worried about it," he says understatedly.

Temporary relief for baseball management came in late 1971 when first a U.S. District Court and then the Supreme Court finally ruled against Flood. But the precedent for challenge to the reserve clause was there and its unchallenged hold would never again be assumed. Ultimately the Flood decision would be a Pyrrhic victory for baseball management and their system of control over players' contracts.

"The verdict was a good thing to hear," recalls Calvin, with evident perplexity. "But what did it mean? I don't know. What good did it do?"

While Flood, ironically, was left asking the same questions, baseball's shift in balance went on inevitably. Another dramatic sign of change came in the spring of 1972 as major league baseball experienced its first extended players' strike. For thirteen days the Major League Players' Association, led by Marvin Miller, held out for greater health and pension benefits.

From his position as a member of management's Player Relations Committee, Calvin was one of the strongest voices of hardline opposition to any concessions. "Let 'em strike," he told reporters. "The players haven't got a dime invested and they want all the profits . . . . The Twins have made enough money over eleven seasons in Minnesota to be able to stand a strike for two years."

Yet owners as a group were certainly not as ready for an extended strike as Calvin was. Settling for contributions of an additional $1 million to pension and benefit plans, management purchased peace at a relatively low price, even if in doing so it had to admit the union's existence as a full-fledged power.

Calvin would bitterly remember this first example, in his mind, of baseball's appeasement to the players' union. "You can't win at anything without competing," he complained years later. "They told me 'No, don't battle anymore, you're never gonna win. You might as well go with the other group!' But I never did vote for anything. I had my own principles about it."

Calvin's uncompromising opposition to union demands could, in retrospect, arguably have netted better results for management—at least in the short-term. Taking advantage of the prevailing atmosphere of concession, the Players' Association in 1973 negotiated several changes in the reserve system that would have lasting impacts. Most important was the addition of salary arbitration, a measure that Calvin claims few owners recognized at the time as a major issue.

"A lot of 'em said, 'Hell, it's not gonna cost you more than $20-25,000 a ballplayer. And what did happen? $750,000 at one trip," Calvin disgustedly recalls an early arbitration decision giving that award to Chicago Cubs relief pitcher Bruce Sutter. "That's what the owners never could visualize—that it would be so extreme. That really rocked baseball."

Ownership's apparent discussion of backup tactics in the face of arbitration, and later free agency, was based on faulty legal counsel, says Calvin. "We were told that if the arbitrator did rule that there was collusion, the most we would be fined would be $25,000. Now it might cost millions of dollars," he says, referring to 1988 rulings that baseball management had indeed attempted to limit players' market values by ulterior means.

Only a few voices of opposition, including his own, Charlie Finley, and labor consultant Dick Meyer, predicted arbitration's dramatic effects. "We had some meetings that shook the rafters, no question about it," Calvin says, especially remembering then owner of the Texas Rangers, Bob Short's outspoken arguments at a meeting in Montreal.

"He really shook the room," remembers Calvin. "And every word he (Short) said has come true. We just gave away baseball to the people that played the game but have no responsibility of paying the debts. We (owners) have to worry about the debts if it ain't making a go."

In fact, it was short-term financial distress that caused owners to reluctantly accept arbitration, concludes Calvin. "Baseball knew better than to accept arbitration, but they couldn't afford a strike," he adds. "There were four or five ballclubs that owed banks so much that the only way they could get their money from banks was to have an agreement with the ballplayers to play ballgames. Otherwise the banks were gonna call the loans in. The other owners felt sorry for 'em. I didn't go along. I voted against 'em."

Ironically, in early 1974 Calvin would be the first victim of arbitration, as pitcher Dick Woodson gained a $20,000 pay raise. Though he later denied the quote, a reporter wrote that Calvin responded to the decision by promising to make the money back in a trade of the offending player. "I'm an ornery son of a gun," he allegedly said. Woodson was traded within a few months.

Calvin would never accept arbitration, although later moderating his position to accept the idea of a panel of former players and management jointly moderating salary disputes. But the imposition of an "outside" arbitrator to rule on baseball issues was symbolically, as well as literally, a threat to his world. Along with other changes that would soon follow on its heels, free agentry and player agents, it would begin to change his personal outlook on the future.

"We had felt we could still exist. We felt we could be in there," he says referring to the Twins success both on the field and at the box office, drawing over a million fans a year through 1970. "But then arbitration and free agency started coming and people started getting a pretty good idea what was going to happen to them in baseball."

A beginning pattern of decline in attendance couldn't have helped Calvin's outlook. The team's collapse in 1971 was witnessed by only 940,984, the first time less than a million Minnesotans had come to Metropolitan Stadium. 1972's quick start after the strike, and the Twins eventual third place finish, might have been expected to increase turnout. But attendance fell even further to 797,901.

Looking back years later, Calvin could philosophically maintain that the attendance decline was predictable. "When we moved from Washington out here we figured we'd have a honeymoon for the first ten years. After the tenth year you'd better have good ballclubs or else you're not gonna make it. That's what we anticipated and that's what happened."

There must have been a growing sense of urgency however as Calvin also watched the Twins decline on the diamond. Though publicly sticking with Rigney's managing through the disastrous 1971 season and into a mediocre start of 1972, Calvin's patience was nevertheless growing thin.

By July he was telling reporters, "I've never said that the manager is sure of his job. A manager's job is in jeopardy all of the time . . . . When we are losing and not drawing, I'd say that everybody on the ballclub, including the manager is in trouble."

Calvin's doubts about Rigney seemed centered on his handling of the pitching staff, although the Twins owner would admit that injuries to key players such as Jim Perry, Tony Oliva, Jim Kaat, Ron Perranoski, and others were clearly tying Rigney's hands. His manager was largely caught in the middle of the owner's more general frustration at the team. "If I have any criticism of Rigney it would be his inability to get along with the players," said Calvin. "But I guess even I have trouble communicating with the players nowadays."

Nevertheless, Calvin was ready for a change by July 6, when he called both Rigney and young coach Frank Quilici into his office. "He told me he wanted me to manage and I thought he meant at Denver, like with Billy (Martin)," remembers Quilici. "But Calvin meant with the big club. Rigney was right there saying it was a good idea. He was a real professional."

Calvin was also remarkably diplomatic in explaining his decision to reporters. "A lot of things had been running through my mind the last couple of weeks. And last night I didn't sleep very well," he said. "On the way to work this morning I made up my mind. The thought about last year went through my mind and I didn't want another 1971. Frank gave us a spark in 1965 (as a player) and I think Frank can give us that spark again. I think he can give baseball back to our fans."

Calvin was clearly hoping that as the major's youngest manager, the 33-year-old Quilici could offer an image of energy and enthusiasm not unlike that which had left with Martin. It was a move many have thought to be purely a public relations gesture, especially in light of Calvin's oft-stated opposition to managers learning their profession in the majors.

But Calvin found other arguments for the move, again referring back to Bucky Harris' managing at a similar age of the Washington Senators to the 1924 World Championship. "Maybe he (Quilici) can perform the same sort of miracle with the Twins," said Calvin to reporters. "I know that he will have better communication with the players. I think that our game will be more interesting for the fans to watch."

A less important precedent that he could also point to in jest was Quilici's ethnic heritage. "Our Italian managers have all been popular in this area," said Calvin. "First

Cookie Lavagetto, then Sam Mele and Martin. Now Quilici. There isn't any doubt in my mind that Quilici can do it."

Minnesota did battle back to finish third in 1972, a position it was to hold for the next three years under Quilici. His management and personality would at least help stabilize the Twins. Though never a true contender, the club would always be respectable, an increasingly difficult accomplishment in the face of the Griffith organization struggle against baseball's changes.

1973's introduction of the designated hitter was one innovation that met with Calvin's approval, however. "Charlie Finley was vehement that he wanted both the designated hitter and the designated runner," remembers Calvin. "I was on the Rules Committee at the time and I told him 'Finley, make up your mind which you want and I'll vote for it. But you're not gonna get both.' I said, 'I would prefer the DH because people get more thrills out of a home run than a stolen base.' So he said, 'I'll go for the hitter then,' and we went into the Rules Committee and League meetings and we passed it."

Calvin's generally traditionalist background might make his support for the designated hitter seem curious. But Minnesota also just happened to be searching for a place to employ the continued hitting skills of Tony Oliva, now virtually hobbled by leg injuries. "He was the type of player we wanted to keep around," says Calvin. "Course nobody ever thought the DH's would be costing five or six hundred thousand dollars (annual salaries). We thought they'd be players on their last legs looking for seventy-five or a hundred thousand."

Other innovations of the era met with less support from Calvin, although he says he was always open to ideas, including those being regularly brought forward by Finley. "He stimulated things," says Calvin with a laugh. "It wasn't always thought of too much. But we brought them into the Rules Committee."

Quickly discarded though was Finley's idea for using orange baseballs. "He didn't know that way back when night baseball got big (in World War II) the Bureau of Standards tried all these balls—red ball, white, orange. But they found the white ball was the best of all," recalls Calvin. "Clark Griffith had all kinds of balls that were demonstrated in his locker. Course Charlie didn't know about these things. But he started a lot of conversation, did a lot of good."

Nevertheless in 1972 Calvin would firmly back Commissioner Bowie Kuhn's intervention in Finley's stalemated negotiations with star pitcher Vida Blue. "Anytime you offer a ballplayer money you've gotta stick with it," he says referring to Finley's attempt to withdraw an increase to Blue. "When you offer something you've gotta stick with it."

Calvin's relationship to the controversial Finley would always be a curious one, reflecting an appreciation of his innovative spirit while rejecting his lack of historical perspective on the game. "I was like an advisor to him," he would say of his efforts to dissuade Finley from his 1976 attempts to sell off key members of the Oakland A's. Kuhn would again intercede, voiding the sales and eventually winning the resulting lawsuits.

"If the sonofabitch had paid attention to me, he wouldn't have got in all this trouble. I told him, 'Charlie, you can't sell all these ballplayers. Make sure you get something for 'em. You can't put money on the mound," says Calvin, who in 1974 would turn down a reported offer of $1 million from the Kansas City Royals for pitcher Bert Blyleven.

Calvin's own economic philosophies would draw increasing criticism however, even as the franchise's troubles at the gate continued. Only 2,000 season tickets were sold going into 1973 and though attendance would eventually "improve" to 907,499, Twins players found that always difficult contract talks were going to be particularly torturous that spring.

The battles were also increasingly public, as both sides took their arguments to the media. "Calvin Griffith is so cheap he throws nickels around like they're manhole covers," quipped Jim Kaat.

"I didn't see any of the players return any of the 35 to 48 percent raises when they had bad years," answered Calvin to reporters, explaining reported cuts to stars including Rod Carew, Jim Perry, Blyleven, and Kaat. "I'm not going to let these guys put me out of business. I've made fair offers to all of them. That's going to be it."

Even beloved Harmon Killebrew was not exempt. "He took a cut this time because we lost money last year," explained Calvin. "But if Harmon has a good year and the club draws well at the gate, he can earn nearly as much as he did in 1972."

An injury-plagued Killebrew would not regain either his lost salary or heroic form in 1973. But with other younger, relatively low-paid stars such as Bobby Darwin, Jim Holt, Larry Hisle, Bill Campbell, and Steve Braun, the Twins would remain competitive through most of the season. On the fourth of July, over 45,000 fans came out to watch bonus baby Eddie Bane (on whom the Twins did spend $55,000) drop a 5-4 game to the front-running Kansas City Royals.

By mid-August, the club was slipping back however, and the decline seemed to be led by Kaat. At almost 35 years old, his pitching days appeared to be numbered. Thus, in another roster move that would earn him the everlasting enmity of many fans, Calvin would let the popular Kaat go to the White Sox for the waiver price of $25,000.

"Quilici was gonna put Jim Kaat in the bullpen," explains Calvin. "I said, 'No you're not. If you put him in the bullpen there's gonna be a revolution. So we let him go and (Chicago and former Twins pitching coach) Johnny Sain got him to pitch inside and made a new man of Jim Kaat."

Unfortunately, while Kaat would rebound to win 21 games for the White Sox in 1974, the Twins would quickly fall out of contention in a division dominated by the World Champion Oakland A's. Only 662,401 fans would come out to Metropolitan Stadium despite the team's strong second half and a final record of 82-80 that slightly improved on the previous two years.

With losses as high as $500,000 and reported purchase offers from several potential buyers, including Minneapolis' Bob Short, Calvin was clearly facing a number of questions in the off-season. One of the most difficult was that of Killebrew, whose playing value had faded to that of a part-time designated hitter platooned with Tony Oliva. By season's end it was clear that Calvin wanted a different arrangement.

But on January 15, 1974 news broke that Killebrew had asked for, and received, his release to join the Kansas City Royals. "We've been dickering for a month," Calvin told reporters. "But I was surprised when Harmon asked for his release in our telephone conversation today. I'm sorry to see him go because it ends an association dating back to 1954 in Washington . . . . I thought I was more than fair with him."

Little appreciated in the storm of criticism that followed was Calvin's offer to Killebrew of either a minor league managing spot at Tacoma or a player-coach position with the Twins at a salary reduction to $50,000. "I begged Harmon not to go to Kansas City," maintains Calvin. "I told him 'You know you're not getting around on the ball and you're a hero. Don't dilute it!' But he needed the money and that was it."

Killebrew's decision to reject the managing position particularly upset Calvin, whose emotions were clearly evident as he told reporters that he couldn't guarantee there would ever be another spot for Killebrew in the organization. "It has been my policy that once a player leaves us, he's gone from the organization unless we want him back."

Years later, the head of the Griffith family organization would still talk of how he had envisioned Killebrew following a course like Billy Martin, from minor league to major league manager. "He woulda become manager of the Twins," maintains Calvin. "If he'd have gone out there and learned a few things I woulda made him manager of the Twins at some time. He knew that. He meant a whole lot to our organization, no doubt about it. He was number one in Minnesota."

That was a title Calvin knew by 1975 that he could no longer claim for his Twins team, especially as the football Vikings grew in popularity. Moreover, Calvin's own personal place in the sun had long since disappeared, with the clouds of popular disapproval growing steadily darker. For many he had become a negative symbol whose public relations short-falls were reinforced by his grim-faced, overweight photographic image of the period.

Though he denies any connection, Calvin's isolation from Minnesota fans would seemingly be mirrored by his growing estrangement from his wife, Natalie. Their differing social lives and outlooks had become increasingly obvious, with Calvin sharing little of his wife's interest in plays or literature.

"I like to look at magazines, read a few stories, read the captions," said Calvin to a *Sports Illustrated* reporter in 1974. "I don't like to socialize too much. You run into people who are not athletic-minded. They're bookworms or symphony patrons, and that's all they want to talk about. I don't mind a musical once in a while, but none of these damn dramas for me."

Calvin remembers often going straight from the ballpark to the lake in the back of their Wayzata home where his fishing line would serve as his companion and diversion. "Every day I used to go out there," he remembers. "I had a nice comfortable chair. I'd go out from the ballpark and the only thing I'd do is change shoes."

By the end of 1974 he'd be changing homes however, moving to a small apartment nearer Metropolitan Stadium and leaving the beloved lakefront house to Natalie. They would never formally divorce, partly from fears that a settlement might affect ownership of the Twins.

"Your personal life you have to keep separate from your work," Calvin still stoically says. "My life really was making bread and butter for the family. It was passed from my uncle who gave me the opportunity and I tried to think more of them than myself . . . . And you can't let things worry you 'til you can't sleep. I always slept good. I still sleep good."

Chapter 13

TOUGH TIMES GET TOUGHER

"From now on, baseball owners are going to have to be associated
with other businesses so they won't have to depend on sports
to feed their kids. Or they are going to have men who were born wealthy,
who have zillions of dollars and are just looking for a team to buy
so they can have something to do with time and money.
But how many guys with zillions are there?"

The Twins improvement in the latter stages of 1974 had given some reason for hope entering the 1975 season, though few Minnesotans appeared to have noticed or, at least, responded by turning out at Metropolitan Stadium. Harmon Killebrew's departure to Kansas City didn't brighten the picture, as many fans, rightly or wrongly, blamed the Twins ownership for losing their local hero.

Calvin's own outlook seemed torn between optimism and despair. "I think our baseball future is great," he told reporters in spring training. "We have more good kids in our minor leagues than ever before. We have a young club here with great potential. But fans are the most important part of baseball. And for the Twins to exist we have to draw better than one million (fans)."

Despite success in four arbitration cases where the Twins were now being represented by his son Clark Griffith, official losses of $462,728 in 1974 confirmed Calvin's long-term financial concerns. The family's dependence on the ballclub was both real and fragile. Yet Calvin's pessimistic public statements elicited less sympathy than speculation about the team's future in Minnesota.

Rumors of sales or moves to cities such as Seattle or Denver began to pop up in media columns despite Calvin's repeated denials. "Our family has made its life in Minnesota," he said in early 1975. "We love it here. If we did move it would be as a last resort."

Not unlike Washington in the late 1950s the additional factor of a new stadium, in this case a domed version, was also being thrown into discussion. Also not unlike Washington, Calvin was giving enough public support to the idea to allow advocates, such as local sportswriter Sid Hartman, to describe him as a supporter. "If we can get a decent place to play we'll be here forever . . . . A domed stadium is the answer," he was quoted as saying by Hartman in April, 1975.

Curiously, years later Calvin and others would describe his original reactions to a dome as more ambivalent or even negative. "I didn't give it too much thought to tell you the truth," remembers Calvin. "The only dome then was in Houston. (Judge Roy) Hoffheinz was a brilliant person to come up with that idea. But when they started talking to me I was not too much for it."

"Calvin was against it, day one against it," agrees Tom Mee, whose recollection is confirmed by Clark Griffith, Howard Fox, Billy Robertson, and others.

Regardless, as the dome issue became bogged down in local politics, Calvin's thoughts turned to the Twins more immediate future. The team completed a fairly successful spring training with Quilici and others dropping hints of a run for the Western Division title. Met Stadium fences were moved in by 15-20 feet in all fields to add excitement, and to help offset the Twins uncharacteristic lack of power.

For those paying attention, Calvin had offered an ominous warning to his manager earlier that year regarding Minnesota's now-departed long-ball legend. "I hope Frank Quilici has his pitching staff pitch Harmon Killebrew right so he doesn't embarrass me and hit some big home runs against the Twins," said Calvin. "I wish Harmon good luck against everybody else."

The Twins pitching staff would often struggle that year, though not against Killebrew. Once again moving slowly out of the chute, Minnesota struggled to 6-10 with five rainouts before shutting down Killebrew and the Royals 4-1 on May 2. Only 2,946 fans came out to see their departed hero's jersey officially retired.

Attendance and the Twins play would pick up in June, as rookie hurler Jim Hughes' hot start would briefly lead them into the heat of the race. But injuries took their toll, including those to Larry Hisle, Lyman Bostock, Bert Blyleven, and Danny Thompson, who was now diagnosed and being treated for leukemia at the Mayo Clinic.

The previous season Calvin had reportedly expressed his bafflement at Thompson's slumping play. "I can't understand what's wrong with him. There must be something on his mind besides baseball."

Calvin clearly had something on his mind as the Twins fell from the race by mid-August. By September rumors were starting to fly about a change in managers. "I've had good rapport with Quilici," he cryptically suggested to reporters late in the season. "But now I'm starting to wonder if he was listening."

The popular Quilici's fate was actually sealed before the 1975 season's final day when the Twins lost in extra innings to finish fourth. Meeting in Calvin's office before the game, Quilici was both fired and hired—as a new Twins radio announcer, fulfilling an arrangement that had been discussed the previous year. "I said 'Calvin, how about that radio deal,'" remembers Quilici. "And he said he'd talk to them (WCCO radio) about it."

Quilici now sounds as if he almost welcomed the change after his three-and-a-half years of frustration in attempting to win with limited talent and other resources. Like every other former Twins manager available for comment, he still praises his former boss's honesty and personal support, if not his financial support.

"Calvin could read people pretty well. And Calvin Griffith did more things than people will ever find out about. He was very open in terms of personal things and I could always tell him things even if he didn't want to hear them," remembers Quilici. "But as for baseball, the economics just weren't there. We just weren't drawing, and he had to do something."

Calvin describes the change as more than economic, though making clear his obvious respect for Quilici. "He was a leader, he was a leader," says Calvin in retrospect. "He'd have been a helluva good manager if he coulda just gotten over one thing. He had to forget that he was a player. A manager can't be associated with the players like he did. A manager has to be in the management part of the ballclub. He could not become a member of the management team."

Calvin's search for a new manager had already begun in fact, with brother-in-law Joe Cronin's nomination of Gene Mauch, the veteran National League skipper. Local writers pushed for Killebrew after he was released by Kansas City, but Calvin made it clear that was not an option he was considering. "I will never again hire a man who doesn't have any experience as a manager," he declared.

The Twins president was willing to renege on another vow however, as he showed in signing Mauch to a three-year pact. "Gene Mauch had the reputation of a good manager," remembers Calvin. "We were going through a period where we had a lot of uncertainties. He had a lot of experience. He knew the area (as former manager of the minor-league Minneapolis Millers) and was well liked by the press."

Negotiations with Mauch would delay his signing until after Thanksgiving, when Calvin would somewhat sarcastically introduce him at a Twin Cities press conference. "It's great to have you, Gene. I'm confident the media people will bear with you—at least until May."

Calvin's own love-hate relationship with the media didn't change during the holiday season. Rumors of a franchise move to Seattle again appeared in local newspapers with Calvin denying any validity, despite making a personal trip to Seattle. "I don't know where these silly stories start, I haven't talked to anybody from Seattle," he said in late 1975, just before renegotiating a Met Stadium lease.

But Clark Griffith II remembers more interest, with the support of some American League officials, from other members of the family who met with Seattle representatives. "Bruce (Haynes) and Billy (Robertson) were hot to trot on Seattle. This is about the time Seattle was suing the A.L. (for the Pilots departure to Milwaukee) and the Kingdome was sitting open," he remembers.

"We had a royal battle, a knockdown, drag-out," continues Clark. "Then I pulled out two maps showing the regions and pointed out that with all the bodies of water in Seattle, the population base was much bigger in Minnesota."

Curiously, Calvin gives credit to Clark Griffith Sr. for the decision against Seattle. "I remembered 'Unc' saying never to put your ballclub near the coast 'cause people can't live on water."

Regardless, both Griffiths now agree, more promising at one time was the possibility of a sale to former Texas Ranger owner and Griffith ally, Bob Short. "I used to go down there and talk to him at the Leamington. He wanted to buy the team and have me run it for him. We would have thought about it, yes," says Calvin, though Short's interest cooled as he began plans for his unsuccessful 1978 run for the U.S. Senate, and shortly after became engaged in a losing battle against cancer.

Calvin's own battles over the winter would include a new adversary, with ace pitcher Bert Blyleven asking for a trade and suggesting that the ballplayers should be paid more instead of having so many Griffiths on the organization payroll. "I have to have a front office, don't I?" answered Calvin. "My family is more important to me than Blyleven is."

Years later, Blyleven would recall mentioning his own pending fatherhood to Calvin during negotiations and getting a very disinterested answer. "He said, 'Well I didn't tell you to get married or have a kid,'" recalls Blyleven. "All the stories you heard about Calvin Griffith were probably true. He was a very tight individual as it came to salaries. But he ran an organization for Calvin Griffith and his family."

Adding to the drama of the Calvin-Blyleven verbal duel was the arbitration ruling announced shortly thereafter in favor of the requests of California's Andy Messersmith and Baltimore's Dave McNally to break their reserve clause chains. The two pitchers thus had gained the right to negotiate with the teams of their choosing, and brought forth the age of free agency.

"Nobody welcomed it," remembers Calvin of owners' reactions to the ruling. "Or if they did, they were damn fools and kept to themselves."

Almost prophetically, Calvin told reporters after the decision that the business of baseball would be forever changed. "From now on, baseball owners are going to have to be associated with other businesses so they won't have to depend on sports to feed their kids," he said. "Or they are going to have men who were born wealthy, who have zillions of dollars and are just looking for a team to buy so they can have something to do with time and money. But how many guys with zillions are there?"

Certainly Calvin was not one of them, despite the Twins "success" in holding their 1975 losses to only $150,000 by increasing ticket prices and cutting out their winter baseball school that year, short-term survival took precedence over new investments, and especially any participation in the free agent market. Along with two other teams, Calvin declared that the Twins would not claim any free agents for three years under the new collective bargaining agreement with the players' association.

With wealthier owners such as George Steinbrenner and Gene Autrey quickly taking advantage of the situation, it was a position even Calvin couldn't continue to publicly hold forever. "We claimed some ballplayers later but it was a damn farce," he admits. "I think we had to do it or really get ridiculed. I had no intention of really signing any of 'em. But for public relations I had to do it."

Public relations would not soon grow better however as a perception of mediocrity, or worse, began to surround the Twins. Despite Mauch's aggressive management, they found themselves off to another slow start in 1976 that included a home opener loss memorable mostly for embarrassing operational problems that saw much of the crowd of over 20,000 either inexplicably delayed at entering Metropolitan Stadium or experiencing an equally mysterious shortage of hot dogs and beer when they made it inside.

Bad timing and press continued to follow the organization, as a dramatic second-half rally that pulled the Twins to a third-place finish and their best record since 1970 (85-76) went largely overlooked. Only 715,394 fans came through the turnstiles all year, despite strong years from Rod Carew, Larry Hisle, Lyman Bostock, rookie catcher Butch Wynegar, and reliever Bill Campbell that kept Minnesota within five games of division-winning Kansas City.

"We still had a farm system," remembers Calvin proudly, noting the team's average annual outlay of $2-3 million, still among major league highs. "We had capable scouts. We had one of the better scouting forces in baseball. (Scouting director, George) Brophy knew every prospect in the country. He wasn't a great computer man, but he always brought us players."

But the Griffith organization's strong points increasingly were overshadowed by controversy, such as the continued early season clashes between Calvin and Blyleven. The contract dispute had continued from spring training with increasing bitterness that at least partly stemmed from Blyleven's introduction of an agent, Dick Moss, in negotiations.

It was another change in baseball with which Calvin would have little patience. "We talked about everything in the world and I finally said, 'What exactly do you want?' recalls Calvin. "You have to be patient. But we were going round and round till I can find out what's what."

By June, the frustration level had grown so great that Calvin was willing to let Blyleven arrange his own trade to any interested major league team. "It was unusual to me. I said find out who wants you," says Calvin, with an explanation that many former Twins might find incredulous. "You have to try to satisfy your player. You can't have an unhappy ballplayer. I don't think deep down in their hearts that I ever had an unhappy ballplayer. There was lots of discussion, but not real unhappy."

It was clearly an unhappy Blyleven who made an obscene gesture to a Minnesota crowd, after being booed on June 1. His trade to Texas, along with unhappy shortstop Danny Thompson, was announced the next day.

"We made a good deal," says Calvin, who received shortstop Roy Smalley, third baseman Mike Cubbage, and pitcher Bill Singer along with $250,000 from the Rangers. "We got some good years out of those guys. And the money was something extra."

By the end of 1976 Calvin was facing a problem that was not so easily resolved, however. Relief ace Bill Campbell, who led the team in both wins, 17, and saves 20, was going free agent after having been turned down on his request for an $8,000 raise to a total of $30,000 at the beginning of the season. "That was the only mistake I made," admitted Calvin later. "I should have given him an extra $2,000."

Now Campbell was the center of a bidding war that Calvin was not about to even enter. When the reliever eventually signed a million dollar contract with the Red Sox, the Twins owner was genuinely dumfounded. "This is the weirdest thing that ever happened to baseball," he said angrily. "You try and keep an even keel and build your club for the future and then this comes along."

While Campbell's disappointing record after that season would vindicate Calvin to some degree, it was the type of dilemma that would be repeatedly played out in coming years.

Even in their most exciting, competitive years, there was an undertone of public skepticism in the face of the Twins continued inability to cope with free agency and players' salary inflation. Fighting a guerrilla war against increasingly stiff odds, Calvin was also losing the battle for the hearts and minds of Minnesotans.

Trying to counteract the trend, Clark Griffith would initiate a number of public relations moves including the hiring of an advertising agency, Martin-Williams, to promote the Twins players, and particularly Calvin, as personalities. It was a concept of marketing that the Griffith organization, remarkably, had never before attempted.

"We decided we had to get Calvin on the air smiling and looking happy. Everybody always saw him frowning or grimacing," recalls Clark. "We also had the thought in the back of our minds that writers and other broadcasters can also be seduced by this. If it's really well done, you can get not only the public, but the media to go along."

One television spot featuring the Twins owner's pleased reaction to catcher Butch Wynegar's assertion that he would play baseball for free became a local classic. "That was a pretty good ad," even Calvin admits with a chuckle. "I've still got a couple of those T-shirts (engraved)—'I Really Like That Kid.'"

Yet despite Clark's claims that the $650,000 ad campaign was beginning to have results, Calvin would balk at the price tag after one year. "Clark wanted to spend like a half million (dollars) a year on marketing and the way I was brought up was that the public would come free if you had a winning ballclub," explains Calvin.

"He (Clark) was an excellent person on his job with the baseball commissioner. He got his ideas on selling baseball there," continues Calvin of his growing disagreements with his son. "But baseball's a different world. Our box scores, our write-ups in the paper, that's all the publicity we needed to let people know we were playing."

Clark took the rebuff both personally and philosophically. "It just wasn't his deal and it flew in the face of everything he understood," says Clark. "I couldn't disagree with his central thesis that winning brings people in. But I also thought that advertising would broaden our base to draw from. You have to be positioned properly."

An argument could have been made for either the father or son's approach in 1977 when the Twins both rebounded at the gate and had their best opportunity to reach the playoffs since 1970. With Carew, now moved to first base and having the best year of his career, and young stars such as Lyman Bostock, Larry Hisle, and pitchers Dave Goltz and Tom Johnson reaching their peak, Minnesota streaked to the top of the A.L. West by the beginning of June.

Minnesota kept up its challenge to Kansas City, while Carew flirted with a .400 batting average throughout the season. With fans beginning to come back to Metropolitan Stadium, the Twins 73-59 record allowed them to stay within three games until September 1.

Always looming in the background, however, was the dark cloud of free agency. Fruitless negotiations with the unsigned Hisle, Bostock, and relief pitcher Tom Burgmeier, who along with Johnson was just making fans forget Campbell, dominated headlines as often as Twins victories. Public allegations and combative descriptions from both sides competed with a pennant race for attention.

Also not helping was a front-page *Minneapolis Tribune* article of September 25 suggesting that the Twins were ready to give up their top players despite a cash reserve boosted to $3 million by the successful season. Only deep in the body of the article was it acknowledged that team reserves had already fallen nearly $1 million since 1971, and that one-time-only shares of new franchise fees from Toronto and Seattle had temporarily boosted organizational finances.

Whether appropriate or not, Calvin's chronic financial insecurities were not eased by 1977's relative success at the turnstile (1,162,727) and in profits (over $868,000). "We didn't feel that secure," he remembers. "We were just going year by year. We had money in the till. But when you lose $900,000 (actually $700,000 in 1980) in one year that hurts. We lost three out of five years and finally got down to where we couldn't declare a dividend. We were seeing the handwriting."

Negotiations continued however, with both Hisle and Bostock acknowledging that the Twins made very substantial contract offers of at least $2 million apiece. At various times it seemed, tentatively, that there might be agreements worked out before the end of the season. Certainly both management and players did not want to damage the Twins morale in the pennant stretch.

Then the bottom fell out on both an overachieving pitching staff and perhaps on the entire Griffith organization. The Twins lineup was unable to pick up the slack as losses in 18 of its last 27 games caused Minnesota to limp home in fourth place. "What the hell happened to us I never will understand," says Calvin. "I thought we were gonna win it in '77. I really thought we were gonna do it."

It was a dramatic collapse that only worsened off-the-field public relations, as Calvin openly gave up on negotiations with free agents Burgmeier and infielder Jerry Terrell. Disparaging remarks about both Hisle and Bostock's late-season contributions did not help the situation. It was increasingly clear that neither would be around for another pennant run with the Twins.

Hisle was always a long shot to return because of his demand for a multi-year contract, rationalizes Calvin now. "I was advised by a doctor that if I signed Hisle to sign him for one year. We had him going to a clinic. He (the doctor) was right because he (Hisle) went to Milwaukee and he played for one year. But he never really did after that. But we couldn't talk about those things then."

Twins physician Dr. Leonard Michienzi confirms that he had warned Calvin of Hisle's physical condition (leg and shoulder problems). "I definitely advised him not to sign Hisle beyond one year. And we were right. We saved Calvin four years of payments."

Calvin says, however, that he always thought he might resign Bostock, "I offered him more money than California," he claims. "'Cause Bostock was a ballplayer that could win games for you. But his agent (Abdul Jalil) wouldn't tell him because he was mad at Brophy over some kind of a fight they had and the goddamn agent never told him about our offer. I saw Bostock after that and he said the agent never said a word. It was a real shame, just like what happened to him."

Bostock's tragic death in a freak shooting accident the next summer and Hisle's career-shortening shoulder problems after a year would, for some, give a macabre merit to arguments against signing free agents. For whatever reasons, few of the Twins departed free agents would make significant contributions elsewhere. But even Calvin realized the Griffith organization had also suffered, as it increasingly appeared to many Minnesota fans that their team would not be able or willing to keep its top players.

"You don't tell the fan that you're not keeping this free agent so you can give the money to your brother," says Clark Griffith, who wanted to keep both Hisle and Bostock regardless of cost or health, but who was again on the losing side of the family debate. "The fan doesn't care about your brother. That's absurd."

For a time it seemed the Twins might not even keep their manager. Gene Mauch was also reportedly negotiating with other teams, notably California, looking for greener pastures. But Calvin refused to let the veteran manager out of his contract, swallowing his pride to a degree. "We had a lot of things shaking down," he recalls. "We couldn't start out with somebody new."

Decimated and demoralized, the Twins would muddle through 1978. Even before the season began, the team's remaining star, Rod Carew, would express anger at Calvin's handling of his contract negotiations, alleging that the Twins owner had rudely treated his agent, Ron Simon. Once play began Carew still sparked a surprisingly potent offense with his seventh batting title, and support from Smalley, Danny Ford, Cubbage and others. But with the pitching staff still struggling, the team quickly fell out of serious contention. The Twins eventual fourth place finish, 19 games back (73-89), while not a total collapse, attracted only 787,878 paying customers.

Even the signing of free agent and ace reliever Mike Marshall to a $1.35 million contract in mid-season couldn't convince many fans that the Twins organization had anything but the most cynical motives. 1978 appeared to be the nadir of the Twins existence.

"It was a bad year," agrees Calvin philosophically. "But we survived. In sports you have good years and you have bad years. When you have bad years you just have to keep rolling and make the best of it. You have ups and downs all the time. In Washington we were down practically all the time, but we still survived."

That philosophy would carry the Griffith family on well beyond the expectations of most sports observers and possibly even themselves. Underneath their clear level of concern ran a vein of optimism, sometimes even naivete, that their understanding of baseball would yet carry the day. Resisting change he disliked, or at least ignoring it, Calvin was both blessed and cursed by his sense of history.

"Baseball became a fast moving world and he really couldn't move fast," argues Clark Griffith, who again saw his influence stymied when Calvin chose to largely disregard an executive committee which in its first activities came up with such innovative ideas as a "Dear Calvin" newspaper column that included letters calling the Twins owner a "fool" and an "old-fashioned idiot."

Clark obviously agreed that his father was too old-fashioned. "Calvin had come to believe that Uncle had told him everything he needed to know about economics," he notes. "And unfortunately, early in the free agent game we got beat where we shouldn't have gotten beat."

Calvin was not about to apologize for remembering the lessons of Clark Griffith Sr. "If my Uncle Clark knew how much money I've been willing to pay these players, he would kick me square in the ass," he told St. Paul columnist Pat Reusse, arguing the continued relevance of his financial ideas. "Some people say that multi-million dollar business has to borrow money. But the way I figure it is if you borrow money, you have to pay it back. And I would rather be collecting interest than paying it."

The Twins owner insisted that baseball would eventually be forced to come back to his position. "Baseball people better come to their senses," warned Calvin, delivering a typical lecture. "A lot of these teams are owned by corporations and those corporations are going to raise hell with the teams for spending so much money. I'm staying in. We might be called something else in the future, but we'll still be in business, and I think the public is on my side."

Public reaction would be quite different however, as Billy Robertson describes. "We thought, 'Who'd want to come out and see ballplayers making a million dollars?' Now you pay them two million and the more you pay them the bigger the attraction they are. It's worked just the opposite."

Even as baseball players were increasingly recognized as entertainers, Minnesota fans were proving increasingly less willing to sympathize with the Griffith family troubles. Calvin's fears that the public would be alienated by the modern players' increased mobility and salaries proved largely unfounded. Ironically, it may have been his philosophical determination to hold the line for the game that eventually helped drive him from it.

Clark Griffith, Montana rancher around 1911

Griffith family

Composite picture of Calvin Griffith, age 9, 1920 (Chattanooga Times)

Calvin Griffith in his youthful days as mascot with the Senators (Chattanooga Times)

Calvin Griffith, mascot of the Washington team

Undefeated Staunton basketball squad

Calvin with the Chattanooga Lookouts

Looking over the local situation from Engel field with "Uncle Clark." (Chattanooga Times)

Calvin Griffith (Chattanooga Times)

Calvin handling the secretarial duties for the Chattanooga Lookouts (Chattanooga Times)

Clark Griffith on the occasion of his thirthieth election as President of the Washington baseball team. With him are Calvin, Vice President (center) and John J. Jachym, part owner (right), January 3, 1950.
(AP/WideWorld Photos)

Calvin Grifith with President and Mrs. Truman, opening day at Griffith Park in early 1950.
(Courtesy Minnesota Twins, Don Wingfield, Photographer)

Farm director Ossie Bluege (left), Calvin Griffith (center), and Bucky Harris (right) discuss the Senators' minor league system in the mid-1950s. (Courtesy Minnesota Twins)

Former President Eisenhower takes a look at a 1956 American League baseball pass presented to him 7 April by Calvin Griffith, president of the Washington team. Griffith holds a handbag for Mrs. Eisenhower. (AP/WideWorld Photo)

Calvin in Washington with Billy Jurges, Charlie Dressen, and Cookie Lavagetto. (Courtesy Minnesota Twins)

Standing beside Senator star Bob Allison, former President Eisenhower throws out the season's opening ball for 1959 while Vice-President Richard Nixon and Calvin look on in the background.

Calvin Griffith in his office at Griffith Stadium, Washington in the late 1950s. (Courtesy Minnesota Twins)

Calvin and son, Clark II (Courtesy of Minnesota Twins, Don Wingfield, Photographer)

Calvin Griffith, owner of the Washington Senators now the Twin Cities team in the American League, waving a cap with the insignia Twin Cities Senators on it. Griffith waved in response to a welcome given him by nearly 1,000 persons at Wold Chamberlain airport. (St. Paul Pioneer Press Dispatch/Spence Hollstadt)

Calvin Griffith with Charles O. Finley (center), President of the Kansas City Athletics, and Del Webb (right), co-owner of the New York Yankees, July 1963. (AP/WideWorld Photo)

Calvin Griffith relaxes with Twins manager Sam Mele in a Finnish steam bath in the club dressing room. The purpose of the steam bath was for post-game relaxation, easing muscle soreness, and weight loss by players and officials. (AP/WideWorld Photo)

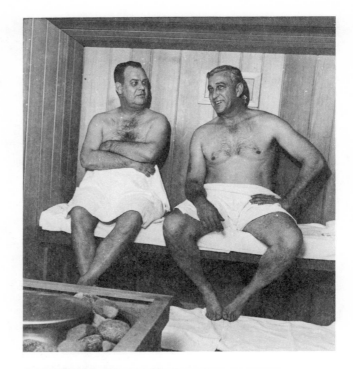

Governor Karl Rolvaag (left), *at a special state-organized fish pond, showed Yogi Berra* (center) *and owner Cal Griffith how to catch Minnesota trout. The pond was set up on the mezzanine of the Radisson hotel, 1965 All-Star Game headquarters. Looking on behind Rolvaag is Joe Reichler, Associated Press baseball writer.* (St. Paul Pioneer Press Dispatch/Buz Magnuson)

Calvin sits in the press box at Metropolitan Stadium watching the Twins on television and awaiting the start of the Minnesota Vikings-Detroit Lions National Football League Game. Griffith was unable to be in Washington to watch the Twins win the American League pennant in 1965 because of a pending lawsuit by a minority stockholder over the transfer of the Twins from Washington. (AP/WideWorld Photo)

Calvin with Jim Kaat. (St. Paul Pioneer Press Dispatch/Buz Magnuson)

Former Vice-President
Hubert Humphrey, with Calvin,
opens the 1968 season
at Metropolitan Stadium.
In the background are
Bob Allison and
Twins manager Cal Ermer.
(Courtesy Minnesota Twins)

Harmon Killebrew with Calvin Griffith
receiving one of his many trophies.
(Courtesy Minnesota Twins)

118

Tom Mee, Rod Carew, and Calvin Griffith enjoy one of Carew's many batting trophies in the late 1960s.
(Courtesy Minnesota Twins)

Jim Perry, Bob Allison, Billy Martin, and Early Wynn try their casting luck at Metropolitan Stadium in the late 1960s. Martin's poorly timed fishing trip may have helped cost him a job as Twins manager in 1969. (Courtesy Minnesota Twins)

Calvin with Ted Williams
(and fish), then manager
of the Washington Senators.
(Minneapolis Star-Tribune/John Croft)

Calvin's 1971 birthday
party is celebrated
by the family and close
friends. (From left)
Howard Fox, Joe Cronin,
Clark Griffith II,
Billy Robertson,
Calvin Griffith,
Phil Howser, Jimmy
Robertson. (Courtesy
Minnesota Twins)

Mike Marshall signs a contract that made him the highest paid player in Twins history while Calvin Griffith looks on. (St. Paul Pioneer Press Dispatch/Sully Doroshow)

Calvin Griffith visits with some of the 80 members of the Waseca Lions Club who attended a Twins-Yankees game in 1979. (AP/WideWorld Photos)

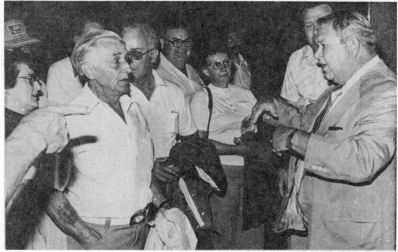

Calvin Griffith thanking the fans for their support after the final game in Met stadium in 1981. (AP/WideWorld Photos)

Calvin surveys the damage done by the collapse of the Metrodome roof in the stadium's opening season, 1982. (St. Paul Pioneer Press Dispatch)

Calvin and Thelma.
(St. Paul Pioneer Press Dispatch)

*Calvin holds back the
tears as Carl Pohlad
takes control of the
Minnesota Twins in a
Metrodome ceremony,
June 23, 1984.*
(St. Paul Pioneer Press
Dispatch/Brian Peterson)

*Calvin fights back tears
after he signed away
Twins ownership to Carl
Pohlad, June 23, 1984.*
(St. Paul Pioneer Press
Dispatch/Brian Peterson)

Calvin laughing. (St. Paul Pioneer
Press Dispatch/Brian Peterson)

Harmon Killebrew. (Courtesy
Minnesota Twins)

Camilo Pascual. (Courtesy
Minnesota Twins)

Jimmie Hall. (Courtesy
Minnesota Twins)

Zoilo Versalles. (Courtesy
Minnesota Twins)

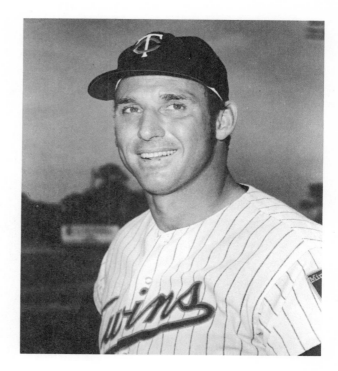

Bob Allison. (Courtesy Minnesota Twins)

Tony Oliva. (Courtesy Minnesota Twins)

127

Jim Kaat. (Courtesy
Minnesota Twins)

Dave Boswell. (Courtesy
Minnesota Twins)

Bert Blyleven. (Courtesy Minnesota Twins)

Graig Nettles. (Courtesy Minnesota Twins)

Rod Carew. (Courtesy
Minnesota Twins)

Butch Wynegar. (Courtesy
Minnesota Twins)

Kent Hrbek. (Courtesy
Minnesota Twins)

Kirby Puckett. (Courtesy
Minnesota Twins)

Gary Gaetti. (Courtesy
Minnesota Twins)

Frank Viola. (Courtesy
Minnesota Twins)

INTO THE LION'S DEN

"It was one of the worst things I ever went through.
I went down there to play golf and go to a dinner. But they got a writer there
that had to be sensational and intimated things I didn't say.
I was shocked as hell. If I had a gun I woulda shot the sonofabitch."

On the map, Waseca, Minnesota is a small dot representing a community of just over 8000. But to Calvin Griffith it meant perhaps the darkest moment of his life, and certainly a damaging continuation of the public relations problems that plagued the Twins owner throughout the decade of the 1960s. To an outside observer it at least demonstrates how starkly different interpretations can be made of the same incident.

It was in Waseca on September 28, 1978 that a small Lions Club group heard Calvin Griffith reportedly address a number of controversial subjects including, but not limited to: the American League's disgrace by the presence of hometown hero and former Twins player Jerry Terrell, the negative effect of Butch Wynegar's recent marriage and bedroom activities on his baseball success, Rod Carew's status as a "damn fool" for having signed a contract for only $170,000, and a comparison of the racial populations in Washington D.C. and Minnesota.

Yet to Calvin the speech remains a baffling example of how misunderstood he has been by the media and many members of the public. Indeed, Calvin would alternately call the entire *Minneapolis Tribune* article either a "frame-up" or just the product of a few drinks and what he expected would be an off-the-record speaking engagement. When a reporter who happened to be in the audience published his remarks, Calvin seemed genuinely astounded. "I was misinterpreted . . . . I almost cried when I read the story," he said immediately afterward.

Years later he still appears genuinely upset at the portrayal and public reaction to *Minneapolis Star & Tribune* reporter Nick Coleman's description of the event, published three days later on October 1, 1978. "It was one of the worst things I ever went through. I went down there to play golf and go to a dinner. But they got a writer there that had to be sensational and intimated things I didn't say. I was shocked as hell. If I had a gun I woulda shot the sonofabitch. I woulda shot Coleman. But you can't do that or you go to jail."

Although he charged that the newspaper had run the article as a means of bolstering sagging circulation, Calvin is hardly a knowledgeable analyst of media marketing or of professional journalistic standards. Yet his arguments of a frame-up would likely have been even more vehement had he known Coleman had neither a tape recorder nor pen and paper with him when he came to the Waseca Lions Club with his father-in-law.

Coleman, now a columnist with the *St. Paul Pioneer Press,* recalls that he was so astounded by Calvin's comments that he began taking mental notes. "After the first couple of comments I just realized I'm gonna have to start salting some of these away because I'd never heard anybody talk like this," says Coleman, who as a Twins fan maintains that he was personally distressed to be forced into a reporter's role at the event.

"I was really disappointed in what he was saying. It was just incredibly vulgar, insulting, denigrating commentary on anything and everything that came up," says Coleman. "I was thinking to myself as I shrunk lower and lower in my seat, 'Just shut up Calvin, please shut up. Don't say anything more. Because if you say anything more, I'm gonna have to tell somebody about this.'"

Coleman made the decision to write the story that evening even though he was approached afterwards by the publisher of a local paper who indicated that the speech was being considered "off the record" by them. "As soon as I got back to the farm, I sat down and wrote down all the quotes," Coleman says. "There were a couple I wasn't quite sure of and I canned them. Everything I was really sure of, that I was fairly confident of, I wrote down . . . . If you're a reporter, you're trained to hear things. Those quotes were pretty easy to remember."

Calvin continues to blame Coleman, however. "So that was it. He ruined my reputation as a man. Certainly it hurt. I still have a lot of episodes and people say things. I'm over it. I know what I said and I didn't say anything bad. But peoples' minds are funny and you don't know if people ever get over it."

Nothing was probably more damaging to his reputation than Griffith's alleged description of his decision to move the franchise to Minnesota when he realized that there were only 15,000 blacks in the state. "Black people don't go to ballgames, but they'll fill up a 'rassling ring and put up such a chant it'll scare you to death. It's unbelievable. We came here because you've got good, hardworking, white people here," he said, according to the *Tribune* article.

"The words were misunderstood, taken out of context," Calvin would claim in newspaper accounts afterward. "I had had a couple of drinks and was trying to be funny."

That account would be supported by the president of the Waseca Lions Club and others at the dinner, who suggested Griffith's words were only said in jest and without malice. "It didn't come out that way in the program," Ken Lenz said. "I wasn't offended and don't know anyone who was . . . . I think Calvin is getting a bad rap out of it. Our community is just reeling. But I'm sticking to my guns—that the story in the *Tribune* was one hundred percent distorted all the way. He (Coleman) didn't write it all."

Coleman would argue that Waseca residents were just embarrassed and angry that the privacy of the Lions Club had been violated. "I felt bad for the community because Waseca was acutely embarrassed for some time," he maintains. "People were sucking breath in the room. He may have thought he was joking, but the people in that room that night did not react like it was humorous."

But Lions Club members who would come to a Twins game at the Metrodome nearly a year later sounded anything but embarrassed. "Everybody knows how to spell Waseca thanks to the *Tribune,*" said the vice-president of the Chamber of Commerce.

"Calvin Griffith is one of the ten greatest Americans of our time," added another Waseca resident. "He is for us."

For whatever reason, Lions Club members were publicly standing behind Calvin's version of the Waseca incident. "It was a real good laughing affair," said another. "Ninety-five percent of us weren't bothered at all."

Certainly there was immediate and negative public reaction elsewhere in Minnesota to the newspaper account, however. A Bloomington state representative called for a full investigation of Griffith by Major League baseball and suggested the Twins might no longer be welcome in Minnesota. The local chapter of the Urban League suggested that the Griffith family and the Twins might be more at home under apartheid in Johannesburg, South Africa.

Calvin's immediate explanations did not lend great credence to his case. Caught by a reporter while on a fishing trip immediately after the story was published, he stumbled. "I thought everything was off the record. I don't even know who the hell Nick Coleman is. I thought he was a state representative or something," Calvin said, mistakenly referring to Coleman's father, then Minnesota Senate majority leader.

"Look, I'm no bigot," Griffith would later tell another reporter. "When we sign a prospect, I don't ask what color he is. I only ask 'Can he run? Hit? Throw?' After this season, I'm going to ask one more question. 'Can he field?' We made so many errors this season . . . ah, never mind."

Calvin's famous candor, despite an often painful inability to fully express his thoughts, is hard to ignore in this and many other cases. "I guess I'm too honest," he said shortly after Waseca. "I was brought up to tell the truth and told that it wouldn't get you into trouble. But it's caused me a lot of headaches. From now on, I'd better start thinking up some lies."

Twins media relations director Tom Mee notes that all attempts to write Calvin's speeches had only worsened matters, however. "He couldn't pronounce a lot of the words. Not that Calvin was dumb, but he just wasn't good with words. Malaprops, I think you'd call it. When you got to know him, you knew that he wasn't dumb—that he really knew this game of baseball. But he didn't have that knack for public speaking."

That night in Waseca, argues Mee, Calvin's speaking foibles were unfortunately mixed with an unfamiliar reporter. "Had anybody been there who'd been around Calvin a little, they would have thought nothing of it 'cause they would have realized Calvin does not use the language like you or I do," says Mee. "Regular reporters would have known it didn't mean anything. Calvin talked that way about a lot of things."

Coleman, who had brief encounters with Calvin during coverage of a handful of domed stadium related events, describes as condescending the idea that the Twins owner needed to be treated differently by the media. "One of the things that shocked me the most in the aftermath was the reaction of some of the sportswriters and columnists, particularly Sid (Hartman). The reaction was, 'Oh yeah, Calvin always talks like that,'" describes Coleman. "The sportswriters all knew this or recognized these attitudes or quotes. They'd say, 'Oh yeah, that's Calvin.' But apparently they were too close to him or felt the situation was wrong to write about it."

Remarkably, a Chicago reporter had written a similar account some 20 years before when he had accidentally, he maintained, found that he was able to overhear a private Major League owners' meeting through listening at a hotel floor vent. Bill Furlong's account in the *Chicago Daily News* had quoted Calvin Griffith as feeling out the possibility of moving his franchise to the Twin Cities because, "The trend in Washington is getting to be all colored."

Minnesota Twins racial attitudes would be called into question, briefly, in 1964 when it was revealed that blacks and whites were being housed separately during spring training in Florida. Calvin refused to apologize for the segregation, arguing, "There are six so-called integrated hotels in Orlando. But they are nothing we would stop at. We are not going to a third- or fourth-rate hotel just to accommodate the civil rights people. If we are going to integrate, let's go first class."

It was an approach that Tony Oliva insists was shared by the team's blacks, who preferred the food and atmosphere of the tiny Statler Hotel to that of the whites' Cherry Plaza. "He put us in the best place available. In Orlando, we stayed in this nice little motel. Then after the World Series (1965) they (Sheraton) want everyone. We weren't too happy to go over there."

Longtime Griffith family employee and handyman Charlie Daniels remembers it was a personal loan from Calvin Griffith that got him his first house in Minneapolis in 1962 when local banks refused to lend to a black man. "Calvin is just a guy who says a lot of things before he thinks," says Daniels.

Thelma Haynes suggests another interpretation of the Waseca speech. "He (Calvin) was trying to be sarcastic. When the people did come to Washington to try and prevail on us to come to Minnesota, they did use the fact that there were not many colored people in Minnesota as one of their selling points. They thought that was a good selling point. They just said there's mostly white people out there, only ten percent colored people."

Calvin doesn't rely on that explanation, however, though agreeing that the low number of blacks in Minnesota was mentioned to him. "But the only thing I said about blacks (at Waseca) was that they didn't go to ballgames. I read it in the paper. And they're still saying it. You read articles all the time. Is that radical, er . . . racist?"

Clark Griffith says that he used to suggest that he was to blame for his father's Waseca errors by having attempted to explain demographics and baseball attendance to Calvin. "Nobody believed me," he says, adding that he was only half-serious. "I think he just got caught. He'd been drinking a little bit and he forgot he was in Waseca in 1978 and not Chattanooga, Tennessee in 1938," he concludes.

"But I really don't think he's (Calvin) racist," adds Clark. "He has some views that are not racial but just his concept of how the world is. Calvin's not dangerous. It takes too much. He doesn't have it in him to hate 25 million people."

Calvin denies that his reported Waseca description of blacks turning out in great numbers for non-baseball events at Washington's Griffith Stadium was racist. "All I did was talk about the noise at wrestling matches," he protests. "I said it was like if you go to an Indian pow-wow they're all over there humming like mmmmm (making sound) . . . . I said that's the way black people were at wrestling matches. They'd be making that noise. Now is that racist?

"They used to have black and white matches and they'd root like hell for the blacks. But I didn't say nothing like that. I didn't say nothing like that."

That Calvin is not consciously racist in his attitudes is unquestionable. "I'm not a racist. If I were a racist I'd say so. I know what it is . . . . A lot of these Northern bluebloods maybe went to college with them (blacks). But a lot of people don't go to college or experience them in real life."

Calvin points with pride to the Griffith family's long association with blacks in Washington, where Clark Griffith had created a special Griffith Stadium bleacher section called "the pavilion" for low-income fans. "We even had a black rooter down there —'Greaseball'. He'd get those people stirred up," remembers Calvin. "The ministers asked him (Clark Griffith) to do it. They didn't have much money, those people."

Rentals of Griffith Stadium to black groups continued even after Clark Griffith's death. "How could I talk about blacks when our ballpark had 350,000 of 'em every year and I practically knew half of them," Calvin says. "They've been good to us. They were our bread-and-butter in Washington. The Homestead Grays (Negro League) brought in money all summer—14 games or so. You're not gonna knock anybody that kept you alive."

All of the family would be obviously defensive about their racial attitudes for years after Waseca. "I had more colored friends in Washington than anybody," said Jimmy Robertson in 1986. "We used to have a lot of fun together. If they were good guys, they were good guys . . . . I used to have all colored vendors in Washington. (But) I fired three or four of 'em because some guy was booing cause a colored guy (player) had popped up and they were all excited. I told 'em if they paid their money they could boo anybody, me, you. I don't care whether they're black, white, yellow, purple, long as they come in the ballpark."

Explanations and protestations did not satisfy many Twins players and fans however. Baseball commissioner Bowie Kuhn publicly rebuked his former Griffith Stadium boss. Twin Cities newspapers called for Calvin to sell the team. Carew would soon demand a trade saying, "The days of Kunta Kinte are over," and "I refuse to be a slave on his plantation and play for a bigot."

Calvin the cheapskate was now in many minds also cast as Calvin the racist. It was an image that contrasts greatly with his own self-image.

"Hell, I went to school with black people in Montreal, Canada and I didn't even know what they were, who they were outside of they were human," protests Calvin. "They talked just like we did. I used to talk with 'em, play with 'em just like anybody else.

137

"In Washington I played ball with them in the backyard. I went into their stores and bought sandwiches, milkshakes from them and every other damn thing."

In contrast with most descriptions of a Washington, D.C., that was still largely Southern and segregationist at the time of his youth, Calvin recalls childhood games with mixed race, neighborhood kids in the Griffith Stadium parking lot. "We used to pick up a game with the blacks and the whites and we just had fun. The funny thing about it was nobody knew, nobody even talked about it, somebody being of the opposite color."

Washington sportswriter Shirley Povich is mixed in his assessment of the Griffith family's racial attitudes. "They had a Southern strain," he says. "I don't think that he was sincerely prejudiced though, nor was Mr. (Clark) Griffith who was a holdout against blacks in the Major Leagues."

Early in the century, the Griffith organization was one of baseball's early pioneers in interracial relations. In 1911, Clark Griffith was among the first to scout Cuban players, signing Rafael Almeida and Armando Marsans for Cincinnati. While not an overt attempt to break the color barrier, Griffith's multi-racial Cubans still represented a risk. American blacks had been known to pose as Cubans in an attempt to slip into the Major Leagues. "You had to have 'em mixed up. You got a Cuban and you got a Castillian, they were white—true Spanish. There's no question that some of the ballplayers Mr. Griffith signed had black blood," remembers Calvin. "But nobody said anything about it. Nobody said nothing about it. So why bring up questions about something that nobody asked about."

Clark Griffith's motives certainly were not all altruistic. "They were good ball-players," points out Calvin. "They could play and they were eager to play because $400 or $500 a month was like a million dollars to them. That's where Mr. Griffith got in with those Cubans way back in those days."

The Griffith organization's success with that strategy lasted until well into the 1960s. But some historians and critics have suggested that Clark Griffith was less progressive in breaking the color barrier with native American blacks despite meeting with Negro League stars such as Josh Gibson and Buck Leonard. "The door has always been open to those boys if they were good enough to make it into the big leagues," he is reported to have said in 1948.

In Calvin's version of baseball history, it is Branch Rickey who is the villain for having preempted more serious change however. "Back in those days there was a Negro League and that Negro League could play ball," he remembers. "And they were becoming as good as the majority of the clubs in the Major Leagues. What they were hoping to do, the owners of that league, was to get so good that they could challenge the white boys."

"There were two brothers that owned the (Homestead) Grays. And they were talking to Mr. Griffith about one of these days they wanted to challenge the Major Leagues for the championship. And that's the only reason Mr. Griffith didn't sign some of 'em," argues Calvin. "But Branch Rickey went out and broke it all up by signing Jackie Robinson. If he hadn't signed Jackie Robinson there could have been in the years to come, a challenge of the black to the white."

It could be argued that Clark Griffith's defense of the Negro League structure was also a convenient means of keeping another tenant in Griffith Stadium. But Calvin disputes that argument as well as any suggestion of plotting by American League owners to delay integration in the years before Jackie Robinson. "I don't remember much talk about it," he says. "It just never came up."

Interestingly, Calvin also rejects the obvious excuse that Washington was too much a Southern city to have pioneered interracial baseball. "Washington at the time was around 89 percent black, so it would have been advantageous to you. I'll tell you how good it was. Satchel Paige used to come to Washington, oh, three times a year, four times a year to pitch against the Homestead Grays. He'd fill up Griffith Stadium, 28,000 a game. I never missed one!"

There seems little but genuine admiration for the Negro Leagues in the voice of the man who would later be derided by many as one of baseball's biggest racists. "Boy I'll tell you what a tough schedule and life they had," says Calvin. "They traveled around in automobiles, sleeping in cars. They couldn't eat in a restaurant on the road. They had to go around to the kitchen and even then the goddamn people might not even serve them."

Calvin even struck up something of a friendship with Homestead Grays catcher, and future Hall of Famer, Josh Gibson. "Gibson was so good if he was in the major leagues they would have to say that we was the best catcher that ever caught," says Calvin. "That's how good he was. He could sit on his ass and throw the ball to second base better than anybody standing up. But I'm not gonna tell you why he died, I'll tell you that!"

Officially, Gibson died of a brain hemorrhage in January 1947.

As a former catcher himself, Calvin's appreciation for Gibson's skills at what is generally regarded as one of baseball's most demanding positions is not inconsequential. Indeed, many critics have forgotten that the Twins later had one of the first black catchers in major league baseball. Earl Battey became an All-Star signal caller for the Twins at a time when most black players were still being relegated to non-leadership positions.

But the stigma of racism that the Waseca speech brought to the forefront grew as critics pointed out the relatively low numbers of black personnel in the Griffith organization. Trades of several outspoken blacks for whites, including those of Ken Landreaux and Gary Ward, would further fuel the controversy.

Though coming a year after the sale of the team, Reggie Jackson's 1985 attack on the Twins for their lack of black faces was the most publicized of several similar criticisms.

Calvin's reply was that any lack of black players was purely coincidental. "I never thought it was gonna be a big issue. If you could play ball we would sign you, that's the way I look at it. Why count? I don't count 'em. When I go down to the ballgame I don't know whether they're black or white. From where you sit you can't tell the difference lots of times, you know."

Explanations for a lack of black players could include the shortage of minorities in the Twins traditional scouting areas. Longtime scouting director George Brophy was himself a native Minnesotan, while other Senator-Twins front-office personnel had obvious Midwestern or rural roots.

It is difficult to say whether it was racism or just the Griffith organization's lack of turnover and reluctance to change that resulted in a pattern not all that different from major league baseball norms. But as Twins executive vice-president Andy MacPhail would note in announcing scouting changes in 1987, "There just aren't a lot of black players in Minnesota, the Dakotas and some places in the South where we've concentrated a lot of time before."

That strategy may have already been slowly changing even before the team's sale to Pohlad, if the scouting and signing in 1982 of a Chicago inner-city black named Kirby Puckett was any indication. Late 1970s American black players such as Larry Hisle, Danny Ford, Lyman Bostock, Hosken Powell, Tom Hall, Darrell Jackson, Danny Goodwin, Dave Edwards, and Ron Jackson were arguments that the Twins had at least temporarily improved their racial quotas.

"We didn't care what color they were," Calvin again protests. "We had five or six blacks on the team at times. We had scouts and the farm director out trying to find the best players available. If he's black, he's black. If he's white, he's white. I never asked questions of Brophy whether he was black or not. I never thought of that."

Clark Griffith also denies that racism ever affected on-the-field decisions, but affirms that the stigma of Waseca never left Calvin. "The two most damaging things that happened to him were (Billy) Martin and Waseca. Martin did severe damage and Waseca just buried him," he rues. "He ceased being able to function as head of an organization that required public support. He could run a manufacturing organization, a financial services corporation, or something else, but he was gonna have a hard time with anything requiring public acceptance."

While unwilling to accept that analysis or suggestions that he step down as president in favor of Clark or Fox, Calvin was clearly aware as his family business entered the 1980s that it had serious public relations problems. Closing out a 1979 roast in his honor, Calvin was able to find humor in his situation. "I have been advised by my sister (Thelma Haynes) not to stay up here too long because I might say something I shouldn't."

But he wasn't about to back off from his position of almost total innocence at Waseca. "You can talk your way around things you know. But I'll tell ya, I didn't say anything at Waseca that I wouldn't say again.

"The only thing I said wrong at Waseca was about that catcher (Wynegar)," clarifies Calvin, referring to his reported suggestion that, "He was playing hands with his wife during spring training, and instead of running around the outfield he did his running around the bedroom. Now love is love. But it comes pretty cheap for young ballplayers these days and I think they should take advantage of that and wait to get married."

By 1988, Calvin realized such public remarks were of questionable taste. "I knew Wynegar wasn't running around the outfield so I figured he had to be running around somewhere. Some comics would have gotten a helluva laugh out of that. That's all I meant. That is the only bad thing I said at Waseca."

Coleman, of course, begs to differ, though conceding that Calvin has probably changed as a result of the experience. "Based on what I heard in that room there's no doubt in my mind that Calvin Griffith was a racist, sexist troglodyte," he says. "But I think he's probably mellowed a lot since 1978. I think he's probably learned a lot from the uproar that followed that. I think he probably got dragged kicking and screaming into the latter part of the twentieth century.

"It's like Campanis," continues Coleman. "It's not that Al Campanis is a bad guy. Nor do I believe that Calvin Griffith is a bad guy. It's just that his attitudes were from the Dark Ages and he got caught in public saying something incredibly stupid. But I think it is what he believed then."

Questioned about the remarks of Al Campanis several years later, Calvin would have obvious sympathy for the fired Dodger executive. "You can't find a better guy than Al Campanis," he said. "And if anybody worked for blacks it was him. He was black motivated. I don't know what they're complaining about."

Yet Calvin apparently had at least developed some doubts about his powers of self-expression. "You're better off keepin' quiet. Some people hit the jackpot and others don't. So I don't say much about that."

Chapter 15

GONE WITH THE WIND

CALVIN AND BASEBALL'S NEW ERA

"We didn't have all these agents in the old days,
and you were able to sit down with the ballplayers face to face.
When you're face to face you can tell them all the facts."

*I*t is an exaggeration to compare the period after the ending of baseball's reserve clause to that of the South after the Civil War. Landless, former slaves still had little collective force and even less realistic opportunity to individually shop for a higher-paying plantation, let alone better commercial endorsements.

Nevertheless, baseball's reconstruction after the invalidation of the reserve clause would similarly require of its ownership a period of adaptation that still continues. "It was a great shock for everyone. No one (general managers) had been trained in collective bargaining," recalls Clark Griffith. "All but Calvin suddenly found themselves in a spot where they had to spend more of their owner's money. Some of them turned it into a plus."

As in the postbellum South, some owners would be in a better position to eventually reap gains from the change. Even Calvin must have noted that the cash-rich Yankees, led by free agent acquisitions such as Don Gullett, Goose Gossage, and Reggie Jackson, were not only winning their third straight pennant in 1978, but that they were drawing fans while doing so.

"Reggie's (Jackson) a ballplayer anybody would have liked to have had," he admits, reflecting a gradual change in thinking. "I'd like to have had him and I would have paid him because he was a ballplayer that drew people. He and Pete Rose were the two players I would have paid my way in to see play. I said that if the day came where a free agent would be the ballplayer I needed to win, I'd go after him."

Calvin would nevertheless be slow to make that leap into an area fraught with both economic and philosophical danger. Free agency was an actual affront to his values, argue associates. "Calvin thought it was a moral wrong for someone to come along and take the results of his minor league program," says Twins media director Tom Mee. "Calvin had put money into this crop, fertilized it and nurtured it, and now somebody's gonna come along and reap it and take it away from him? To him, it was a moral wrong."

Calvin would spell out his philosophy in 1980 to a local magazine, *Twin Cities*. "You spend money developing these players in your farm system . . . then you make them a star, and bingo, they get their release and become millionaires. The way I look at it, sports owners don't owe an athlete anything. The athlete owes everything to the sport he's participating in."

Calvin's disgust at the collapse of the reserve clause and the coming of arbitration, free agency, long-term contracts, and fringes such as hospitalization, pension funds, termination pay and grievance procedures was expressed in particularly sarcastic form to *Sports Illustrated* in 1983. "Ballplayers used to sit in the dining car and discuss baseball when they traveled by train," he remembered. "Now they get on a jet plane and 80 percent have attache cases and some kind of musical box with earphones on. The money is so easy they don't have to struggle or become students of the game. The talent has become watered down. The players today wear gloves that are like nets—they just look at the ball and it's caught. They were better hitters back in the olden days, too, because they would stay after a game and take batting practice. A player today wouldn't think of staying after."

Yet the old order was gone, and Calvin's rear guard action could not entirely disguise some grudging accommodation. "It was hard for him to see the player's view. He thought they owed him," notes Mee. "But as free agency became a factor over the years, Calvin gradually came to accept it. It still galled him, but he would attempt to make sure they (Twins players) didn't become a free agent after '77 or '78."

At the urging of manager Gene Mauch, Calvin re-signed Mike Marshall in 1979 to a 1.65 million dollar contract over four years. Even then, he gave the controversial screwball pitcher a rather backhanded compliment in telling reporters of his decision. "I check around with the other owners Marshall played for and they told me that I have had worse S.O.B.'s on my club."

Today, Calvin remembers the decision as a mistake. "I didn't like any part of it at all," he says, still reflecting the psychological strain that the issue must have provoked in him. "Mauch and (Howard) Fox talked me into it. They got very close together. He (Marshall) was a great pitcher for one year then went downhill. It was the only time I ever let myself be talked into a long-term contract."

Calvin's adaptability to changes in modern baseball had already faced a more serious test, however, with mixed results. Rod Carew had been waiting for the opportunity to test the market and Calvin's will. With memories of Waseca and his 1977 signing for only $177,000 in mind, it was an almost personal confrontation that Calvin claims he tried to avoid, both publicly and privately. But his attempts were perhaps too little, too late.

"We did our best to make him happy," Calvin says, noting that he voluntarily gave the American League MVP a $100,000 bonus at the end of the season. "That was hard to do and we didn't have to," says Calvin. Carew however, would focus on what he considered Griffith's rude and insulting attitude toward his agent, Jerry Simon, during attempts to renegotiate Carew's contract after 1977. Ill-feeling would be as apparent as the dollar signs when Carew got his opportunity for revenge, two years later.

Calvin denies that any particular clash with Simon occurred, but readily admits that dealing with agents was another change in the game he had great difficulty accepting. "We didn't have all these agents in the old days, and you were able to sit down with the ballplayers face to face," he argues. "When you're face to face you can tell them all the facts. 'Cause the facts are right there in black and white on paper. What you did, how much you helped the ballclub and every other damn thing."

Calvin argues with vehemence that agents' main concern is their own share of player's profits, rather than their client's best interest. "A ballplayer today is a damn fool in my opinion," he charges. "They've been to school, at least high school. And every one of 'em knows the dollar. Every one of 'em. I'd say they'd get more if they argued for themselves.

"And don't give me all that crap, 'We don't wanna hurt your feelings,'" Calvin continues, mocking another common ballplayers' argument for hiring agents. "That's baloney. You tell the agent what you want. He's just your stoolie."

Calvin's low opinion of agents had early roots. "One of the first agents I talked to said, 'We're gonna have you out of baseball in the next two years,'" claims Griffith. "He said, 'We're gonna get you out of baseball. We don't want you around.' He mighta been right, but I hung in quite awhile more."

Perceiving baseball's rapidly inflating salaries as destructive to players' incentive, Calvin came to resent everything that agents represented. "Everybody can be a morning glory—you pay the S.O.B.s and they become daffodils," he said in describing negotiations with Twins infielder John Castino. "Three agents came in to negotiate for Castino, and who the hell did the talking? A woman! It was one of the damndest things I ever heard of."

Interestingly, Carew was the only Twin whose negotiations Calvin had not turned over to Howard Fox by 1979. Perhaps still hoping his past, close personal relationship with Carew in the player's early years might save the day, Calvin was willing to make an extra, if fruitless, effort to keep this free agent. Though he would again fall short, this time he makes clear the decision was made more on the weight of financial than personal values.

"We had meetings with his attorney. But there was no hope at all. He was such a goddamn superstar," explains Calvin. "For me to pay that kind of money, he'd have had to be a Killebrew or Tony Oliva—a fellow who could drive the ball. Carew got all kinds of hits, he set the pace for you to score all kinds of runs, and he was one of the greatest hitters in baseball, no question about it, but he didn't drive in that vital run."

Negotiations continued for months, rather meaninglessly. But with Carew's contract running out at the end of 1979, Calvin proved he had learned at least one lesson in dealing with free agency. Carew would not depart Minnesota without bringing the Twins some form of compensation before his contract ran out. Word went out that the first baseman would be available to the highest bidder.

Playing off interest in Carew from both the Yankees and Angels, Calvin thought he had worked out a sale to California by early 1978 only to be foiled by a former employee. "We had it all set up to get $400,000," he remembers with a scowl. "And then I got word that the Commissioner (Bowie Kuhn) wouldn't allow it. That was really a stinker. That could have gone a long way with our organization."

Stymied much like Charlie Finley had been in the early '70s, Calvin nevertheless took defeat at his one major attempt to trade a player for cash stoically. He continued shopping for the best possible deal from either the Yankees or the Angels before spring training opened. A reported deal with New York for Chris Chambliss, Juan Beniquez, and Brian Doyle fell through when Carew publicly announced his reluctance to play for Steinbrenner. "Steinbrenner said the hell with him," remembers Calvin.

Despite being virtually limited to talks with California, Calvin made on February 3 what he felt was still a good deal, picking up four promising young players plus $200,000 in cash. One of the ex-Angels, outfielder Ken Landreaux, would lead the team in hitting that year with a .305 average and 83 RBI.

Yet the deal was clearly an unpopular one with many Minnesota fans who added the name of Carew to those others sent into economic exile by the Griffith organization. A cloud seemed to once again hang over the Twins organization.

Almost forgotten were two other off-season trades, including one that brought a pair of useful and inexpensive players, Ron Jackson and Danny Goodwin, from the Angels for Dan Ford. The other with the Mets resulted in relatively high-priced Jerry Koosman coming home to Minnesota in return for two young prospects. Calvin would later maintain that he had intended a return trade for Jesse Orosco, one of the two, but that the deal fell through.

Regardless, the Twins defied nearly every prediction in 1979 by jumping out to a quick lead in the A.L. West. With shortstop Roy Smalley hitting near .400 for most of the season's first half, Minnesota fans began to set aside some of their anger. Koosman also got off to a quick start and with Marshall anchoring the bullpen, Minnesota was a contender until mid-September with attendance rebounding to 1,070,061 for the year.

But in the end they would finish fourth, although improving their record to 82-80 and finishing only six games out. "Smalley had a fantastic first half of the year, he started in the All-Star game and everything," remembers Calvin. "We figured if he hit .250 in the second half we'd win the pennant. He didn't even hit .200. He really fell of the table."

In 1980 it would be the entire Minnesota Twins team that would fall off the table for most of the season. Once again free agent flight set the tone as Dave Goltz signed a $3 million, six-year contract with the Dodgers in the off-season. That Goltz would prove a major disappointment in La-La land didn't lessen the public displeasure directed toward Calvin and the Griffith organization.

Nor did a brief players' strike during the last week of spring training ease the level of tension between the Twins owner and union leaders. Calvin had again been among those owners calling for a hard line. When reliever Mike Marshall was released on June 6 with a 1-3 record and one save, he would claim it was due to "union activities."

Marshall's formal grievance would not be upheld, and Calvin would deny any anti-union feelings ever affected his player personnel decisions. "Why would I throw away a player who was helping us?" he asks rhetorically. "We had a guy, (Doug) Corbett, who was throwing the ball like nobody's business."

But the Twins would never seem to recover from the early season trauma, and Minnesota fans were similarly dispirited with watching the futility of a team symbolized by outfielder Willie Norwood's struggles to catch flyballs. For all purposes the season was over by June 1 with the Twins already ten games out at 18-29. On that date only a little over 8,000 fans would come out to see one of the season's highlights come to an end along with Landreaux's 31-game hitting streak.

Landreaux's bat cooled soon after as well as his desire for the game, it seemed to Calvin. "He had some kind of problem. I can't say it," hints Griffith. "But I went down on the field once and he took a baseball bat and was poking it at me like it was a bullfight or something. And I looked at those eyes . . . . It was a shame. He was a goddamn good-looking ballplayer."

As the long summer wore on, personnel problems seemingly provided the major excitement for the Minnesota public as a major league attendance low of less than 770,000 fans found their way to Metropolitan Stadium. Rumblings of discontent ran throughout the team as the punchless Twins sank in the standings.

On August 24, with his team at 54-71 and 26 1/2 games out, manager Gene Mauch dropped the inevitable bomb with announcement of his immediate resignation. At root, several sportswriters had already reported, was Mauch's belief that Twins management would, or could, not make the personnel improvements necessary to improve the team.

But despite rumors, the former Twins owner says he was taken totally by surprise by the criticism and Mauch's resignation. "He never asked me to make a trade that we didn't try," maintains Calvin. "Unfortunately somehow Mauch and (Howard) Fox got very intimate due to they used to play golf all the time. And they may have done talking I didn't know anything about."

By the time he spoke to Mauch it was too late, says Calvin. "He (Mauch) said he had a chance to do this and that. I never denied a person a chance to better himself. He wanted to go and when people are that way you have to let them go."

Arguably, the departure of the iron-handed Mauch may have relaxed the Minnesota team. With well-liked third base coach Johnny Goryl now at the helm, the Twins went 23-13 the rest of the season including a 12-game winning streak to finish third.

Nevertheless, Calvin could hardly have felt very positive about the organization's losses of nearly $700,000 in 1980 or the presence of three more free agents, Geoff Zahn, Jose Morales, and Mike Cubbage ready to jump ship. Rumors of the team's imminent sale abounded once again with Minneapolis sportswriter Sid Hartman predicting new owners before the Twins moved into the Metrodome in 1982.

Early in spring training of 1981 Calvin did have a meeting with a most unusual prospective buyer. Country and western singer Conway Twitty and several partners, who Calvin met through his longtime friendship with the Oak Ridge Boys, met to discuss what he believed to be their interest in buying out Gabe Murphy's stock. "It turned out they wanted to buy us out and move the team to Nashville," recalls Calvin. "We had a good talk. But I didn't take it too serious."

Despite its financial troubles and the threat of a major league players' strike looming over baseball, the Griffith family was not ready to give up however, Calvin even found another reason for optimism entering 1981 after making the difficult decision to leave Metropolitan Stadium.

"I was thinking sentimentality would bring people out, to tell you the truth," he remembers. "Knowing that that was gonna be it, and there wasn't gonna be any more Met, I thought we'd do okay."

But the Met's potential gate attraction was nullified by first a terrible start and then a total shutdown of the season. While the official strike was put off until at least the end of May, the Twins got an unofficial early start. Losing five of their first six games, they quickly dropped out of the race. By mid-May the situation was even worse as injuries to stars such as Butch Wynegar, Roy Smalley and John Castino took their toll—helping embark the team on an eight-game losing streak.

On May 23, Calvin finally acted, reluctantly replacing Goryl with coach Billy Gardner. Once again the explanation was that the Twins manager was too easy-going for the position. Despite being fully aware that there might be a strike within the next week, Calvin took on a second manager's salary partly, several sportswriters reported, out of concern for Goryl's deteriorating health. "Johnny Goryl was a helluva good baseball man, one of the best coaches we ever had," praises Calvin. "But the pressure got to him that's all there was to it. I think he even asked to be relieved. It was one of those things and we were lucky to have Gardner handy."

It may have also been the organization's good fortune when the player's strike finally got underway on June 13 with the Twins buried in seventh place at 17-39. Ironically, the stoppage of play became a financial boon for the Griffiths due to the subsequent payment of strike insurance benefits, for which the owners had paid premiums in anticipation of a strike.

"It messed things up," concedes Calvin of the strike generally. "But we had insurance. That was a godsend. We didn't lose anything. We got like two million bucks, I think, out of insurance and I don't think we would have netted $2 million if we had played."

The Twins were one of the few major league teams in such an unusual situation however, with higher payroll organizations now feeling the pinch from the strike. As Calvin recalls, "Strike insurance only covered teams like the Twins, maybe Texas and Seattle, teams like that. Steinbrenner's the one who got hurt by it (the strike). No telling how much money he had to keep spending on guys who weren't ready or were over the hill as major leaguers. He was sending them all down to Columbus. I think he had ball teams down there in Columbus he was paying more for than I was paying any club here in Minnesota."

Calvin's unexpected boon only furthered the hard-line position he had made clear on national television early in the spring. "For the betterment of baseball, the owners should let the players strike on May 29 for the season over free-agent compensation," he outspokenly argued. "If that happens though, I'm broke."

Calvin would later be forced to retract that personal prediction in testimony before a panel of the National Labor Relations Board considering whether major league owners should be forced to open their books to prove their claim of financial hardship. "I don't think I'm about to become extinct," he testified at the hearing, ignoring his long-range concerns.

Other major league teams, as well as players, were of course actually losing considerably more money during the 57-day strike. As the debts and public displeasure mounted in late summer, both sides finally had enough.

Federal mediators, and to a lesser extent Commissioner Bowie Kuhn, helped facilitate the final settlement, which included a modified compensation plan for teams losing free agents. Clark Griffith II would play a major role on the owner's Player Relations Committee that approved the deal and ended one of major league baseball's most trying ordeals.

Yet to Calvin the agreement ending the strike was an unfortunate lost opportunity and his one major grievance with Kuhn. "I was hoping it would be a longer strike," he says candidly, shaking his head. "But the Commissioner stepped in. The owners themselves have never been given a true opportunity to express their full pleasures about the union. And they should because they're the ones paying the bills, not the Commissioner or the president of the league."

But even Calvin could see the resolve of the owners weakening as the strike wore on. "Everybody was unified until we started voting on sheets of paper (secret ballots). Then they'd change their minds so you didn't know what in the heck was what," he recalls, admitting his confusion at the weakening of resolve. "It was kind of a hush-hush thing. None of the owners wanted to be put on the spot with the ballplayers and fans."

Regardless, Calvin's argument has remained consistent that owners should not only have hung tougher beyond demanding a free-agent compensation system. He maintains that they should also have pushed for a revision of the arbitration system that he saw as baseball's principal problem. It is an argument that other owners have increasingly seconded.

"In the final analysis it was a joke," Calvin says of the strike. "Nobody accomplished anything. We have to do something about arbitration. They gotta work out some way for a ballplayer to get a hearing but not a $1 million increase in salary."

Calvin's feelings remained so strong that he even voted in the minority against the strike settlement his son had helped negotiate. It was a decision that Clark bitterly describes as an example of his father's deliberate undercutting of his efforts—even while admitting he had often been fearful during the strike to discuss the status of player negotiations with the outspoken Twins owner.

"I voted against everything one hundred percent, which hurt him (Clark)," agrees Calvin. "It hurt his pride and his feelings and everything else, I know that. It was a real kick in the tail for the boy. But I didn't know what he voted for and what he didn't vote for. He couldn't talk to us as far as I remember. I voted that way all the time and never changed my mind. It wasn't good for baseball and that's how I looked at it."

Calvin's opinion did change on the major leagues' split-season continuation of the 1981 schedule in August, with each of the half-season "winners" meeting for a championship series. "It turned out to be a farce," he concludes, though admitting his initial attraction to the idea. "I liked it at first because everybody started out even. If your ballclub was starting to come, like ours, then you had a better chance in the second half. We almost won if I remember correctly.

"But when you're in the big leagues you should play for a season and don't need the fringe stuff," says Calvin, reflecting his purist side and contrasting baseball with football. "Two divisions is enough. In a little short season anything can happen. A lousy team can win in a short season."

Minnesota almost became the proof of that observation. Coming back after the strike to post a 24-29 record, the young Twins actually made a run at the second half title and were not eliminated from the possibility of post-season action until late September. It was then, coincidentally, that a trio of rookies named Kent Hrbek, Gary Gaetti and Tim Laudner all made major league debuts with home runs in their first games.

But the real landmark of the 1981 season was more somber, as nearly 16,000 Minnesotans came out on a cold, rainy October 2 to see the final baseball game ever to be played at Metropolitan Stadium. As a promotional device, Calvin gave out special certificates of attendance, hundreds of which he autographed for fans during the game. Following a final ceremony, many of the faithful stayed, stomping their feet and calling in semi-organized cheers for Calvin to return to the field again. It was a touching response that he neither expected nor would forget.

"I'll tell you the truth, it was a sad, sad situation because the Met reminded me so much of Griffith Stadium because the seats were so good for everybody in the infield," sighs Calvin. "And the angles from left and right field were sloped into the diamond. It was just a pleasure when the moon was out or the sun was out to see a game at the Met, no question about it. You can't beat natural grass and we had one of the really great groundskeepers in Dick Erickson. They could fix that diamond to make it as smooth as a billiard table."

But nostalgia and traditionalism had lost out to the bottom line and external pressures, as Calvin admits regretfully of his move to the Hubert H. Humphrey Metrodome. "Knowing that you weren't going to have the same composure at the new place as the Met, it was a tough deal, no question about it," he says "But it was something that we couldn't help. They told me to move downtown or get out of town. That's the way it was and there was no place for me to go."

Chapter 16

GIVE ME SHELTER

"Knowing that you weren't going to have the same composure
at the new place as at the Met, it was a tough deal, no question about it.
But it was something that we couldn't help.
They told me to move downtown or get out of town.
That's the way it was and there was no place for me to go."

They raised the roof on the Hubert H. Humphrey Metrodome the day after Metropolitan Stadium saw its final baseball game. Calvin was not in attendance, although Clark II was, as one of the select 450 invitees. But the Twins were now locked in as one of the primary tenants in the stadium that they hoped against hope would revive their economic future in baseball.

Nevertheless the conversion had not come quickly or easily, especially for Calvin, as the Griffith family was forced to weigh its options and survival instincts against its traditional values. Often accused of being inflexible, the Griffith organization's tortured debate over the Metrodome in a sense mirrored their battle between links to the past and future. On few issues would Calvin be as frustratingly enigmatic as in the heated debate over the pros and cons of moving baseball indoors for the 1982 season. His private agonizing would be distrusted and resented by both sides in the highly controversial issue.

The delay caused by Calvin's indecision in signing a lease would be a major surprise to most of the stadium's well-heeled Minneapolis backers, who had seemingly overcome every hurdle in their decade-long battle to build a domed stadium. The simple lure of cash, in the form of promised season-ticket increases and other incentives, was assumed to be enough to lure in Calvin and the financially strapped Twins organization. Opponents received no formal show of support in their arguments for remaining at Metropolitan Stadium.

Moreover, with Clark Griffith II making clear his support for a downtown Minneapolis dome at an early point and *Minneapolis Tribune* columnist Sid Hartman steadily reporting that Calvin held the same view, there seemed little room for doubt in early 1979. But the reality was that Calvin's opinions were as mixed as those of the general public.

Clark had appeared before the Metropolitan Sports Facilities Commission in the late fall of 1978, with Calvin in the audience, to offer an almost rapturous description of indoor

151

baseball's economic beauty. Reflecting his appreciation for the organization's increasingly strained financial situation, Clark offered one side of Griffith family views that saw the downtown dome as a protection from persistent Minnesota weather problems as well as a marketing opportunity of great potential.

Increasingly however, the young executive vice-president's views were without the support of his father. "Clarkie was always over there doing all kinds of talking," Calvin remembers. "I was trying to get from him what was going on and he was talking too much. He was doing a lot of talking, no doubt about it. I don't know why."

Clark, of course, claims his father should have been well-apprised of his activities even without being told directly. "Calvin knew what I was doing. He absolutely knew when I was going over there or making speeches. We shared the same secretary. Sportswriters would tell him," Clark replies, while curiously adding, "Several times in our lives he understood that I was doing things I couldn't possibly tell him about."

Clark does agree that Calvin always showed a basic dislike for the downtown dome concept, however. "I remember where during one of the lease negotiations at the (Twins) board level he told me to shut up," bitterly recollects Clark. "He just wanted to hear the negative stuff."

Griffith organization decision-making on the issue appeared to slow to a crawl during 1979, whether a result of baseball traditionalism, tactical delay, or just personal differences. Billy Robertson and Bruce Haynes took on more of the negotiating responsibilities, along with Calvin himself, as deadlines passed throughout the spring.

"I didn't think we were gonna sign a lease. Calvin took a very negative view of people wanting to go indoors," remembers Billy. "We wanted a retractable roof. Our feeling was that in this part of the country people like to be outside in the limited number of days we have. But we also couldn't afford to lose games."

Balancing that important concern against the Met Stadium's outdoor attraction was a difficult task. "People in Minnesota are different than anywhere else," argues Calvin. "They'd go out there and tailgate and sit in snowmobile suits and everything else. They really enjoyed it, that's all there is to it."

No doubt his own traditional definitions of the sport also made him hesitant to enter the Metrodome. "Baseball actually was developed to play in the afternoon, and the true game of baseball is played on natural turf and in the daylight where everybody can see the ball very plainly," said Calvin to a reporter in 1981, even after having made his decision. "The hitters can see the ball better. It's more realistic to them, the perspiration and everything else in the afternoon."

Calvin also was well aware of the continuing unpopularity of the dome proposal in many quarters. "We had to always worry about what the people of St. Paul were gonna do," says the man often accused of having no sense of marketing. "The people of Minneapolis aren't enough to support a ballclub. We were worrying our tail off over how they would feel about it."

Calvin suggests that a remodeled Metropolitan Stadium might have remained his preference even without the popular opinion factor. "The Met was one of the greatest places in the world to play a ballgame," he says. "There's no question about it. Perfect sight lines and everything. Easy access. All kinds of parking space. Christ you've got everything right there under your nose. Terrific. But they just didn't fix it up."

Harkening back to his own investments in the stadium during the team's relatively affluent 1960s, Calvin would always bemoan the Stadium Commission's reluctance to make more improvements, including clubhouses for both teams, more storage areas, and permanent left field seats. "If they had made the left field like right field we might still be out there," he maintains. "We offered to spend the money if they'd give us credit for it."

Eventually the Vikings would build temporary left field bleacher seats with the blessing of the Minneapolis-controlled Stadium Commission, although Calvin considered the addition a mistake. "That's a difference with football," he says. "People go to baseball games to sit back and relax. They couldn't do that at the Met. But they wouldn't listen to us."

Calvin would also bitterly remember a dispute at the start of the 1962 season between the cities of Bloomington and Minneapolis over unpaid stadium taxes that resulted in the Twins being threatened with a loss of their concessions and beer licenses until they made a $40,000 payment in escrow. "Then after I got things straight with Minneapolis I went back (to Bloomington) and they laughed at me, said they spent it," claims Calvin. "What can you do? They had me by the tail. When you're dealing with politicians you're in jeopardy."

It was Met Stadium's deteriorating condition and costs of repair, which he recalls including an estimated $750,000 for fireproofing, that eventually convinced Calvin. "One of the reasons I had my mind changed was that I walked around the Met," he recollects. "And what do I see, but lo and behold railroad ties holding up those seats (left field). And I said well that can't last very long. Deterioration of the wood and concrete that could really be trouble. That's one of the reasons I just gave up."

Calvin eventually saw his options as limited, whether because of sabotage or unintentional poor planning. Metropolitan Stadium remodeling did not appear to be a possibility that he could take seriously. Reluctantly, the downtown Minneapolis stadium became the focus of Calvin's attention and hopes.

"You had to be hopeful, you had to," explains Calvin. "You know it wasn't exactly what you wanted. But you said to yourself, 'How many times have we had people from Bismarck, Fargo, Minot, and all those places come in here (Metropolitan Stadium) and get rained out. I used to get criticized for delaying games too long. But I said, 'If I let them go now I may never get 'em back.' So we kept trying to play the games, and sometimes we got 'em in, sometimes we didn't. In the dome we knew we'd always get 'em."

Even with Calvin's psychological commitment, the issue was far from settled however. Other snags developed, particularly personal ones between Calvin and negotiators for the Stadium Commission. "I said I wanted to talk to (Dan) Brutger cause he was the chairman," says Calvin. "I didn't want to talk to (executive director, Don) Poss 'cause he told us all kinds of crap."

Poss replies that it was the confused state of the Twins negotiating team that led to misunderstanding. "It took a while to understand the politics of the Twins organization," he notes. "But I came to the frustrated conclusion that no one could speak with any authority," he said. "I'm not sure that the details of negotiations in herky-jerky fashion were well understood by Calvin."

Personal suspicions and ill-feelings were only slightly lessened by Brutger's assumption of a negotiator role, as other disagreements developed with a Stadium Commission straining to come in under a $55 million bonding limit. "We wanted a (club) room like the Halsey Hall room at the Met," recalls Calvin. "'No way, no space for it.' We wanted a restaurant so people could watch the game. 'No way, we don't have the money.'"

But the most controversial issue would involve the Twins role in concessions and novelty operations. After sole control of both enterprises in all their years at both Griffith and Metropolitan Stadiums, the Griffith family at first sought similar deals in the Metrodome. "That's how we made our living here and in Washington," notes Calvin. "Concessions is what saved us many, many years."

Stadium Commission negotiators seeking to maximize Metrodome profits through the use of subcontract vendors had different ideas however. "They said it was gonna cost us four to five million for the setup," remembers Calvin. "No way we could afford that. We kept novelties but they acted like it was a big deal when they offered a share of the concessions."

In retrospect, Calvin would be especially embittered by the agreements reached with his successor, Carl Pohlad. "We eventually got 30 percent (actually 25 percent in the first year). We had to accept it, that's all there was to it," says Calvin. "Look at what's going on now and not a goddamn word is said," he justifiably complains, referring to Pohlad's demands for 40 percent of the Metrodome's lucrative concessions revenue, plus rent decreases, after record-setting attendance years.

As negotiations dragged on late in the summer of 1979, Calvin was increasingly portrayed in the media as a greedy obstructionist holding the Metrodome hostage. A *Tribune* cartoonist parodied him as Star War's Jabba the Hutt, while Hartman used his column to deliver thinly veiled threats of business community retributions if the Twins did not soon agree to a lease.

Calvin, who normally insists that he isn't influenced by sportswriters or other critics, admits he was feeling the heat from Metrodome supporters. "There were a couple of writers who were continually writing about what a lousy organization the Twins were," he remembers. "That could have been the ruination right there. The newspaperman can just knock you right out.

"I've stormed bad publicity," Calvin continues. "I could have bought space in the paper. But it could just continue too long and I couldn't overcome it. You could read between the lines."

Calvin's other options were few despite highly publicized suggestions, ironically coming mostly from Metrodome backers, that the Twins might move to New Orleans, Seattle, Denver, or elsewhere if not given a satisfactory stadium situation. "We wasn't ever serious about moving to Denver," debunks Calvin. "It's a nice city, beautiful city up there in the mountains. But the traveling over the mountains, I questioned it.

"Now if you played all afternoon baseball like they do football on Sunday afternoons then you don't have to worry about the fans," continues Calvin's unusual analysis of

Denver. "But when you play night baseball it gets kinda dark going over those mountains. And I would never go into a thing like that at all because the mountains would take their toll."

Seattle was also quickly ruled out with Calvin again remembering his uncle's warning against coastal cities. "We thought about going to Seattle until we started analyzing the situation and the water," he repeats. "There was more water than land and people don't live on water."

Calvin also made a visit to the New Orleans Superdome but came away less than favorably impressed. "We gave that up for the fact that the sightlines were so bad," he says. "And New Orleans is a football town. It's not a place where you can have games twelve days in a row. There's not enough money there. Cleveland, I think, had a Triple A club there once but it was only 'cause they thought some major league club was coming in and they'd get some money. That's the way that was. Double A was the best they could get (in New Orleans)."

As summer headed toward fall, negotiations took on a more frantic pace. Citing construction and bond sales deadlines, the Stadium Commission put further pressure on the Twins to accept a lease. "They came up with some 24 hour deadline or something," remembers Calvin. "Then the Vikings didn't sign for a week later. That really irked me. That's the reason why they come up with more things."

Twins attorney Peter Dorsey, who would later represent Brutger in unrelated business matters, disagrees. "Calvin is a man of absolute integrity. If he said he would do something that's exactly what he'd do," Dorsey says. "But sometimes he would hear things or interpret things a little bit differently than they may have been said. I never felt there was bad faith or anything."

Clark Griffith agrees. "We just waited too long to make a commitment. Calvin didn't want to move into the dome. That's why we didn't get as much as we should have."

Calvin and attorney Peter Dorsey did come up with one very important addition, however. Quietly but firmly, the Twins demanded and received an escape clause in the thirty year lease that allowed what would prove to be several very useful escape routes for the team. If attendance could be proven to suffer from the dome's lack of air conditioning or if the Twins could prove a lack of profitability after three years, also measurable by an average attendance of less than 1.3 million, they could void their commitment at the end of the fourth year.

"That was one of the best things I got," says Calvin of the clause. "I never bribed anybody. I never talked to 'em about it or threatened anything. But I knew it could happen for the simple reason that there was no air conditioning. They must have really thought we were neophytes. And that was why we protected ourselves that way."

On August 11, 1980 the Twins finally signed the agreement that put them in the Hubert H. Humphrey Metrodome. Calvin and the Twins had made their commitment to the future of baseball played indoors. Publicly, they would begin to join the boosterism that surrounded the stadium's opening and its hoped-for financial benefits.

But privately, Calvin was far from convinced. Despite a certain level of optimism that the indoor facility might bring stability to the Twins economic fortunes, it was a shotgun marriage, as Calvin now tells it. "We got a lot of pressure to come in here. And we got taken on the contract. I should never have signed it."

DOMEBALL

BIG TRADES, SMALL CROWDS

*"We were trying to develop. We had Gaetti, Teufel, Hrbek, Laudner,
Puckett coming up. You could see what we had in the farm system
and it was time to visualize what was coming."*

The opening of the 1982 season was surprisingly unemotional for Calvin Griffith. While most of the Twin Cities greeted the Hubert H. Humphrey Metrodome's inaugural game with either elation or disgust, Calvin remembers being more blasé about the gala affair.

"I wasn't too nervous and I wasn't too excited about it," he says. "'Course knowing when I woke up that there was gonna be a game regardless of the weather was a relief. But I wasn't too worked up."

Yet under pressure to describe his feelings, Calvin admits he felt a mixture of optimism and fear based on his continued concerns about public response to indoor baseball, and on the dome's recent collapse under a snowfall. "I felt it could prolong our years in baseball, no doubt about it," he says of the Metrodome. "At least that's what I was hoping."

An opening night crowd of over 52,000, the largest ever in Minnesota baseball history to that point, could only have encouraged that hope. While the Twins 11-7 defeat at the hands of the lowly Seattle Mariners raised questions whether the team could live up to all the expectations the Metrodome opening had created, Calvin was initially optimistic, at least publicly.

"This is great," Calvin was quoted as saying after the game, while also suggesting to *Minneapolis Tribune* columnist Joe Soucheray that a moon and stars could be painted on the Metrodome roof. "The ball travels here. We didn't know what the ball was gonna do. But it's gonna travel. The fans are gonna love it. Now all we got to do is learn how to catch it."

Problems in that part of the game, as well as pitching and sometimes hitting, would be particularly accentuated by some of the Metrodome's peculiarities. Within a few games it was apparent that an already slow-footed Minnesota team was going to be even further handicapped by the ridiculously lively artificial surface of the Metrodome. "I just couldn't believe it," says Calvin of balls bounding over infielders' and outfielders' heads. Problems picking up flyballs against the roof further handicapped fielders. "I said this is really gonna be a goddamn farce, this kinda stuff."

With his team facing what already appeared to be a difficult adaptation and another long season, Calvin decided to make a major move. On April 10 he announced a trade sending shortstop Roy Smalley and a minor league pitcher to New York for reliever Ron Davis and then minor league shortstop Greg Gagne.

Calvin would continue the housecleaning with back-to-back trades in May that sent reliever Doug Corbett and second baseman Rob Wilfong to California in return for rookie outfielder Tom Brunansky and reliever Mike Walters. The following day he announced another trade with the Yankees, this time sending catcher Butch Wynegar and pitcher Roger Erickson to New York for pitchers Pete Filson and John Pacella, and infielder Larry Milbourne.

The trades were greeted by outcry from local media, fans and others, including the ever-marketing-conscious Clark Griffith II, who was left out of the decision after having signed both Wynegar and Smalley to multimillion dollar, long-term contracts before the 1981 season. Clark and Fox would actually become involved in a physical confrontation after a heated dispute concerning the deal. "I don't think any punches were thrown," remembers Calvin. "But they grabbed each other and they were wrasslin'."

Enmity between the two had been obvious long before the incident, though each deny any jealousy of the other. Fox's rise in influence with Calvin was only part of the changes that were negatively affecting Clark. "I once told Clark, 'The problem you've got is not with me,'" remembers Fox. "'The problem you've got is with Bruce Haynes.' Because Bruce and Thelma controlled 26 percent, as did Clark and his father."

Regardless, the trade and its aftermath made clear that Clark's influence in the Griffith organization had virtually disappeared. It was both a personal and professional schism that left the Dartmouth graduate almost totally isolated. Clark's urbane speaking manner, his fashionable dress, and even his book-lined office clashed with the style of his father and uncles. Clark's own strong ego and sometimes less than tactful insistence on new organizational tactics had the same effect.

"We'd all been pretty well indoctrinated in working together. I wasn't trying to push myself, Sherry wasn't trying to push himself, (Joe) Haynes wasn't trying to push himself, we all worked together for the good of the ballclub," contrasts Billy Robertson. "Clarkie saw things differently from Calvin and some of the rest of us, which was only natural. He was a lot younger and times had changed with marketing and advertising as focal points. There was a great difference in views."

Only one view would now survive, as the Smalley-Wynegar trades symbolized. "Clarkie always felt you had to keep your stars to keep your ballclub up," recalls Calvin, who had bowed to public pressure and Clark's logic in agreeing to Wynegar and Smalley's contracts. "But were they stars? That's the biggest question you have to ask. They haven't proved it since. They're not stars in my opinion," he said in 1987.

In a brief period of time, Calvin had unloaded most of the experience on his team, and, it was noted by critics, his five highest salaries. By saving $1.62 million in one year, and salary guarantees of $3.14 million in future years, Minnesota now had the lowest payroll in the majors.

Many Minnesotans well remembered Calvin's outspoken defense of his low payroll in the late '70s. "It shows I'm not a horse's ass," he said then. "These other owners, they're all egotists. They've got so much money. But nobody knew who they were before baseball. Who the hell ever heard of Ted Turner or Ray Kroc? Or George Steinbrenner? If Charlie Finley ever gets out, you know what he'll miss the most? The publicity."

Curiously, Calvin would later turn his thinking around to praise Steinbrenner as "a big spender in a big-spending city. He's what you need in New York. He really gets his nuts off on that team."

But Calvin still insists his 1982 trades were based more on baseball logic than money. "We were certainly looking at the ups and downs of our finances, ain't no question about it," he admits. "But we weren't in the position to pay money to ballpayers that we didn't think were gonna help us. We could see these guys (traded Twins) losing a little bit and we figured we might as well get something for 'em."

Timing was also a key factor, Calvin notes, with personal loyalties to players becoming secondary to team needs. "When you come in the Dome you try to add more speed to the team. I made a mistake with the club in '65. I kept some of 'em too long. But they were all favorites. You get criticized because they were favorites. But you've gotta realize that when guys get traded newspapermen lose access."

Calvin maintains that it was his own personal sentimentality that had kept the fading Wynegar on the team 'til 1982. "I don't know what happened to him," he says of the 1976-77 All-Star catcher. "He shoulda been an All-Star catcher year after year, he had that ability. 'Course the only reason he got on the All-Star team the first year was through Calvin. I got the president of the league, Joe Cronin, to put him on because it would be good publicity for me. So Joe put him on."

Smalley's defensive inadequacy on artificial turf and Wynegar's suspect health, along with the rapid progress of minor league star Tim Laudner, made the pair vulnerable. Similarly, the trade for Davis made Corbett expendable. "But we never worried about selling ballplayers to stay in business," insists Calvin. "We made good deals."

Few, other than Yankee owner George Steinbrenner and the generally happily traded Twins players, publicly agreed at the time. New relief star Ron Davis added to the controversy with his outspoken criticism of the May trades. "What is he?" asked Davis of his employer. "74 years old? They out to put him in an old folks' home. Trade the owner, that's what they oughta do."

Calvin, of course, couldn't resist responding. "Davis is a New York counterfeit, a New York counterfeit," he charged. "I'm a goddamned real guy."

Remarkably, Calvin would not retain any bad feelings against Davis, even after the reliever had outlived his welcome amongst most Twins fans. "Davis and I became real close friends," says Calvin straight-facedly. "You can't take that conversation and believe it right off the bat. You gotta let it sink into his head and let it sink into my head. It came out to where he didn't mean what he said. I've said things I wished to heck I hadn't said."

The passing of time would confirm many of Calvin's arguments, if not always his tactfulness. But in 1982, all-rookie lineups, even those including such future stars as Kent Hrbek, Gary Gaetti, Brunansky, and Tim Laudner, were almost as unpopular as the Twins major league high admission prices.

One local television station reported that 90 percent of polled fans thought Griffith should sell the team. "Trade Calvin" signs and buttons began increasing in the Metrodome while attendance fell noticeably after the stadium's initial attraction faded. Public support for the Twins was at an all-time low, while media accounts highlighted the success of former players with their new teams.

At the end of the season Calvin would tell a reporter that the speed with which the trades developed had even surprised him. "Honest. At the start of spring training I had no idea of trading off our veterans. But as we started the season and played into May, I saw a repeat of the 1981 season where we finished last overall with Wynegar, Smalley, Erickson and company," he explained. "I decided we could do worse than by turning to our promising youngsters."

Calvin is still unapologetic for the trades. "We were trying to develop. We had Gaetti, Teufel, Hrbek, Laudner, Puckett coming up. You could see what we had in the farm system and it was time to visualize what was coming."

That visualization would be difficult in 1982 however as the team began by stumbling through the second-worst May in baseball history at 3-26. With the dubious achievement of other negative team records for most consecutive losses, 12, and lowest winning percentage, .370, the Twins would limp their way to a final 60-102 record—a major league worst. Attendance would also be baseball's worst, though improved to 921,186 because of the Metrodome's initial attraction.

Adding to the tragic atmosphere was the plight of another young Minnesota prospect, centerfielder Jim Eisenreich, of whom Calvin had already gone on record as being "doomed to be an All-Star." Batting .303 after 34 games and fielding magnificently, the prediction seemed ready to hold up until Eisenreich began to suffer from a nervous disorder, Tourette Syndrome, that included hyperventilation. It was an affliction he could never overcome in three years with the Twins, despite numerous team-sponsored physical and psychological treatments.

Later asked about the Baltimore Orioles 22-game losing streak to start the 1988 season, Calvin would compare it to that disastrous 1982 Twins season. "It's really a drain. You're embarrassed everywhere you go," he recalls. "You just don't go socializing. You get in your car and go from the office right back home and forget about what's going on at night. You go to the theater and everybody says, 'What the hell you gonna do?' You're changing faces and hoping the ones you bring in are better than what you sent out."

It would have been a dark time for anyone. But Calvin at least had a historic precedent to fall back on. "It was something like in Washington," he recalls. "We tried young ballplayers and tried to balance them with a couple of older ones in the clubhouse. You saw the earmarks of potential. The only way you're gonna learn is to play 'em. And the mistakes they made they profited by them. The next year they didn't make as many."

It was true, though Minnesota's improvement to 70-92 in 1983 wasn't noticed by many. Under Billy Gardner's patient tutelage, the young Twins slowly became more respectable, even staying near .500 through the first half of the season. Yet a pitching staff that included one starter, Terry Felton, whose career 0-16 mark set a major league record for futility, eventually took its toll in a second half nosedive. Even so, Calvin's low-budget team averaging only $67,500 in salaries still tied Gene Autrey's free agent dominated California team for fifth place.

It was only a small silver lining on what was an increasingly black financial cloud however. With attendance again falling to 858,939, the team's tenuous financial situation was clearly not improving despite the Metrodome's vaunted recuperative powers.

A frightening incident in which the stadium's roof partially collapsed during an unexpected windstorm in mid-1983 added to Calvin's doubts. "Yes it did. When those lights and speakers started twirling around out there I said, 'Oh, my God. Please let them hit in the infield area, not where the people are,'" he remembers. "Finally it all calmed down and everything was okay. But it was a worrisome time because nobody ever thought something like that could happen. I was worried what people would think coming in there again."

Yet the biggest negative factor for many fans was the Metrodome's lack of air conditioning, which was determined to be unnecessary because of the stadium's unique "breathing" design. "The people were so damn smart that you didn't need air conditioning," says Calvin, recalling his disagreement with stadium architects. "I was saying to myself, 'Well, listen to 'em talk. But what in the hell is gonna happen with all that concrete in there for the grandstand?'"

By early 1983 the answer was undeniable as sweltering humidity at times made the roof of the Metrodome nearly disappear in a cloud. "I raised hell," Calvin says, his voice rising at the memory. "If they didn't give us air conditioning, I was gonna move out. 'Cause people didn't enjoy coming to a ballgame to sweat—not unless the sun was out. If the sun was out people would enjoy it. But when you're covered up and you can't get a sunburn nobody enjoys it."

Air conditioning's installation in mid-1983 couldn't change all the team's economic problems however. Calvin had officially managed to scrape out a profit of just over $100,000 in 1982 but the next year's financial losses of over $1 million helped erase the Twins savings almost completely. In fact, the Twins were forced into a short-term $750,000 loan at the First National Bank until the next year's television revenue arrived. "Finally we were able to pay it off," remembers Calvin. "But we weren't gonna keep doing that and get killed by interest."

Payroll expenses were only certain to grow as his young players matured. "That started to really worry me," says Calvin. "I said, 'Jesus, we got a lot of ballplayers that are gonna be stars. I don't have the capital to take care of them.'"

Ironically, Calvin's public cheerleading for his team may have hurt his own pocketbook. During the 1982 World Series, he declared that he preferred every one of his regulars to those of the world champion-to-be Cardinals except for St. Louis shortstop Ozzie Smith. Then when the American League rookie-of-the-year award was given to

Baltimore's Cal Ripken, Jr. over Minnesota's Hrbek, Calvin expressed his outrage by calling it a "travesty."

Asked by reporters about the possible impact of his assertions on contract negotiations with many of the young Twins, Calvin hardly blinked. "When I feel somebody's entitled to something, the money doesn't matter,'" he maintained. "Hrbek isn't going to hurt me in salary. I'm going to give him a helluva raise—as far as I'm concerned."

It was plenty of ammunition for any agent, and Hrbek's showed up asking for the same amount as Ripken, who had recently signed for $185,000. Calvin balked, but after a one-day walkout in spring training, Hrbek received a raise from $40,000 to $110,000.

Calvin now shrugs at recollection of the incident. "It couldn't hurt me too much cause he couldn't go to arbitration. I had him where I wanted him," he says candidly. "But I think I was fair with him. He was as good as Cal Ripken and that's all there was to it. I said what I thought about the boy."

Arbitration also struck with a vengeance, first in 1982 as Davis won a $475,000 salary, and then in 1983 when Hrbek signed for $375,000 just before the hearing. Calvin was less than diplomatic in his public comments on both results, giving further fuel to critics' charges that he was an economic neanderthal.

"I'm so sick about Davis winning that I almost vomited," he told reporters. "He is no more entitled to that kind of salary than I am being President of the United States."

A year later Calvin even seemingly turned against his former favorite, Hrbek. "Kent Hrbek is not worth $375,000," he said. "Here's a guy who's been in major league baseball two years, and we tripled his salary even though he had a poorer year last year than he had the year before. We'd better draw a lot of people or we're going to be in trouble."

Equally troubling for the long-term health of the club and public relations would be the Twins increasing difficulty in signing top draft choices. In 1982, top draft picks Tim Belcher of Mt. Nazarene College, Ohio and University of Maine pitcher Bill Swift would fail to come to terms after lengthy negotiations. Griffith stubbornness in refusing to meet their signing bonus demands received most of the blame in media accounts.

"The agents got in on it and kept raising the ante," argues Calvin, with backing from Brophy and others in the organization. "I said the hell with it. If they can't keep their words, I don't want them around."

The pattern was repeated in the secondary draft of 1983 when highly sought-after Arizona State outfielder Oddibe McDowell wouldn't sign with Minnesota. "They (media) yelled at me for not signing this kid," remembers Calvin. "But they didn't say we were about the fifth team to want to draft him and his mother said he was gonna finish college. And besides, we've got an even better one in Triple A at Toledo (Kirby Puckett) coming up. Course, I didn't know he'd (Puckett) be this good."

A siege mentality had clearly set in with the Twins owner. Never shy with his opinions, Calvin was now almost too outspoken to be credible. "Money isn't going to drive me out of baseball," he said in mid-1983. "I live baseball. If I get out of the game I'll become a real old man. Calvin Griffith is going to be a part of this ballclub any place it operates. Look at Bear Bryant. He said that once he retired he was going to grow old in a hurry. He died shortly after he retired. I don't want to die."

Yet despite confident descriptions of how he planned to be running the team at age 85 like his uncle Clark had, Calvin must have known he was facing his last stand. His strategy of holding on until the free agent and arbitration situation stabilized, or until television and particularly cable revenue swelled, was running out of time.

Particularly disappointing was the outcome of the Twins cable television venture, Twinstar, which began in 1980 as a joint undertaking with the Minnesota North Stars hockey team. Looking at the experience of other markets, the Griffiths were cautiously optimistic that the deal might provide their survival edge.

"It was something new. It was something extra," explains Calvin. "Look at what cable did in New York. What do they make now, $20 million a year? Look at L.A., look at the Cubs, Atlanta. But I wasn't holding my breath. It was a potential. It might help carry you over in a bad year."

Once again timing would work against the Griffiths however, as Twinstar's beginning coincided with the decline of both sports teams. Even worse were terms of the agreement which saw the still relatively more popular Twins giving up fifty percent of their revenues to the North Stars until the year 2010, even while bearing more of the costs from a lawsuit filed by a local commercial television station. While unsuccessful, the suit would cost the Twins over $1 million in legal fees.

"That thing really got balled up, there's no question about it," says Calvin, admitting he should have kept a closer eye on the details. "I told Billy (Robertson, in charge of negotiations) that there's no way the Twins would agree to give them fifty percent of our share when we play so many more games. I definitely didn't want that in there and wouldn't accept it. I figured that was it and that we didn't do it."

Efforts several years later to renegotiate the contract also failed, mysteriously in Calvin's opinion. "I still say that if Fox had allowed Billy and Walter Bush (attorney) to talk to the Gunds (owners of the North Stars) they would have gotten out of it," argues Calvin in response to later Pohlad organization complaints at the agreement. "But Fox said, 'No, I'm not gonna do it.' I don't know why they didn't get together, but Fox didn't want to."

Regardless of responsibility, the contractual arrangement meant that the Twins would see little revenue, while bearing legal costs that were even more immediately crippling. "That really hurt us. That was most of our savings," remembers Calvin. "I felt then that they did it just to get us out of baseball . . . . And it got down to where that bill I received was a factor. 'Cause you can always get sued and if you don't have an extra pocketbook you can be in trouble."

Combined with the team's still shrinking attendance, the Twins financial bottom line looked bleak. "It gave me the thought of selling," admits Calvin. "I thought we'd see after the start of the season. You get very concerned. You could see the handwriting."

Clark Griffith suggests that Calvin began receiving family pressure to sell the team after the cable television deal went sour. "I think the Twinstar deal had a very big effect on Billy, Bruce, and Thelma," he argues. "Here is Bruce's first big public venture and he'd fallen flat. I think they were running away from that. It was a terrible deal."

Regardless, by mid-1983 the family was already accepting feelers about the possibility of a sale. "I'll listen, but that doesn't mean I will sell, or I won't sell," said Calvin in June. "I've listened to a lot of prospective buyers."

Included was the not-so-quiet approach of a group of Tampa investors for whom the purchase of the Twins to play in their as-yet-unconstructed stadium was an alternative to seeking an expansion franchise. On August 1, a still noncommittal Griffith confirmed to reporters that he had been offered "the biggest offer ever made for a major league team, bigger than the $30 million recently paid to purchase the Philadelphia Phillies."

Sports Illustrated soon after quoted a Tampa spokesman as saying that Calvin was so close to signing the contract that he was "down to where he's selecting the spot for the toilet in his private office."

Calvin would, at the time, vehemently deny that negotiations had ever reached that point. "I can't believe they would print that," he said of the *Sports Illustrated* article. "They (Tampa) did show us plans for the Tampa stadium. We told them about some of the mistakes that have been made here (Metrodome). Some of our offices are too small and so is the conference room. We haven't made any commitment to anybody and won't until after the 1984 season."

Years later he would admit he had been highly impressed with the Tampa plans, including those of the bathroom-equipped offices. "We spent many an hour sitting with them going over architectural plans," says Calvin. "If I had sold the ballclub anywhere but to the people here in Minnesota I would have sold it to Tampa, because they're good people and the stadium they were gonna build would have been the greatest stadium in the United States for baseball."

But despite his attraction to Tampa, Calvin was clearly not yet committed to the sale of the team. "We were hoping we never had to do it," remembers Calvin. "But we wanted to get in a position where if the time came we would know exactly what we could do and what we had to do."

That family decision would come without the input of one previously central figure. In August of 1982, Clark Griffith would announce that he was essentially leaving the organization to go to law school, in part because of his lack of involvement in team sale discussions. "I would like to be a lot more involved with the team," he complained. "I don't know what's going on. I haven't been told anything about the offer from Tampa to buy the club."

Calvin's response was less than apologetic. "He (Clark Griffith) is chairman of our salary committee and he is treasurer of the team. If he has an idea I listen to him. But if I don't like the idea, I am not going to carry it out."

Perhaps in light of later events, Calvin now sounds more appreciative of Clark's ability, which would be lost to the organization in the upcoming crucial months. "Actually Clark had the better sense of all of them in the organization. In business he was very, very intelligent," recalls Calvin, though with a qualification. "But he didn't have the baseball sense that would have come with experience . . . . He decided he wanted to do other things."

Both within the family and with others, including Metrodome officials, Calvin was not about to surrender his power easily. "I'm not going to do one thing until our three year lease runs out," he explained to reporters in late 1983. "At that point we are going to be in a position to get a lot of things straightened out. When our lease expires we will find out what we can get and what we can't get. We will be in a position to do the dictating then."

Chapter 18

AN OFFER
HE COULDN'T REFUSE

"You go into the office and you start analyzing and thinking and
making evaluations and you can see things weren't too good.
We didn't have any second pocketbook to fall on . . .
that really puts a grindstone around your neck."

1984 would be a year of scrutiny for Calvin Griffith. Ironically, even as his organization faced its worst financial situation since the mid-1950s, the Twins owner was enjoying as much political and personal leverage as he had ever known since his move to Minnesota.

The attention of numerous civic leaders and business investors, in addition to Metrodome officials, would only increase as speculation grew on the Twins future. Minneapolis' Chamber of Commerce formed a Major League Task Force in late 1983 to help the Twins attract 2.4 million fans and, of course, eliminate that contractual escape route.

Their concern for the Griffith organization's troubles emerged after the Twins attractiveness to other cities became apparent. Tampa was interested, as were bidders from Indianapolis, Denver, and Vancouver. Several Twin Cities businessmen had already made clear their interest.

"We haven't approached any other city about moving," Calvin told reporters in March, 1983. "They are coming to us trying to buy the club. I'm not going to move the franchise myself. It will be moved by other people, not by the Griffiths and Hayneses."

That distinction aside, the family had certainly welcomed the attention. "They came to everybody," recalls Calvin. "My brothers, Brucie (Haynes), I imagine Fox, myself. People really wanted the ballclub, though I don't think some of them knew what they wanted to do with it."

One particularly memorable offer would come during a late 1983 visit to New York, when Calvin met with real estate and gambling tycoon Donald Trump. "I had the thrill of my life going through Mr. Trump's towers there and seeing all those million dollar condos he had," remembers Calvin with almost child-like innocence. "Whoooeee! It was so superb it was unbelievable. Johnny Carson has a condo there."

Even more unbelievable would be the financial discussion that followed, with Trump making an offer reported at $50 million. "It was a lot of money no question about it," says Calvin. "I never thought I'd get in a room talking about the kind of money he was talking about. It was more than Pohlad ever offered, definitely."

Twins attorney Peter Dorsey, who went along for the meeting, also has a strong impression of Trump's interest. "We met up in his office and he said, 'I've got something that a lot of other people have and I don't have something that a lot of people do have. I don't have a board of directors or shareholders. And I do have a helluva lot of money,'" says Dorsey repeating Trump's sales pitch.

When the two sides disagreed on a price, the multimillionaire real estate developer got the chance to prove his wealth, recalls Dorsey. "Just like that he said 'I'll up it $3 million.' Just like that. In a second."

Part of the reason for the Twins increased value was the major league's new television broadcast contract with NBC that greatly increased each team's annual revenue. Front-running Tampa's offer of $24 million shrunk in importance after the 1984 agreement, remembers investor Earle Halstead. "Our tough break and Calvin's good break was that they got that $1 billion TV contract and suddenly each club's value went way up."

Vice-president Bruce Haynes would tell reporters in March, 1984 that the Griffiths had received more than one offer of $50 million for the Twins. "The price of clubs has gone skyrocketing in recent months," he said, noting that the Detroit Tigers had been purchased the previous year for $50 million. "And we can match it. We have a better organization and we have no debt."

The inexperienced, but likeable, Haynes took on an increasingly prominent role in negotiations, much as he recently had in the organization. "I had been contacted by some people interested in buying the club and I guess that's what started it," he recalls. "We were just at a point where we couldn't see any light at the end of the tunnel. It was strictly a business decision by the family."

Selling the club was also a highly emotional decision that did not come easily for anyone in the family. But Thelma Haynes, who was also the lowest paid member of the board of directors at $50,000 a year, had made increasingly clear her willingness to give up the uphill fight. "I think my love for baseball runs as deeply as it does for Calvin," she told reporters. "After all, my father (Clark Griffith) is one of the founders of the team. But I have children, friends, other things that are important too. What can be more important than friends?"

Baseball was clearly still the number one priority in Calvin's life. But by spring training of 1984, he now says, he had already come to read the handwriting on the wall. "You go into the office and you start analyzing and thinking and making evaluations and you can see things weren't too good," he explains. "We didn't have any second pocketbook to fall back on. We couldn't expand or do this or that or we'd go broke. In three years we'd lost around two and a half million dollars. That really puts a grindstone around your neck."

Calvin's admittedly old-fashioned business values, that included an almost moralistic dislike of credit, limited his options. "I always was told, 'Don't spend more than you can get,' he explains. "Fortunately for us, we kept that going. Baseball was our only business. And I always said I was gonna get out my own way—without owing a fortune."

But there were other factors relevant to Calvin's eventual decision to sell he now says. "There was a lot of inner fighting in the family starting to get in there, no question about it," he admits. "And if you couldn't have harmony in the organization, you gotta get out of it. I didn't want that. I was getting into an age where I had had enough."

Calvin's clash with his son was only the most obvious example of the tensions tearing at the Griffith organization. "Bruce and Clarkie, they were really enemies," he says, despite the denial of both parties. "My sister caused some of it because she felt Clarkie was getting too much of it in the business and her son wasn't getting any."

Thelma places the blame for most internal problems on Clark, but agrees that she felt it necessary to defend her son's interests. "Clarkie had a lot more done for him than Bruce did just like Calvin had a lot more done for him than I had done for me. I just think Clarkie thought he could do what he wanted to do. But you have to have a captain of the team, and Clarkie wasn't happy to have Calvin as captain of the team, that's all there was to it."

Thelma was apparently willing to let Calvin be the captain regarding the sale decision. "It was all me. Mrs. Haynes gave me permission to do what I wanted," he remembers. "She never expressed exactly what she wanted. But at times she looked like she wanted to have it easier—to be able to do this or that and relax without having to worry about paying the bills."

There seems little question Calvin was seeking his own relief. At age 72, fatigue was a factor, he admits. "I've been on the circuit traveling and worrying about things since 1923. I've gone by bus, train, airplane. I done every darn thing and I was just getting fed up with it."

Calvin was even growing tired of the attention that the team's potential sale was bringing. "I was talking to people from Tampa, Denver, Minneapolis, Vancouver, Indianapolis for two years," he recollects. "All these places wanted baseball. I listened to them and when I got all the information I wanted I finally turned them over to Bruce (Haynes). I got tired of all that."

Yet Calvin remained happily in charge of day-to-day operations, giving few outward indications that he was ready to part ways with either baseball or its controversies. "Nobody else knew what I was thinking about. When you keep a secret, keep it to yourself," says Calvin solemnly.

His December 7, 1983 trade with Texas certainly appeared to show a commitment to improving the team over the long haul. Sending outfielder Gary Ward to the Rangers for pitchers John Butcher and Mike Smithson gave desperately needed strength to the starting rotation.

Critics, including Ward and several Twins players, suggested however that Calvin was trading not only the team's veteran leader but also the only black man in the starting lineup. "He's been treated like royalty, a royal king," answered Calvin of Ward's attacks. "That should have been the furthest thing he should have ever thought of. I wish more blacks would come to the ballpark."

It was a controversy that also overshadowed the re-signing of star infielder John Castino and reliever Ron Davis to multi-year, million dollar contracts. The Twins owner had

169

faced strong criticism from media as negotiations dragged on before Calvin gave in to the expensive commitments.

"I wish the writers would leave me alone so I could negotiate my own way," complained Calvin later when Castino's back problems worsened. "I felt I should be a little more cautious in my negotiations with Castino because of his back surgery. I signed him because I wanted to eliminate the negative thinking and help the task force sell tickets."

Calvin would react more sentimentally when Castino was forced into retirement after the 1984 season. "That's one of the great tragedies. If he had a good back and was able to play we would most likely have won two or three pennants. We just didn't have the one guy to do the trick. I remember so many times in the 7th, 8th, or 9th innings when Castino would get that hit," says Calvin of the player who once left his office in tears during contract negotiations. "He had the guts of a lion and the intelligence of a Winston Churchill, I would say. He was a good boy, really a nice person."

Calvin's re-signing of Castino and Davis would gain less notice however than his refusal to give $125,000 to the Minneapolis Chamber of Commerce. Their Major League Baseball Task Force's attempt to help the Twins depended on the team kicking in additional funding to staff season ticket sales to corporations and groups they purportedly represented. Image, rather than ballplayers, was their major concern.

The Task Force had earlier compiled a lengthy report that was critical of the Twins sales efforts, noting that, "to be a fan of the Minnesota Twins is synonymous with being a loser," and recommended a new, "merchandizing" approach to promotions. Interestingly, in light of later events, the Chamber itself refused to offer any financial support to the season ticket sales efforts, noting that to do so would create a "charitable mode."

It was hardly a strategy likely to win over a man with Calvin's long-term suspicion of marketing efforts. "We spent a helluva lot of money doing things they asked us to do," he says. "I couldn't see it did much."

An April 3 opening night crowd of 34,381 didn't change Calvin's impression of the marketing efforts. "It's not a bad crowd," he said. "But I would have thought we might have had 50,000 the way everybody was working. They were hustling this and hustling that. Everybody was hustling someone."

More encouraging to Calvin was the team's quick start on the field, as they did their own part to change the Twins "loser" image. With a young southpaw named Frank Viola finally beginning to achieve the pitching success long predicted for him, and another product of the Griffith organization, centerfielder Kirby Puckett making his major league debut in early May, the Minnesota team quickly jumped into the thick of the A.L. West race.

But it was an effort that would be overshadowed nearly all season by events off the field. Sale discussions and rumors would become a regular part of local news, with area newspapers displaying attendance statistics more prominently than the Twins standings in the league. With little likelihood that the team would naturally draw 2.4 million fans, it was assumed by most commentators that the team would leave the Metrodome after the 1985 season.

A local sense of alarm grew in late April when it was disclosed that Twins minor owner H. Gabriel Murphy had sold his 43 percent of the club to the Tampa investors for $11.5 million. It was a surprise as well to Calvin, who apparently was not entirely pleased at the Florida city's new strategy of gambling on getting enough leverage through the Murphy purchase to gain a major league franchise in the future. "He got very irritated," remembers Cedric Tallis, a member of the Tampa group. "That helped blow the deal."

"All this means is that I have a new partner," responded Calvin publicly, while also calling off a fishing trip to British Columbia for fear that it would be seen as part of plans to move the team to Vancouver.

"They were trying to get us to go up there (Vancouver) all the time and I didn't want to go up there 'cause that would be too evident," explains Calvin. "I didn't want to go anywhere to give any person the impression that we were ready to sell. But we were thinking about it."

Calvin had in fact already begun serious negotiations with Minneapolis businessman Carl Pohlad, who was then unidentified. "If they will meet our price, we will sell to the local group," he said to reporters on April 26. "We may be close to making a deal."

It was a relationship that would surprise many observers, but had stemmed from conversation between Calvin and Pohlad almost a decade before. "He called me up and said that if the day came that you ever want to sell your ballclub I'd be very much interested," remembers Calvin. "He was the first one and I always thought if you're first it means something. I kind of cater to them. So I kept my word and gave him first shot."

Yet just two days later, on April 28, a group of Twin Cities corporate leaders met in a so-called "crisis atmosphere" to discuss how they could purchase the Twins at an amount lower than the $30-35 million Calvin was known to have considered his minimum. "I think Calvin's a few million high," said Curtis Carlson, himself a multi-millionaire whose companies rank among the largest U.S. corporations.

On April 30 Griffith met briefly with businessman Harvey Mackay, one of the organizers of the earlier meeting, to reject his offer of only $20 million for the franchise. Calvin's infuriation was heightened when he learned that Mackay's lawyer, Sam Kaplan, had already released a letter concerning the offer to the press.

"They are a couple of foul balls," Calvin said after first learning of the letter from a reporter. "They should never have showed up. They embarrassed the hell out of us. Bruce Haynes told them that if they didn't have a bigger offer, not to show up. But they told Bruce they had everything worked out and would satisfy us. They didn't have a thing worked out. It was just a publicity stunt."

Haynes agreed, saying, "This is about as rotten a move as I've seen in a long time. I don't know what they are trying to do. But they didn't help anything . . . . I hope the others locally interested in buying the club don't get upset. This isn't good for the Twin Cities at all."

But Mackay wasn't about to stop at that point, having already developed a second plan to force the Griffith organization to remain in the Metrodome—a structure his lobbying efforts had helped create. On May 4 it was announced that a number of Twin Cities corporations were well on the way to pledges of $6.4 million aimed at buying enough

171

tickets to reach the 2.4 million in attendance figure for 1984 that they believed would eliminate Calvin's escape clause and force him to sell the team to a local buyer.

Many of the same groups who had recently rejected giving "charitable" financial help to the Twins marketing efforts were included as contributors. Included were the Minnesota Vikings and several corporations that had significant real estate investments in the stadium area, such as Control Data Corp. and the *Minneapolis Star & Tribune.* In addition, the Stadium Commission and the Minneapolis City Council would find significant financial reason to make funds available for the buyout which they hoped would insure the Twins sale to a local buyer.

"I would have a different feeling about those people . . . if they were for us before," Calvin said to a reporter. "But they have always favored the Vikings."

It was a strategy that was again masterminded by Mackay, but which he would later claim in his best-selling book was spawned by telephone conversations with Calvin's baseball nemesis and salesman extraordinaire Bill Veeck. Mackay would claim that Veeck (deceased by the time of Mackay's publication) had waited since 1961 to get revenge for Griffith's about-face in American League ownership debates over who should head up the replacement franchise in Washington when the Minnesota Twins were created.

It is an interesting interpretation of history in light of Veeck's praise of Griffith during his last years and his fond reference to the two of them as examples of baseball's battle against catastrophic changes. "We are doomed. We are the last dinosaurs in a forest where there are no more trees to feed on."

Calvin seems genuinely baffled by Mackay's characterization of his relationship to Veeck. "We were asshole buddies," he insists. "We were asshole buddies."

Veeck's fondness in his final years for Calvin is confirmed by his widow, Mary Frances Veeck, who notes that her late husband had greatly respected Calvin's efforts to keep the team going as a family operation. "He had great respect for Calvin," she says of Bill Veeck. "He thought he (Calvin) had been an honorable man."

Regardless, Mackay's strategy certainly had a major flaw in its equating of the ticket buyout with keeping the Twins in the Metrodome. While 2.4 million fans might meet the attendance provision of the escape clause, it failed to address a provision allowing the team to void its contract if they could prove financial losses over a three-year period.

"I read about it in the paper," remembers Calvin. "I said, 'Well, that silly so and so.' He (Mackay) didn't seem to know that the attendance is just secondary. I got a clause in there that if I lose money I can move. That's the easiest thing in the world to do. The Twins right now (1988) have the same thing in their contract and they're claiming they lost money three years in a row. We had accountants too.

"He (Mackay) didn't screw Calvin Griffith," continues Calvin. "He screwed the banks and the corporations up there. He no more kept us from moving than the man in the moon."

Yet Mackay continued with the ticket buyout through June, 1984, to widespread publicity, and the tune of over $6 million. "He's that much of an egotist," charges Calvin. "He's a big man around Minneapolis. He gets invited to all the big things so he must have an in with all the big shots. Of course he owns a very lucrative envelope company. The only time I really talked to him was when he came out to Seattle to try to buy the ballclub.

"He thought he was the big man to keep Calvin in the Twin Cities," concludes the former Twins owner of Mackay. "I laughed about it because he didn't know what the score was."

Calvin wasn't laughing at the immediate effects of the ticket buyout, however. Mackay naturally sought the most economical method of reaching the 2.4 million attendance mark, regardless of impact. "He would buy tickets, no question about it," recalls Calvin. "But they were all cheap tickets. He'd get the $3 tickets and stuff like that, which really irritated me, cause he was taking it away from other people that only had $3 to buy a ticket."

In an even larger sense, Calvin objected to the ticket buyout's effect. "It wasn't good for baseball," he still argues today. "If baseball has to have someone to proselytize it's not good. Baseball has to live on its own. It has to entertain the fans and if you can't entertain the fans then you shouldn't draw. I never begged anybody to come to a ballgame. I think it's a terrible thing to say, 'Please come to a ballgame, I need your help.'"

Yet despite threatening legal action, for public relations reasons, the Twins couldn't refuse to sell tickets to the buyout group. "We couldn't," says Calvin. "If you did a thing like that then they'd say, 'Well see, he's gonna move out. He doesn't want help.'"

Instead the Twins offered to renegotiate their Metrodome lease, voluntarily locking themselves into the stadium for another four years. In return, they asked for a reduction in rent and for local buyers to underwrite the annual sale of 6,000 season tickets during a four year period.

It was an arrangement that was estimated to cost about $8.5 million, or only $2.1 million more from business and other buyers than the $6.4 million raised for the ticket buyout. Moreover, the next Twins owner would put even more costly demands on Metrodome officials. Yet Mackay and the rest of the Task Force decided to go ahead with the nationally publicized buyouts on May 15, resulting in a series of "sold out," but near-empty stadiums.

"What a way to do business," said Calvin, who still seemed almost puzzled at the ticket buyers' nearsighted approach. "I'm not only concerned about this season. I'm concerned about the year after that and the year after that," he added, noting that the team still had not been drawing naturally despite its first place status. "Something like this just seems to be a move to drive you out of town."

Calvin certainly still had interested buyers in other cities, including Trump's offer of $50 million. "He didn't lose interest," says Calvin, recalling spring, 1984 meetings with a Trump representative that largely focused on acceptance of Griffith's major requirement that members of the family be continued in management positions. "He was gonna keep us on and me as president of the ballclub, and he'd be chairman of the board."

Even Trump's background as an Atlantic City casino owner would not have been a negative factor, argues Calvin, noting the Yankees' Del Webb's previous ownership of Las Vegas gambling interests, and George Steinbrenner's current horseracing involvement. "Major league baseball couldn't reject him," he concludes of Trump.

But Calvin would ultimately reject a life in Trump Towers. "The reason why I wouldn't sell it to him is he wanted to move the club up to the Meadowlands (Stadium) in New Jersey," says Calvin. "I said, 'Hell no.' That'd be three clubs up there. That'd never be approved. There had been three before. But things have changed now. They wouldn't allow three ballclubs within 50 miles of each other."

A more subtle factor may have been Calvin's great distaste for the thought of living in the Big Apple. "I despise New York. I'm petrified there," he admits. "I get in an elevator with someone I never push the button till they get up. I don't go into my room unless I have a bellboy. I've gone in and had people in my bed. That scares ya."

Geographic concerns largely ruled out another long-term suitor—multimillionaire real estate developer John Dikeou of Denver. "He's one of those Forbes 400 guys. They had the money. They'd show up at the All-Star game and everywhere else. We'd always talk to him and consider what he had to say," says Calvin, who nevertheless would again rule against moving the team to the Rocky Mountains.

Indianapolis also remained in the running with promises of large amounts of guaranteed season ticket sales if the Twins moved there. But Calvin's dislike of their new, domed stadium proved fatal. "The stadium they built just wouldn't suffice for major league baseball," he describes. "I think it would have cost Indianapolis about another $8 million more to recondition it (the Hoosierdome) for baseball and then it wouldn't have been a good stadium."

Representatives of Vancouver's Molson Brewing Company made a particularly attractive pitch for that city, recalls Calvin. "They were rich people. When you've got brewing you've got money, and wonderful people—a very good deal."

But another domed stadium and Canadian ownership laws were discouraging, particularly as they affected future employment with the team. "They were gonna keep me on in management," he explains. "But up there you had to be a Canadian citizen to get a job. I would have had to be accepted, but you would have problems with the rest of your family."

Another of Calvin's major concerns was the effect any sale announcement might have on attendance during the team's remaining time in Minnesota. Especially in the case of Tampa, which couldn't even begin construction of their own stadium until they had a tenant, it could be a particularly difficult time.

But the Florida city even solved that problem to remain at the top of the list of cities outside Minnesota, says Calvin, with confirmation from Tampa investor Earle Holstead. "They were even willing to pay the losses if I'd have said I was moving to Tampa. It was something I didn't have to worry about. They were first class people and they were gonna keep me on to run the ballclub."

Despite the contention of Bowie Kuhn in his 1987 autobiography that he would have never have allowed the Twins to move to Florida, Calvin remains convinced that he would have gained league approval for the shift. "If you prove that you have done your utmost in trying to win and you lose money and your attendance is not comparable to other clubs in the league, then you can do anything you want money-wise."

Calvin's faith in that quasi-legal opinion was unshaken despite the doubts of others in the organization, including Fox and Clark Griffith. But it did suffer a relapse in 1982 when the football Oakland Raiders were temporarily held in place by the California Supreme Court. "I don't know how the court could allow six women on the jury to decide whether it's fair for a ballclub to move," he said. "Who were the women? What were their capabilities? Most likely they went home and caught hell from their husbands."

Ultimately Calvin's faith in his own options rested less on court rulings than on a simple analogy. "It's the same thing with any store, you know. If Dayton's (department store) don't like to work here they can close their store and move out to Southdale or Burnsville or someplace else," he argues. "It's the same way in baseball if you can prove you can't make it and you've done your job."

Regardless, Calvin had already decided his first wish was really to keep the team in the Twin Cities. "Minnesota has been so good to me, I never did really want to move out of Minnesota," he declares. "The only way I woulda was if I couldn't have done something here in this state. 'Cause they accepted us in 1961 with open arms and we had a lot of wonderful years here.

"So we weren't gonna come in here and be turngoats, I mean turncoats," Calvin says with seeming sincerity. "We came in here and appreciated what they did for us and we did our utmost to give them the best baseball humanly possible—the way we had to operate."

Holstead confirms that Tampa was aware of Calvin's desire to remain in Minnesota if offered an acceptable deal. "Calvin really didn't wanta move," he says. "We always knew that. Calvin got a bum rap up there from people who didn't know what they were talking about. I realize he left Washington but he had to. Minneapolis got a real break."

Chapter 19

A FOX IN THE HENHOUSE
AND THE DEED IS DONE

"In the baseball business you always made a deal by shaking hands with someone.
Pohlad wasn't in that kind of business. He was in a cutthroat business.
We were in different businesses."

By mid-May, 1984 the Griffith family was both ready to sell and had made known their preference to sell to a Twin Cities buyer. Even before Harvey Mackay launched his much-hooplahed ticket-buyout scheme, purportedly to keep the Twins in Minnesota, negotiations were well underway with a local prospective purchaser.

"We are making good progress with (Carl) Pohlad," Calvin told reporters on May 12, explaining the only holdups. "We hope before long we will get a report from our tax attorneys so we can work on the sale. We're going to sell the club even if we wind up with the $6 million for the tickets. But we plan to continue in the management of the team. Everybody we have talked to about a sale has asked us to stay on as the managing directors."

Calvin's confidence at both his family's continued role with the Twins and in Pohlad's sincere interest in the team seemed to hold up well through initial negotiations. "We've pretty well agreed on the price," he told writers on May 17. "We're hopeful that the deal can be concluded in the next 10 days."

$32 million in payments and salaries over 20 years would be the amount finally settled on after Pohlad had spent several months going over the Twins account books. He would even hire the team's auditing firm, Arthur Andersen and Co., to help make a detailed assessment of the tax and other implications of the purchase for himself. The baseball team would be judged for its value as an addition to the chain of banks, transportation and soft drink bottling institutions of which he already had ownership control.

"The way I looked at it, we were determined to get the $30 million I was offered by Tampa," says Calvin, explaining his simpler arrival at the sale price. "That was always our starting point."

More complex would be the several month discussion of other terms. Tiring of the process after several initial meetings with Pohlad, Calvin turned over direct responsibility for negotiations to Bruce Haynes. "I started it all," he says. "And I talked to Brucie every time. I told him what to talk about. But they did all the negotiating, the nitty-gritty work." Entrusting the negotiations to Haynes was an act of faith which Calvin would later regret.

But Calvin's bargaining position grew even stronger in late May with the addition of another prospective local buyer. Twin Cities real estate developers and future owners of the Minnesota Timberwolves NBA basketball franchise, Marvin Wolfenson and Harvey Rattner, made a reported $27 million cash offer through Minneapolis banker Harold Greenwood, who had a long association with Calvin through his purchase of the Twins television broadcast rights.

After Greenwood set up a short personal meeting, both sides emerged with praise for each other, though no agreement. "I have a lot of respect for Calvin Griffith and his family and would retain all of the present personnel working for the club," Wolfenson pledged through reporters, continuing his flattery. "I don't know of any better baseball man than Calvin."

Years later Wolfenson was more candid and angrily recalled being rejected in a brief meeting with Calvin. "I think he's a smart baseball man and a dumb businessman," he concludes. "If it had been a real estate transaction and I had offered $8 million more (including interest) than the next guy I would have got it. But he didn't want to work for me. He wanted to work with Pohlad, which turned out to be a grievous error cause he treated him like crap . . . . Griffith was probably second to none in judging baseball talent. But he wasn't so good at judging people sometimes."

Calvin remembers being impressed with Wolfenson and Rattner, despite the brevity of their meeting. But he admits that his definition of fair play perhaps overrode business sense. "Like I said before, Pohlad was the first one to approach me and that was it."

Several persons, including Clark Griffith, noted that the Wolfenson and Rattner offer would yield a better return than one with extended payments. "I told Calvin he was making a bad deal (with Pohlad); that if he was intent on selling he was better off taking the cash offer from Marv Wolfenson and Harvey Rattner," Clark said years later to *Star & Tribune* columnist Pat Reusse. "I told Calvin he would be treated better by those gentlemen.

"But there was no swaying Calvin," adds Clark. "I knew it was a lost cause early that June. I went in Calvin's office one afternoon. He told me Bruce had convinced him it (the sale to Pohlad) was the best deal. You know what Calvin said? 'Bruce Haynes is a genius.'"

Loyalties were certainly being twisted and strained in many directions as Calvin chose to prefer Bruce Haynes' advice, and that of Howard Fox and the Arthur Anderson accountants, to that of his son. "They tell me now that was the better deal," he laments of the Wolfenson and Rattner offer. "I should maybe have given more consideration to Hal Greenwood since I dealt with him all these years. He never went back on his word. That's something you always relish if you can talk to people and they keep their word to you."

(Ironically, Greenwood would several years later be the subject of an FBI investigation and be forced to step down from his presidency of the financially troubled Midwest Federal Savings and Loan.)

Yet, in addition to not going back on his own word, Calvin preferred Pohlad's offer of extended payments for his own rather curious financial reasons. "If I got all that cash at one time there's no telling what I might do with it," he says. "I might go buy a castle in Spain or Scotland, or this or that. If you travel around and live like you want to, it costs a lot of money. So I said, 'Let's leave it for the children.' I got enough the first trip in to take care of me for the rest of my life. When I die payments will still come in to the children or Mrs. Griffith. They won't have to look for their bread and butter someplace else."

It is a particularly curious logic for a man often alternately described as either cheap or gluttonous. Yet Calvin was passing up a larger amount of cash, as well as tax advantages, in what could either be described as naivete or a genuine obsession with the long-term security of his family.

"I figured 'Hell, I can't even spend it the rest of my life,'" explains Calvin. "Why should I worry about how long it takes? As long as nobody's worrying about their next meal, that's the thing. Everybody should be happy on what they got."

On May 25 Calvin announced that he had reached an agreement in principle with Pohlad. "We had a great meeting today," he told reporters. "I don't think there is any chance that the deal will fall through."

It was Pohlad's concern for maximizing all financial angles that delayed the sale for another month. The multimillionaire not only began his own successful negotiations for a more favorable Metrodome lease but also negotiated with Mackay for suspension of the ticket-buyout and the eventual diversion of the remaining funds for future Twins season ticket sales.

Remaining negotiations with the Griffiths largely focused on non-financial matters. "The other terms were the most important," Calvin recalls. "We finished talking about the money and then we got down into the particulars and the people you have working for you—so they can be free of mind."

Continued Griffith family roles with the Twins as a precondition to the sale was "discussed quite regularly at meetings," confirms Bruce Haynes. "We thought we had an understanding."

Calvin's often-stated demand to remain active in baseball operations appeared to be accepted by Pohlad, who in repeated public statements praised the Griffith family. Without such assurance, Calvin told reporters on June 9, "We'll cross them off the list. I'm not going to sign my death warrant. If you're inactive, your mind becomes inactive."

Yet Calvin, who was personally less than actively involved in negotiations with Pohlad at this time, made clear his desire to hurry up the process of giving up team ownership. "I hope it doesn't go on all summer. I want to live a normal life," he said, while summarily turning down another purchase offer by the investment house of Merrill Lynch Pierce Fenner and Smith.

Haynes was by now entirely in charge of negotiations with Pohlad. Seeking moral support, Haynes invited Twins vice-president Howard Fox, with whom he had often worked, to also attend meetings. It was another act of arguably misplaced trust that would haunt the Griffith family when Fox, surprisingly, was named the first Twins president under Pohlad and then, shockingly, presided over the firing of his former employers.

Calvin makes clear his regard for Fox's hiring as part of a sellout. "He (Fox) was going with Bruce Haynes down to Pohlad's office, which I didn't know a damn thing about until we had already agreed to sell it to him," says Calvin angrily. "I didn't know Fox was there and he didn't have any authority. It wasn't any of his business what we were doing. He got in so good with Pohlad that he was assured of a job."

Fox vehemently denies the accusation, with one qualification. "Until Carl Pohlad bought the ballclub, I never knew what my role was going to be," he maintains. "However, once I was told, not by Carl but by somebody else, that if he bought it, I was going to run it."

Certainly Fox was adept at finding niches to fill, as Calvin admits with a certain amount of condescension. "Howard Fox was a person who you needed in life to do what had to be done," says Calvin, using hotel accommodations and travel reservations as examples. "I'd say, 'Howard, I need this and that and that. Go ahead and do it.' And he would do it. Or at least I thought he had done it."

But Calvin has since grown to distrust the man who was once arguably his closest friend and advisor. "Now I find out there were a lot of things he didn't do. That's what hurts. But it took me ten years to find that out. I didn't find that out 'til after I sold the ballclub. That really irked me."

Fox continues to protest his innocence. "I never did anything that Calvin wasn't apprised of. I felt it my responsibility as a friend and so on," he says, while noting that it was Bruce Haynes who officially was responsible for bringing details of sale negotiations to Calvin and the Board of Directors. "I wasn't in on it."

Calvin even suspects that Fox had planned to use the gullible Haynes as his springboard. "I think he knew when he went out negotiating with Brucie that he was gonna have more of a chance if he got together with Brucie," he speculates. "He would get more conversation, more inside information. That was it."

Haynes gets little sympathy from Calvin, however. "Brucie didn't get fired," he notes. "He just didn't want to work, that's all there is to it. He was too much interested in playing golf and getting into other business. Fox took advantage of it."

Fox does agree he had developed some form of relationship with Pohlad as a result of his ability to fully describe the Twins organization in detail. "In negotiations I met with Carl, along with Bruce, several times because Carl wanted to know about things. I think I met with Carl on two occasions without Bruce and I came back and reported to Calvin. I wanted him to know what I was doing because that's the way I operated all my life."

Calvin angrily denies that Fox ever told him of his private meetings with Pohlad. "The only thing he (Fox) told me was, 'I'll take care of it for you on the (Chris) Speier thing," Calvin says, referring to the Twins ongoing attempts to pick up an extra infielder while negotiations were taking place.

Yet Fox's version of events suggests that he was even given a recommendation for the Twins president position by his former boss. "Carl told me that," says Fox.

"Pohlad never asked me for a recommendation," replies Calvin, twisting his face in disgust. "Pohlad just told me he was gonna make Fox president and I said, 'Well, all right.' I was surprised as hell. But what could I say? He'd already made up his mind. Fox didn't have enough intelligence to do it. Why in hell Pohlad made him president I can only imagine.

"Course he (Fox) only stayed one year," notes Calvin with a sarcastic smile. "What went wrong, I don't know. He did a good hatchet job on my family."

It was a sequence of events which would leave Calvin increasingly embittered as he looked back. "It was very bad. If I'd have known Brucie needed help I'd have had Clarkie go down," he says, momentarily forgetting his estrangement from his son. "Or else I could have gone down. To me, negotiations were all over except for lawyers putting final touches on."

By mid-June 1984 most of the final touches had been added and approved by Peter Dorsey, representing the Twins. A joint agreement was announced, and after privately signing letters of intent, an official signing ceremony was scheduled for June 23 in the Metrodome. It was a touch of drama that apparently pleased both Calvin and Pohlad.

But the last few days leading to the ceremony were not easy ones for the head of the Griffith family. With the Twins fighting for the division lead, second thoughts naturally kept pounding into Calvin's brain, despite being convinced of the long-term hopelessness of the situation.

Once again, Calvin remembers turning for private reassurance from the most influential figure in his life, the deceased Clark Griffith. "I said, 'Unc, I'm sorry but I can't continue any further.' He made everything possible for me and my family. But with the changing times I think I didn't let him down. He woulda gotten out of baseball way before I did. He couldn't tolerate the players' union and players telling you what to do. I think Clark Griffith would have understood what I was doing, what I had to."

Even feeling secure of his uncle's acceptance couldn't entirely ease the torment of awaiting the June 23 ceremony, however. "I guess my mind was blank all day long," says Calvin, leading in to description of a flood of memories. "So many things enter your mind you just couldn't believe it, knowing that it was your last farewell days as an owner or president. The name of Griffith was carved into baseball history from 1920. I just kept thinking about it as I was getting ready to get in a car and ride around the ballpark."

That Friday night's ceremony at home plate lasted only a half hour. But to Calvin it would seem like an eternity. "I was nervous as hell," he recalls. "I couldn't get the thing started and over with soon enough."

His edginess showed during a pre-game press conference when he uncharacteristically refused to answer questions from a particular television reporter. But the ceremony itself went without a hitch despite the obvious emotional reactions from both Calvin and Thelma. With 21,919 fans, a local television audience, and the Twins and White Sox squads watching, the pair symbolically signed over the team to Pohlad.

"It was fantastic," Calvin remembers of the ceremony. "It was really outstanding. You don't get those kind of opportunities to say thank you to the people and for them to say

181

'thank you' for what you did. It was really outstanding. They really gave me a wonderful farewell."

The aftereffects would be harder, however. "It was a helluva shock to do what I did," concludes Calvin. "I was sad for a week or ten days, I guess. Maybe longer. Oh hell, yes. But eventually it was a relief where you could say, 'Now I don't have to worry about a payroll or anybody ridiculing you or any other damn thing. You're a free man.'"

Of course Calvin did not want to be totally free of any responsibility with the Twins. Almost in the same breath with telling reporters he planned to be a "good-time Charley," he would outline ambitious personal plans for helping the team. "I'm going to have something to do with player evaluation and development," he said on the day of the sale. "It's what I wanted to do. I'll be working with George (Brophy) and getting out around the system and watching other major league clubs. I think between us we can make some pretty good judgements on our younger players. As long as I don't become senile and can do the company some good, I'm sure Carl Pohlad will put up with me."

Pohlad, while already being more cautious in his statements about Calvin, was still promising a role for the 72-year-old. "Mr. Griffith and I still must have some further discussion," Pohlad told Sid Hartman on the day of the signing ceremony. "He has told me it is now time for him not to step out but step aside and let young management assume some responsibility.

"I don't know exactly what his role will be," continued Pohlad. "His role will be whatever we can work out that he will be most productive at. Not what we think, but what he thinks."

While using an analogy that would prove ironic, Pohlad noted however that he hadn't yet made an evaluation of Twins management. "I can't say now whether we will step outside. If necessary, yes. If we need a shortstop and we don't have one in the farm system, we will have to step outside."

Calvin would be the one actually looking for shortstops and other players who could help the team for most of that year however, as he officially continued to own the Twins for over another two months until the contract wording could be completed and approved by the American League. In the interim, he would continue operating the team as it enjoyed its best opportunity to win the Division since 1977. Along with the other members of the Griffith family he continued his same work schedule and habits.

Calvin's daily trips to the office would be interrupted by only one more celebratory event before he officially handed over the team. An early August trip to Cooperstown, New York for the Hall of Fame induction of Harmon Killebrew would be yet another trip back down memory lane. It was 25 years earlier that he had insisted a young, rough-edged third baseman be inserted into the Washington Senators lineup, leading to a career that would be recognized as ranking with the greatest in the game's history.

Just a couple of days later, Calvin would receive the recognition of his own peers during a meeting of American League owners to approve transfer of the team to Pohlad. "I had to make a speech to tell them what a great guy the sonofabitch was," Calvin would later bitterly recall.

Pohlad, for his part, again publicly pledged that Calvin would continue to be a part of Twins baseball operations. "I could just say, 'Calvin, good-bye,' and send him into a corner," said Pohlad to reporters. "But he really can do a good job in baseball."

The highlight of the meetings for Griffith would be a minute-long standing ovation he received from men with whom he had often been in philosophical disagreement. "It was moving," Calvin said to reporters afterward. "It showed that people agreed with what we have done in baseball and that we've always been honest. All the criticism I took for trying to develop a ballclub, and now we have a club winning."

With the Twins taking a surprising lead in the A.L. West Division in mid-August, another of Calvin's youth projects was clearly blossoming. Energized by the excitement of the pennant race but without financial worries for the first time in over a decade, in his final days as an owner he was finally able to enjoy himself.

"I didn't have to get up in the morning to come to the office and get the pencil out and multiply this and divide that to find out if we're going to have enough money to pay our bills or pay the ballplayers and everything like that," Calvin remembers.

With his $10 million down payment from Pohlad, Calvin personally had wealth he had never dreamed of. "I wrote out a check for $200,000 a couple of weeks ago," he told then *St. Paul Pioneer Press* columnist Reusse. "I didn't think I'd ever be able to do that and not flinch. Maybe I did flinch. The first time I wrote it, I screwed it up. I had to write 'cancel' across it and get another check."

Locally, his star was again rising among Twins fans as the team, so recently the butt of jokes, began to mature. Calvin's belief in young players such as Frank Viola, Kent Hrbek, Gary Gaetti, Kirby Puckett, Tom Brunansky and trades for Ron Davis, Mike Smithson, and John Butcher paid off on the field and in the stands. Attendance figures once again reflected an interest in the team that did not depend on ticket buyouts.

Attempting to give the team an extra edge, Calvin completed a trade bringing veteran shortstop Chris Speier from St. Louis for $100,000. Commentators such as Hartman praised the move as indicative of Pohlad's commitment to winning in 1984. Yet even before Speier's injury, the new multi-millionaire was objecting to the price.

"Pohlad wanted to call the deal off," Calvin remembers of the new owner's real feelings. "He wanted to call if off. So I had to call up Commissioner Bowie Kuhn and he said, 'Well you're still the president, you're the say in my opinion. The deal stands.' So we kept him because we felt he could help the club. Gardner was looking for an infielder down the stretch."

Minnesota pennant fever would however eventually be cooled by a reality as undeniable as the coming of the Griffiths' final days in baseball. After Calvin officially turned over the ownership reins on September 7, the young club fell apart in the final weeks— losing its last six games, including a memorable game in Cleveland where the Twins had led 10-0.

It was a collapse that puzzled many baseball men, including Calvin. "They should have won the pennant that year," he still says with the sound of a man feeling cheated. "I am wondering what happened to management after I turned it over to them with a five and a half game lead (on August 22). I never will find out. 'Course the '64 (Philadelphia) Phillies had something like a seven game lead with ten days to go."

But few, including Calvin, were truly disappointed with the Twins surprising season. Spurred on by his own sudden popularity that included repeated cheers from the crowd at an airport reception on the team's return from Cleveland, Calvin was clearly basking in both the team's and his own redemption.

"I feel we're right on the threshold of coming into a ballclub that could be very domineering," he said just a few days after the 1984 season. "We've improved the last two years 20 or 25 games. Next year if we improve 10 games we're gonna win it . . . . I think over the winter the ballplayers will wash all of this stuff out and mature. A guy will become a man over the winter. We have a few ballplayers I'm just hoping will become men over the winter."

Speaking personally, Calvin was equally optimistic. "I hope I'll be remembered as someone who did his best to give the people something they can be proud of," he said. "I think the ovations I've received at various places lately, like out at the airport the other night, have been most appreciative. It makes you know that you're not too bad of a guy overall."

Calvin would even begin to project himself as something of a prophet to baseball owners. "I want to try to say I was right for a change," he told another reporter. "I don't want to brag about anything like that. But in life, if you don't try something, you're not going to gain anything. We tried it and I think now the club owners themselves are saying the only sensible ones in the business are the Griffith, the Haynes and the Robertson families."

But the reality was that the winds of change which had already swept by those families were now about to totally sweep them out. Even before the season's end, Clark Griffith would already be dismissed from his job without a reason given or even a direct contact from new club president Howard Fox.

Calvin's initial reaction was to defend Fox and shrug it off as another outcome of Clark's arrogance. "I've been telling him all along he's got to be a little more humble," he said.

But as the pattern repeated itself, Calvin would finally cast the blame toward Fox. "He got rid of Clark 'cause he knew he was much smarter than he was and knew more baseball. He would have been embarrassed to have a man of Clarkie's ability around," says Calvin after reconsideration of the two men.

Officially given the title of chairman of the board, Calvin and farm director George Brophy would both be excluded from Fox and Pohlad's first post-season meeting to consider the team's future on-the-field direction. Other Twins employees reportedly received directions to exclude Calvin from sensitive information and decisions. He would never again be seriously included in any trade or personnel decision.

Fox agrees the relationship with his former boss had begun to change, but argues it was never vindictive. "Certainly in running the business I didn't feel like I had to confide in him on everything," he says. "But I tried to keep him as comfortable as possible."

Nevertheless Calvin's trust in the promises of Fox and Pohlad began to erode even by the end of the 1984 World Series. "He (Pohlad) wasn't too cordial already," he remembers. "I guess I should have seen it coming. He talks and then he writes memos. And memos I don't read too often.

"In the baseball business you always made a deal by shaking hands with someone," adds Calvin. "He (Pohlad) wasn't in that kind of business. He was in a cutthroat business (banking). We were in different businesses."

Chapter 20

DEMISE OF THE DINOSAUR

"They've taken everything out of the stadium, everything connected with
Griffith family history. I guess they don't want to be reminded."

Calvin Griffith still occupied a tiny office in the Metrodome, at least until September, 1989. As part of the sale agreement that included a salary for five years, the office is his only remaining official connection to the game. The few plaques and photographs decorating the walls are the only remaining physical evidence in the Metrodome of the family's role in Twins history.

"They've taken everything out of the stadium, everything connected with Griffith family history," points out Calvin sadly, leaning across the desk still covered with fan mail, minor league and Japanese scouting reports, and assorted baseball paraphernalia. "I guess they don't want to be reminded."

But Calvin has nothing if not a memory. He and Fox have had virtually no communication since the firing of his son Clark, his brothers Billy and Jimmy Robertson, traveling secretary Mike Robertson, George Brophy, Bruce Haynes, Tommy Cronin and others in that first year after the sale. His conversations with Pohlad have generally been limited to mundane matters of health or the weather.

Promises of a continued role in management disappeared shortly after the team sale. "That was a joke, all that talk that he'd bought the greatest management in baseball," scoffs Calvin, who is no longer even listed in the Twins media guide. "He (Pohlad) said, 'We're gonna make you chairman of the board.' Hell, I never went to a meeting in my life. I never had another meeting with him. I'm never consulted.

"He said he was gonna keep everybody in the family five years. Fox took care of that in a hurry. Fox fired Clarkie, he fired Mike Robertson, he fired my two brothers. They had the best public relations in the state of Minneapolis. They knew every bartender around. They used to bring them in by busloads," continues Calvin, his tale of betrayal perhaps overcoming his memory of attendance realities.

In his usual fashion, Calvin isn't shy about his feelings. "Pohlad didn't tell us the truth," he says bluntly. "He didn't tell the truth. He said he bought the best management in baseball for the next five years. We were supposed to have something to do with the ballclub. That only lasted a few days."

Billy Robertson accepts the family's dismissal more graciously. "Calvin heard something and he more or less accepted without having it in hard writing," he says, rationalizing that he and his twin brother Jimmy had been fortunate to stay in baseball until their retirement age. "It wouldn't have been a happy relationship anyway 'cause our philosophies are really different."

Not so diplomatic is Clark Griffith, who sees the firings as part of a concerted management strategy. "Calvin never checked on Pohlad's record. (But) I had a friend tell me about how Pohlad bought up this family concern in California and hired this friend of the family to run it and *that* guy gave them the axe . . . . One of his techniques was to find some guy who'd worked for a family forever 'cause he'd be so glad to move up. So I wasn't surprised at all. But other people really were."

Pohlad did not respond to numerous requests for interviews. But others defend his position as a natural one for any new owner of a business—wishing to bring in his own management or personnel. Especially with the reputation and stigma attached to the Griffiths, the argument goes, it only made marketing sense to clear away negative reminders as soon as possible.

Fox denies that his role as the hatchet man pleased him, even while he recognized the necessity. "Here are people that you've known for 37, 38, 40 years and you've got to make changes that you know are going to hurt these people. It's not an easy job. It's tough enough keeping friends much less losing them," he says, taking off his glasses to wipe his eyes with a handkerchief.

"(But) when changes are made in companies and somebody puts out a big outlay there's change," says Fox, regaining his composure. "There always has been and always will be. All you've got to do is look at any business. If somebody puts out a whole lot of money there's gonna be changes made."

The clash in personal styles may have also made change inevitable. The Griffiths' unrefined, earthy approach would stick out more prominently in a corporate board room than Jimmy Robertson's red and white Twins beret. "Billy and Jimmy Robertson had a lot going for them," agrees former Twins attorney Peter Dorsey. "But they would tend not to make a good impression on Carl Pohlad."

Certainly Calvin and the family's impressions of Pohlad have changed. "I thought he was honest and then I found out otherwise," concludes Calvin. "He never keeps his word. He can't keep his word."

As another example, Calvin cites the 1984 Chris Speier trade, which Pohlad four years later used as the basis for withholding $150,000 plus interest from his scheduled payments to the Griffiths. Legally, Pohlad can point to wording in the sale document that prohibited Calvin from "devaluing" the team between the signing ceremony in the Metrodome and Pohlad's actual takeover on September 7, 1984.

Calvin angrily insists that while he didn't actually read the document he signed at home plate that June 23, he finally got oral approval of the trade from Pohlad. "I asked him. I asked him before I signed the papers. I said, 'What about the Chris Speier thing? He said, 'Oh, forget about it,'" maintains Calvin. "If he'd have said, 'We'll talk about it later on,' I wouldn't have signed the papers that night. And I wouldn't have been embarrassed, he'd have been embarrassed."

Calvin's only embarrassment may be the accusation of having made a trade that devalued a baseball team. "Did I devalue his ballclub?" he asks, noting that Speier would be named the MVP of the San Francisco Giants several years later. "I didn't devalue his ballclub as much as Fox did when he let (Tim) Teufel go and then made a deal with Cleveland and let (Richard) Yett go. Do they have any of those players (gained in the trade) left in their farm system? If he (Pohlad) questions my judgement on a ballplayer, I am really in bad shape to have a nincompoop like him say something like that."

Calvin's contempt for Pohlad was made greater by his eventual realization of the new Twins owner's relative lack of baseball knowledge. "He eats at seven o'clock when the game starts at 7:05. I don't understand that," says Calvin, shaking his head. "I understand he wanted to see Syracuse and Penn State on TV the other day, the first game of the (1988) World Series. He wanted to see a football game instead of the World Series. I wish the hell I knew all these things. I wouldn't have sold it to him if I knew all these things."

Recalling Pohlad's initial expressions of interest in the Twins as both a baseball fan and a civic gesture, Calvin soon learned he had other priorities. "I was surprised as hell when I heard him (Pohlad) say, 'I've purchased the club to make money and if I don't make money I'll sell it.' I was dumfounded," remembers Calvin, scoffing at Pohlad's public image. "He was all peaches and cream. 'I'm doing this for the city. I'm doing it for this and that.'"

Calvin describes another, higher priority than mere profits that he somewhat naively believed Pohlad shared. "I thought he was a sportsman. The only people who should get into these big games are sportsmen who get into it for the fun of it."

But even Calvin is forced to admit that love of the game is generally replaced by profit and ego as motivation for involvement in professional sports these days. "These Fortune 400 guys, how many of them get their names in the news? Baseball gives you an entree. Look at Pohlad. Somebody told me I was selling to a good man 'cause he'll never try to publicize himself. Then he spent millions of dollars getting his name in print. He's sure not been low profile."

Despite his own obvious wealth and relatively high profile, Calvin still sees himself in a populist light. "You know, the more you have, the more you want. That's the unfortunate thing," he says with a shake of his head. "Those millionaires, shit, all they do is 'Gimme, gimme, gimme.'"

"He (Pohlad) owns 50 banks for chrissakes, and you don't run a bank and lose money. But you just wonder how he's losing so much money running the ballclub," Calvin continues, referring to the Twins claims of losing nearly $20 million since 1985. "He took in $31 million last year (1987). We had a good year taking in $13-14 million and their (player payroll) salaries ain't ten times ours . . . . Now we're catching hell from Sid Hartman for ruining Pohlad. Ruining a man who has 40 banks. What a joke!"

Ironically, after so often being accused of exploiting fans and players himself as Twins owner, Calvin would observe his successor's financial maneuvers going largely without criticism. "What really irked me was when we raised ticket prices and the press raised so much hell. It was uncalled for," he says, drawing a comparison. "They raise the price on the newspaper. They charge more if you get it delivered to your door and everything else. They charge you more for ads.

"I go up a dollar for my tickets and they almost run me out of town. Then here comes Pohlad and after he wins the pennant (1987) he goes up, and after setting a record for attendance (1988) he's gone up $3 in prices," concludes Calvin. "I guess if you have money you can do what you want and you don't have to worry about the press. But we had to worry."

Calvin's comments to the media about Fox's performance in his one year as Twins president earned him his only real meeting with Pohlad since the sale. "Pohlad called me in last year (1987) and told me not to talk about his employees," recalls Calvin. "He made me wait a long goddamn time. If I'd have had any sense I shoulda waited there a half hour and gone. But I was trying to be decent even if he wasn't . . . . You could see that he wasn't real calm. But he's the owner. The owner can do what he wants."

Fox would counter that Calvin was only expressing his frustration at no longer being Twins owner. "He's got an ego. He likes the attention of the fans," he says. "And anytime you have a change in a family there will be innuendoes and talk. This family (Griffiths) lived off this ballclub all its life and all of a sudden they don't have it. It's got to be emotional."

In agreement is Peter Dorsey. "I think Calvin didn't fully grasp the idea that he wasn't going to be running that ballclub. Nobody was deceptive about it. But he had been in the driver's seat so long I don't think any other seat was going to be happy, and he seemed to develop a kind of paranoia about it."

Certainly it is true that everything in Calvin's psychological makeup pointed to difficulty in adapting to a diminished role in baseball. "You have to have a uniform on or own the ballclub to be the big man," he said himself to *Sport Magazine* in 1984.

Calvin's continued attention from fans and old friends hasn't replaced the thrill of making decisions that affected the entire Twins organization. "I liked to be the head guy," he admits. "I'd talk to people before I made up my mind. You'd get seven or eight opinions and you had to be the one to make the final decision."

He remembers the results with an obvious pride that has never been daunted by criticism. "You have to make mistakes to learn," argues Calvin with obvious resentment at his forgotten successes. "But I think I've become a pretty good executive."

Yet Calvin's understanding of the executive position clearly did not fit in the new Twins organization. In contrast with the Griffith formula which called for generally informal meetings among top family members and team executives on most topics, the Pohlad reorganization called for more formal separation of duties and decision-making.

"They've all got these fancy titles," argues Calvin of the specialization. "But I always figured titles didn't really mean anything. You still gotta come into the park and do the work."

Similarly, Pohlad's reliance on highly trained marketing and sales personnel with little or no background in baseball is a foreign concept to Calvin. In the Griffith organization responsibility usually followed more from personal familiarity and trust than from formal expertise.

Dorsey notes as an example the team's unsophisticated financial operation when it first arrived in Minnesota. "Ossie Bluege was his business manager, an old baseball player. Ossie didn't know the difference between a checking account and a savings account, literally. A nice, nice man, loyal as the day is long. But just over his head," suggests Dorsey in drawing a contrast. "Jim Pohlad is a CPA."

Even after a more sophisticated accounting system was developed under Twins comptroller Jack Alexander, the organization was still not oriented toward full pursuit of economic opportunities. "I don't know anything about all this high finance and (player) depreciation," readily admits Calvin of major factors in the modern world of baseball.

With the Twins coming to Minnesota in 1960, Calvin might well have followed the example of other teams, such as the Los Angeles Dodgers, in demanding more real estate and Met Stadium area development rights from their Twin Cities suitors, argues Tom Mee. "Calvin could have had here what O'Malley got at Chavez Ravine. They wanted him so bad he could have had almost anything, industrial revenue bonds, land, anything. He was just too nice and he didn't like to think about high finance. He thought about ballplayers."

Billy Robertson agrees, noting that even later the organization's baseball priorities conflicted with its business success. "That's probably where we made our big mistake," he says. "We could have diversified in the early 1960s when we were making a whole lot of money. We could have developed that whole area (around Met Stadium) if we'd been alert to our business opportunities. But we always just stuck to baseball and had fun."

The Griffiths' refusal to change their priorities may have been a fatal flaw agrees Wheelock Whitney, who served on the Twins board from 1961 'til the sale to Pohlad. "It was a family enterprise and Calvin ran it that way. "But on the other hand he was willing to have a compensation committee and let me run it and we wrestled with the salaries. He was also willing to adopt a profit-sharing plan. Calvin wasn't totally rigid. But there were some old values he had a hard time yielding on."

While the Griffith organization had developed great expertise in baseball over the years, its development in other areas was often limited. "The problem with the family," says Mee, "was that they had all grown up in the baseball world. They had always been on the inside looking out. They had never been outside looking in like you and I. As a result they had no concept of the attitude of the public. It was a foreign thing to them. They'd always been the nub of the organization. As a result they couldn't really feel the population."

Much like marketing, business networking was another concept with little meaning to Calvin, argues Whitney. "He didn't make a lot of friends in the business community. His whole life was baseball. His friends were Harvey (Dr. O'Phelan), George (Brophy), his brothers, (Dr. Leonard) Michienzi and the other people that sit in his box."

Calvin's independence did not gain him many points with the Twin Cities social community. "I'm in the caliber of those people but I don't associate with them," he says frankly. "I don't suck-ass up to them to get on their boards or anything."

What might have been an asset in human terms was probably a liability to Calvin in business terms, Brophy agrees. "He was an old shoe. He's common folk. There were no pompous actions on his part. As a matter of fact, anybody that was stuffy was not gonna be around him too long."

Calvin's public comments during years of declining attendance didn't help, notes Whitney. "He was critical of the business community because they just quit coming and gave up their seats. It wasn't until after he sold the team, in fact until the World Series last year that I started seeing people that I knew at the ballpark," he says with obvious sympathy for Calvin.

"Everybody goes to the football games, the Vikings, that's the thing to do, and for awhile it was the North Stars (hockey) and it will be the Timberwolves (basketball)," notes Whitney. "But the business people deserted us. We were down to 1700 season tickets. That isn't much support from the business community, so why shouldn't Calvin get down on them . . . . But it didn't help."

Other factors may have limited the Griffith organization's ability to adapt for survival. Fox argues that the family structure often stifled upward mobility among employees. "You've got to realize that in this family operation all of the good jobs were taken up by members of the family. In corporations it's tough to get good people when they come in and say, 'I've got no future' and so on . . . . We lost Herb Heft (public relations director) and the reason we lost him, he told me, was because he said, 'Look, I've got no chance here.'"

Those that stayed sometimes had to deal with their resentment. "I'd experienced some successes in the business world on my own and some setbacks," says Fox, referring to the Virginia peanut sales business he ran with his father until forced out by the Depression. "I made baseball my life. (But) I know this, I know I was never allowed to make more money than Clark."

Calvin denies ever having limited Fox's options, while Clark's eventual fall from the inner circle of organizational leadership speaks for itself. "I never denied a person an opportunity to better himself," says Calvin, while noting that no other major league organization ever showed any interest in Fox. "He was just lucky to have the freedom he had around me."

At least one former player, Jim Kaat, agrees that a lack of change in the Griffith organization may have hurt the team, though not for the reasons Fox noted. "I really think if Calvin had surrounded himself with brighter people . . . . How can I put this diplomatically? I don't think Howard Fox was a good influence on him. Howard's link between the team and Calvin was strictly personality. No matter how the guy performed, if his personality was not the type Howard liked, the guy had a tough time. And he had a lot of influence on Calvin. I think that hurt the ballclub."

Calvin insists he was always in control of the Griffith organization, however. "I did practically everything by myself," he says, forgetting his own description of the sale to Pohlad. "I made the major decisions and everybody knew what they were supposed to do and not divert things."

Bitter rivalries and competition for Calvin's ear were an increasingly obvious fact however. Whether based on family or friendship, the old Twins management style often led more to political decisions than logical ones. "You have to remember the organization came out of Washington, and in Washington everyone thinks politically," reminds Tom Mee. "There were a couple of people who'd always look around and no matter what the issue they'd take the other side . . . . Generally Calvin would only listen to one person."

But if Calvin's loyalty was often unquestioned and sometimes abused, it generally also meant security for even lower-rung Twins employees. "We hardly ever had any turnover. People stayed on with us for years, not like what you see here now," says Calvin with pride.

"Everybody was loyal to him and he was loyal to everybody," agrees George Brophy. "Consequently there was a firmness to the operation. Whether you were blood family or not he treated everybody as though they were family and everybody—the scouts, minor league managers, and everybody looked at it that way, not like now . . . . Too many owners now feel that they're qualified to step all over their baseball people."

Personal contact was another casualty of the change in organization. "Under Calvin and the family there was great feeling of brotherliness, I guess you could say," remembers Mee. "Under Pohlad it's much more impersonal. Each person does his own job. The Twins have a lot more employees now and there's no real contact with the top brass, not Jerry Bell (Twins president), but the owner.

"Under the old ownership there wasn't a day gone by I didn't have some contact with Calvin," adds Mee. "I don't see Pohlad now except maybe to say 'hello' two or three times a year, which isn't to say that's bad. It's just the way he runs his empire, he can't get down to everybody."

It is a contrast in styles born from a contrast in business approaches. "Calvin is primarily a baseball man not a business man. Of course baseball has been declared by the U.S. Supreme Court not to be a business," points out Dorsey tongue-in-cheek, referring to baseball's antitrust exemption since early in the century.

The Twins owner always looked out for all the members of his organization, even if his dealings with players were sometimes hostile, says Mee. "The image of Calvin being cheap was undeserved. With the employees, while we didn't work for very big salaries it's true, Calvin always laid it on the line. 'When I hit it big you'll share.' And the years when we hit one million (attendance) we always got a big bonus. The fringe benefits were always excellent. But he got his cheap reputation with the players. Those were the guys the public sees."

Even there, notes Mee, reality is somewhat different from the stereotype. "All the players from the 60s, not so much the 70s, whenever I talk to them the first thing they say is 'How's Calvin?' He could be tough as nails with them and he had to deal with 40 of them every year. But they want to know about Calvin."

Several former Twins admit that they have called on Calvin's generosity since the end of their playing days. Zoilo Versalles describes his loans from his former boss as something of a "makeup" for earlier underpaid days, but agrees Calvin was under no obligation. "I was down and he just give me money knowing I couldn't pay him back. I don't even know how much I owe him."

For others such as Dave Boswell, Calvin's assistance would be in the form of a badly needed, short-term scouting job in the organization. "He was very tight with the buck," recalls Boswell. "But he was honest with his heart."

Tony Oliva would warrant a longer-term payback as a hitting coach in the Twins organization. "I remember 1976 when my knee was very bad and I no want to play no more. He call me to the office and say, 'Tony, we have to talk about your future,'" describes Oliva. "I know that if I have any kind of problem, I can come to Calvin Griffith and he is ready to listen."

Calvin would even keep several players of questionable talent on the Twins' roster in order to complete their eligibility for major league pensions. "I didn't brag about it. But I took care of guys like Karl Hardy, Bill Pleis, and Julio Becquer."

Time would pass by that relationship with the players, just as it would pass by the entire Griffith organization. "I would doubt seriously whether there will ever be another family in baseball because the whole world has changed," concludes Fox. "We can see in the franchises over the last decade where the first thing the banks do (after a death or change in the family situation) is to say, 'get rid of it.' It's not a good investment for an estate or whatever."

Thelma draws larger comparisons. "It's like every family company," she notes. "I get a little peeved when I see these companies, these corporate raiders. I think that's one reason why nothing is as good as it used to be. It used to be a family built something up and they had a certain pride and produced until somebody comes along and grabs it up and thinks 'Oh, what difference does it make, it's just money.'"

Despite attacks on the quality of Twins teams in the late 1970s and early 1980s the overall history of teams under Calvin Griffith confirms an acceptable level of competitiveness. Certainly there was always a continuous level of personal involvement in the product far beyond that of other owners with more extensive investment portfolios. Like craftsmen, albeit sometimes with limited materials, the Griffiths sculpted their work with undiverted pride and care.

Whether the analogy is correct or not, Calvin and Thelma's roles as the last owners whose livelihood revolved solely around baseball would finally come to an end, although their influence may still be felt. It could be argued that many of Calvin's approaches to dealing with baseball's labor changes have lived on in recent ownership strategies. "I think now some of 'em are starting to wish they'd listened to me earlier," he says proudly.

"As the numbers have multiplied beyond reason," said Milwaukee Brewers owner Bud Selig, "Calvin's approach is more and more logical. He may turn out to be the smartest man in our industry."

More accurate may be to say that Calvin's holdout against free agency and arbitration created a model, of sorts, for other owners pressed by the disparity in baseball markets. His unsuccessful struggle for survival would be pointed to, rightly or wrongly, as an example of how organized labor was creating a dangerous imbalance in the sport.

Yet Calvin was also a distinctly different animal than other modern baseball owners. His battle with change in the game was based as much on history and moral beliefs as financial analyses. Whether based on stubbornness or principle, he was the last holdout from an era of baseball that will never return.

Calvin has certainly never resented being an anachronism. "I don't mind being called a dinosaur," he said to a *Sports Illustrated* reporter in 1983. "A dinosaur, from what I've seen on TV, is a pretty powerful person. A dinosaur usually pushes himself around to where he doesn't get hurt."

That conclusion might be highly debatable. But former White Sox owner Bill Veeck, who hung the dinosaur tag on Calvin years ago, may have best described the paradoxical nature of the former Twins owner. "It's not just that he marches to his own drum. I don't even think he hears anyone else's. He doesn't identify with the fans—never has. He doesn't do things because they're good p.r. or politically smart. It's a strange thing to say, with that big, fat belly of his, but in a perverse way I find him gallant."

Calvin takes such critiques in their most positive light. "Maybe it's a compliment for a man who didn't have a second pocketbook to stay around baseball as long as we did," he says. "There never will be another family or group that stays in baseball as long as the Griffiths did without having a reserve somewhere. When you go from 1920 to 1984 with a fellow named Griffith as president of a ballclub, nobody else will ever attain that."

Chapter 21

LATE INNINGS
AND LATE THOUGHTS

"I think I'm a person who looked out for the fan.
I think I was always honest with them. I don't lie. I tell the truth and
that's what got me into a lot of trouble . . . .
We made mistakes. But my mind has always been open for the betterment of baseball."

Calvin's place in history is important to him, as evidenced by his pride at being listed three places in baseball's Hall of Fame and at his 1989 selection by *The Sporting News* as recipient of the Pioneer Award. Calvin's place in Cooperstown is still likely less meaningful than keeping his seat at every Twins home game. "That box is mine," he says emphatically, in response to a question about the end of his five-year contract with Pohlad in 1989. "I'm going to have to get that confirmed with (Minnesota Vikings co-owner) Max Winter if he's not too senile."

With his brothers Jimmy and Billy Robertson and a few remaining Twins employees or oldtimers visiting with other teams, the Griffith enclave still also holds down a small corner of the lunchroom buried deep in the Metrodome. They appear to be much like they were in their glory years when Bill Veeck described the exchange of scouting secrets in the seductively hospitable Minnesota lunchroom as the key to Calvin's baseball success.

With diners now spending more time watching "Wheel of Fortune" on an overhead television while smacking down one of dining room cook Sherm Seeker's meat and potato meals, the Griffiths' time warp struggles to keep in focus.

"Look at that Vanna turn those numbers," Calvin says in between bites. His napkin is attached, like a bib, to his plaid suitcoat by a diamond-studded tie clasp that is a memento from the 1924 World Series. "Did anybody hear how Oakland came out this afternoon?"

Perhaps keeping in mind his own predictions of how he might shrivel up and die if denied an active role in baseball, at age 76 he spent the 1988 season as much as possible like those in his past—coming to the office to open his mail, eat dinner, take his daily nap as he learned from his uncle Clark Griffith, and brush his teeth before game time.

Though he still studies the daily minor league reports and other Twins organization memos that come across his desk, Calvin's principal business concern now is the backlog of requests for support that his newfound millionaire status has naturally increased. "I get on their sucker list," says Calvin of the human service and health organizations that regularly call on him. "I'm gonna start keeping track of who I give to."

Curiously, Calvin can admit his ignorance of personal tax benefits from charitable donations ("Can you deduct that stuff?") and in almost the same breath praise the eased estate tax law changes of the early 1980s which could save his heirs thousands of dollars.

Calvin's generosity is again oriented toward the familiar and trusted, even if far-flung. "I've got a few regular ones," he says, recounting projects in Montana, Virginia, and even Mexico. "Most of 'em are Indian reservations. They need the money except for the ones in Oklahoma who have oil wells."

Closer to home, Calvin's Scrooge-like reputation was dealt a blow with a spontaneous gift of $2500 to the curious Shriners group, the Royal Order of Jesters, to which he has belonged since the early 1940s. "I know a lot of people and even guys in the lodge thought he was a selfish tightwad," says his old friend, Gerald Moore. "But he wants to be one of the boys, he really does."

Cheerfully greeting various Twins employees, media, and even ballplayers passing through the Metrodome hallways, on the surface he appears generally unaffected by the change of circumstances that has made him almost a ghost amongst the machinery that now runs the organization. His public comments run along the line of, "I'm just goldarned happy not to have my name in the paper. I'm enjoying the hell out of life."

In his glass-enclosed private box, Calvin with his brothers, George Brophy, and other close friends now generally on the outside of Twins organization decision-making, still holds a form of power. Their analysis of players and comparison with stars of the past is a pastime that will never be limited to former owners of baseball teams. But the Griffiths are both blessed and cursed by their lifetime of experience in a world that no longer exists.

"I keep saying Hrbek would hit better if he'd stand up and hit more like he did in high school," says Calvin with a frown as he watches the hunched-over Twins first baseman at the plate. "This thing of looking at the pitcher upside down is for the birds. But I'm sure I couldn't tell him anything like I could Oliva."

Recalling his ability to evaluate talent, Calvin harkens back to a conversation with former Chicago White Sox general manager Hank Greenberg several years after negotiating the 1960 trade that brought Earl Battey and Don Mincher to the Senator-Twins in exchange for Norm Sievers. "He used to say, 'Goddamn it, all you do is take advantage of us,'" laughs Calvin.

"That's the only thing I miss. Oh, that was fun," he says of trading players. "There's an art to it. You can't be too anxious. When you start dealing never tell what you want right off the bat—the names usually change five or six times."

Without keeping score, and seemingly without paying attention, the Griffiths are later able to recall virtually any play or at-bat in a game. "I don't need these scorebooks," says Calvin, "You're around this so much you can keep it in your head. I used to go home and fill out a scorecard better than my wife used to keep at the game."

Conspicuously absent from the Griffith box on most occasions is Clark Griffith. Usually seated with his wife and son in seats behind the backstop, he often still passes in front of the other family members without giving any visible acknowledgment of their presence.

Yet, if relations are still cool, they have at least begun to thaw in the years since Clark's estrangement from Calvin and other members of the family in the early 1980's. Mellowing and maturity that came with age on both ends has combined with the perceived presence of a common enemy to help bring a father and son to at least a level of personal cordiality.

Neither is ready to concede on their basic philosophical differences, however. "Clark was always willing to gamble," recalls Calvin. "In sports you can't gamble. Who'd have thought Kansas could beat Oklahoma? Who'd have thought the Vikings would beat San Francisco? Who'd have thought the Twins would be World Champs?" he asked about some of 1987-88's major sports upsets.

Looking back on their conflict, Calvin is perhaps more appreciative of Clark's ability, yet vestiges of suspicion remain. "Clark was very useful, very useful," he says. "But I always felt he was looking for the old man's job. He thought he was obsolete, he had the old ways. Well, what are the new ways? Machinery? Is that gonna do all your thinking for you? You have to have a certain experience that's how I always looked at it."

Thelma Haynes also comes to her brother's defense in discussion of those years. "Clarkie had a drinking problem. And when you have a drinking problem you're not yourself. I think he (Clark) had a lot to do with the bad image that Calvin came up with. He wrote articles (advertisements) about his father, about how he ran the ballclub like the Dark Ages, that sorta stuff. Clarkie caused a lot of problems. But I'm glad he's got himself straightened out now."

Yet Clark, who successfully completed alcohol rehabilitation treatment in 1976, notes that more of his family problems came after he adopted sobriety than before. "She likes to blame things on my drinking," he replies testily. "But what she doesn't like to say is that the rest of them were drinking their heads off for a decade after I stopped."

An age-old mixture of joy, pride, resentment, and sadness comes through in Calvin's discussion of his son. In an almost stereotypical bragging-father fashion he describes his son's schoolboy athletic exploits. "He was a very capable ballplayer. He could hit it as far as Harmon Killebrew or anybody else, and he hit them from both sides of the plate.

"And he was an outstanding football player," continues Calvin of Clark. "He scored something like 16 TD's in eight games, something like that. George Marshall (Redskins owner) saw him at Sidwell Friends High School and wanted to sign him as a kicker. He could kick the ball 60 or 70 yards."

Yet Clark remembers Calvin's interest at the time as only being to criticize or even discourage his efforts. He repeats the story told to a *Sports Illustrated* reporter in 1983 of how in one high school game he scored the winning run after getting three hits, stealing second and third, then scoring on a suicide squeeze. Afterwards, Clark remembers his father's only comment being to growl, "How could you let that pitcher get you out that one time?"

"That's a lot of bull. I never said nothing like that," replies Calvin. "But he's that way. He's got a mind that just won't forget."

As far as encouragement, Calvin insists he merely wanted Clark to make his own decisions. "I didn't have to encourage him. He was a natural. I didn't say anything to force him" Calvin says. "he went to all the private schools he wanted to. He went to Sidwell. He wanted to go to Dartmouth, he went to Dartmouth. I just paid the bills for him, that's all."

Clark vigorously insists that he paid for much or most of his college education after finishing a U.S. Navy stint in the early 1960s.

Later communication problems were worsened by the almost Balkanized atmosphere of the Griffith organization, both men agree. "It was a shame I was misled so much by things that my son is supposed to have said. After a long time, after we really had a knockout blow for he and I, I finally talked to him and he said, 'Well, I didn't say this, I didn't say that.'

"Fox didn't tell you the truth," Calvin continues his explanation. "Like arbitration (hearings). Fox told me that Clarkie wanted to give up arbitration because he could see it was gonna get him in more trouble with ballplayers and he didn't want to get that kind of reputation as a hard-nosed battler.

"Well, finally later on he (Clark) told me he wanted to do it! And he was good at it," praises Calvin. "He won cases we didn't think we'd win and you're lucky to win anything in arbitration."

Clark's bitterness at Calvin's belated appreciation shows through even as he calmly describes his father's life in terms of learning disabilities and phobias. "So he thinks Fox lied to him," he says sarcastically. "He lied to him every day of his life and he loved it. He didn't want to hear the truth if it came from me . . . . He's just in his revisionist period now."

Still his father's harshest critic, Clark continues to argue that the Griffith ownership was unnecessarily scuttled before he got his own chance at leadership. "Calvin likes to talk about how there's been a Griffith in baseball for a hundred years. What he doesn't say is that he's the one that made sure it didn't last for 110 years," Clark says, suggesting that he might have been able to salvage the family enterprise.

One close observer finds fault with both parties. "There's blame on both sides," says daughter and sister Corinne Griffith Pillsbury. "Each of them had a role. Clark thought it already was his team and acted like it, and my father wasn't about to give it up."

To a degree, Calvin is now willing to admit his own errors in dealing with his son. His embarrassment of Clark in opposing the 1981 players' strike settlement that his son had helped negotiate, is a prominent example. "It was a helluva blow," admits Calvin. "It sure didn't help anything between us. It hurt him no question about it."

But Calvin, with some good reason, also remains doubtful that it is entirely within his power to fill the gap between himself and Clark. "We're closer. But not to where you can say we're buddy-buddy. Not yet," he concludes. "He can't get certain things out of his mind, he brings them up all the time and I just don't like it. If the time comes when he doesn't bring up this and that, I can give in a little more. You'd like to get closer to your family, no doubt about it."

Calvin's relations with his daughters have also been limited, though not as overtly hostile as those with Clark. "Father was never around," Corinne says matter-of-factly of her childhood years. "Clare says she can't remember him at all in Washington. He did sit with us in the box then. But baseball was really his whole world."

Like so many fathers, Calvin's definition of service to his family did not necessarily match that of the members, and hard feelings developed on both ends. "My father really doesn't understand, that's the sad part," adds Corinne. "He doesn't see what happened. It's too bad."

Calvin's pain and confusion was evident in his 1983 description of family problems to *Sports Illustrated.* "Love . . . . Love is a funny word. My love was to try to put bread and butter on the table for my family. Clark says I wasn't a good father. Hell, if I wasn't a good father, I'd have let him go to public schools and learn the hard way. He was spoiled more than anything else. I had to work day and night. He always felt he could run a ballclub better than me. Hell, I played catch with him and every other damn thing . . . . I can't understand it. I can't understand a lot of things."

Calvin often puts his conflict with Clark in his most familiar, if minimizing, frame of reference. "It's just like my uncle and I had a few arguments over this and that," he says with a shrug.

Natalie Griffith's battle with cancer finally ended with her death on January 1, 1989. Calvin returned from Florida for the funeral, both to honor her and to spend time with his children in hopes of mending fences. It is a hope not likely to be easily fulfilled.

"My family has been important," maintains Calvin. "My children don't believe that I love them. I don't know what else you have to do for them. I stayed broke putting them through schools and everything else. Back in Washington I didn't have any money or time . . . . When I came up here (Minnesota) the children weren't around much. I would've liked it due to the fact I had more time."

Perhaps not coincidentally, Calvin's taste in entertainment, aside from any sort of sports activity, runs strongly toward television dramas of the Falcon Crest, Knot's Landing, and Dynasty variety. "I've gotta watch Dallas tonight," he insists one night at his Orlando hotel where he still stays during the Twins spring training. "I don't know if J.R.'s gonna get a screwing by the family or what."

Yet Calvin often seems honestly to forget the level of conflict that dominated his family and business. "I don't have maybe two enemies right now," he says. "Well, maybe four. Four enemies right now—I'd say that's pretty damn good with all the people I've known."

One person Calvin will doubtless never be close to again is former best friend, Howard Fox. "I'm sure you know that Calvin and my closeness lessened all the time to the point that now we don't speak to each other," says Fox. "I wish him well. But it's hard for me to have anything to do with him now after the things that he said about me in the newspaper."

Wealth and leisure time don't always aid family relationships as the Griffiths have found out since the team sale. With Bruce Haynes' parked boat in a garage at Calvin's Florida condominium as the bone of contention, Calvin and Thelma have recently concluded either a minor sibling squabble or a power struggle that had been brewing over thirty years.

"That's what the whole thing was about. Thelma was never really happy," argues Clark Griffith.

"Why should we take a back seat?" says Thelma Haynes, defending her son's position in the garage affair. "It's different with a girl. They have to take a backseat. But he (Bruce) doesn't have to take a backseat. Calvin's just used to getting his way."

Calvin, who would settle the affair by moving to another condominium in the spring of 1989, has his own view, of course. "She's (Thelma) the one causing all the trouble . . . . I just wish she'd get out and enjoy herself more, maybe travel and see the world."

It's a philosophy Calvin has tried to follow himself, taking an Alaskan cruise in 1987 and considering Caribbean and other international jaunts. His first visit outside of the U.S. and Cuba had been to England in the early 1960s where he was more struck by the epicurian attractions than historical ones such as Stonehenge ("a pile of rocks") and the Tower of London ("Dang, those hallways were narrow. I was afraid we wouldn't make it out of there").

"I really liked those pubs," Calvin remembering his favorite part of English life. "They got that food all piled up. But I said, 'What's wrong with the refrigerators?' They don't like to give out ice cubes over there."

In 1979, along with Clark and an American League All-Star team, he traveled to Japan—where he enjoyed the baseball, if not the hotel beds. "They asked if I wanted a Western bed or an Eastern bed," remembers Calvin. "I said I wanted a bed like they have in the United States. They have those Geisha girls or somebody in their Western beds."

There were no complaints about the Alaskan cruise however. "It was really something," Calvin says of the trip with his brothers and B.J. Block, his female companion for over a decade. "They had all kinds of movies and things on board (the ship). And the water was so clear—it was like we used to have at the house on Minnetonka. The kids used to go down there and wash their hair in it. Now it's not that way any more."

Calvin ceded the nearly million dollar home to Natalie when he moved into a suburban Edina condominium, though the two never legally divorced. "Every time I talk to her she says, 'Now remember we're still married,'" he would mimic before her death. "I say, 'Yes, Natalie, I remember it.'"

His relationship with B.J. since meeting her at a Christmas party in 1978 is only another part of Calvin's mixture of tradition and change. "I'm living with her, but we're not married, and some people have funny ideas about that," he says, giving his moral dislike of divorce as the reason. "But I'm not a saint. I'm not trying to be a priest or a nun. I'm just a regular guy," he says. "The worst thing is you don't know how to put it in the paper. You can't say she's a lady in waiting."

It is a relationship that defies understanding in other ways. An independent-minded 59-year-old ballroom dance instructor and macrobiotic food fanatic, B.J. admits she has little in-depth understanding of baseball. Yet, she describes their personal links as strong enough to survive their obvious differences.

"It is strange," she agrees, describing his courtship as Victorian and formal. "But I can talk to Calvin about anything. He's so open-minded about anything. He's changed. When he owned the Twins, he felt such responsibility as the oldest child, and I think he felt he had to save the team for his family . . . . (After the sale) suddenly it was like he didn't have to worry about it or being in public. He did things just because he thought he had to."

B.J. remembers years when Calvin would come home after ballgames and go straight to his room, taking the phone off the hook. "He was so disturbed. He was sick inside and had such torment—more than anybody knew," she remembers. "He seems to have been trained just to carry those things around. He's learned to carry them inside since he was very young . . . . He wanted to win the pennant so bad while he was still owner."

Now B.J. describes Calvin as more concerned with other preoccupations such as watching tennis players out of the window of their trophy-filled living room. ("I like to watch these young people move," Calvin says) or feeding her parrot in the kitchen while reading the newspaper out loud as she prepares his morning eggs. "He's so lucky," she says of his diet. "If I had eaten like he does, I'd have been dead twenty years ago. But he seems to thrive on it."

Twins physician, Dr. Harvey O'Phelan agrees that despite his weight and stress Calvin has remained amazingly healthy since his recovery from prostate surgery in 1987. Recurring knee problems since Calvin had his "cartridge" removed in 1983 haven't stopped him from occasional trips to the golf course in the off-season.

"His blood pressure has always been normal and he's slept," says O'Phelan. "I think he went to bed every night thinking he did the right thing. Most people would have at least had an ulcer."

O'Phelan's orders to cut down on drinking came not from fears of alcoholism, but from concerns about the calories in Calvin's daily pair of vodka tonics. "I never really saw him where I thought he had too much to drink," says the doctor and close friend of Griffith.

Interestingly, Calvin maintains that it was his problems with phlebitis that led him back to drinking in the early sixties. "I started drinking these glasses of Dubonnay Red," he remembers, citing the pain-killing effect. "Then eventually I started drinking vodka tonics. Maybe if I'd never started I wouldn't be so fat!

"But I always tried to keep it to two," Calvin says emphatically. "And if I had to think I didn't do no drinking . . . . Well when I go to the All-Star game or something like that I might have three. See, I can stand three 'cause they don't put any alcohol in the drinks anyway."

Many of his friends argue that, contrary to popular opinion, if Calvin ever had a dependency it was on food not alcohol. Eating was his way of relieving stress, argues Wheelock Whitney. "He's pretty into himself. My guess is his way of handling crisis is to have something to eat. Eating has always been important to him. He medicates his feelings by eating."

Calvin scoffs at such pop psychology but continues to wear the copper bracelets that were suggested over ten years ago as treatment for the arthritis in his wrists. "I was at

Toots Shors (restaurant-bar in New York) and there was this English golfer and he had four of 'em for his elbows." remembers Calvin. "But he told me if you're gonna wear a copper bracelet, get one out of Iowa. I didn't even know there was any copper in Iowa. Doctor O'Phelan says its mind over matter. But hell, it did me some good."

Perhaps it is simply baseball that keeps Calvin Griffith healthy, as he has long suggested. "I love baseball so goddamn much—it's like a dessert," he offered a fitting analogy for *Sports Illustrated*.

That conclusion hasn't changed despite the intervening heartbreaks. "I love baseball that's all," he still says. "Ever since I was a little kid playing on those sandlots in Washington. There's nothing like being at the game. The comments from the fans are priceless, the sights and sounds and smells."

Walking through the Metrodome hallways, his waddling, rotund form is identifiable to even the most uninformed fan. A 25-yard walk from the Twins office to his private box can take half an hour as he wades through the autograph seekers and well-wishers. His round figure and familiar jowls act like a magnet for anyone old enough to have a memory.

A locally produced one-man play, *Calvin* by Ken LaZelnik, was a hit with both viewers and its subject.

"People that used to despise me say now that I was a good businessman," Calvin says proudly. "I go to Lunds' (grocery store) or places and people look at me and talk. I can't hardly go anywhere but people want to come up and talk about baseball or something."

Billy Robertson confirms that his brother is recognizable at every remote fishing outpost in Minnesota. "Calvin's more popular than he's ever been. Everywhere he goes people recognize him. They say, 'Are you Calvin Griffith? What are you doing here in Bemidji? What are you doing in Brainerd?"

Calvin no longer gets obscene gestures from other motorists as he drives his Lincoln Continental to the ballpark. "I used to get crucified a lot. But you can't take that stuff too serious. I think a lot of things get said that people don't really mean," he says philosophically. "And to tell the truth I think I always had the real fans behind me," Calvin adds, perhaps unaware that Twins media director Tom Mee used to screen out his negative mail.

But Peter Dorsey insists there was always a solid base of support for Calvin. "I used to travel around with him and I would say he was probably the best known man in the state of Minnesota with the exception of Hubert Humphrey. He was a man that history passed by, but baseball fans always liked him."

Certainly most local media has softened its treatment of him, though Calvin claims not to have ever noticed. "I don't pay any attention to those guys," he says. "You have to realize they have to make a living . . . . I wouldn't want to be a newspaperman and sit down on my tail there and drum out a column day in and day out. Where do you come up with all the ideas?"

Though there have been exceptions, Calvin's openness and patience with the media over the years has been widely known. "He really was almost too honest for his own good sometimes. We used to play him off against the manager for information," remembers former Minneapolis baseball writer Tom Briere.

"Calvin is such a forgiving guy," notes Wheelock Whitney. "I can't imagine the things that Hartman and other writers would say and then that night he'd (Hartman) come in the box. If I were Calvin I'd say, 'Get the hell out of here.' But Calvin, I think, showed tremendous patience with the treatment he got from the press too."

Better days have certainly come for the popular image of Calvin Griffith. As time has passed by, old grievances fade and the positives remain. No better example can be found than Rod Carew's virtual recanting of old criticisms upon his return for a jersey retirement ceremony in mid-1987. Praising Calvin at both a press conference and in his public speech, Carew thanked the man he once accused of racism and exploitation for his continuing patience and friendship during his maturation years with the Twins.

Griffith, who was not included as part of the ceremony, was visibly touched by the gesture. "People don't know you 'til he (Carew) says something like that," said Calvin between sniffles. "It made tears come to my ears to hear something like that. Those things he said before were in anger and you know down in your heart that he didn't mean it. A lot of things are said in this world and you know that it's not the truth, that's all there is to it."

But little could compare in Calvin's mind, as in the minds of many Minnesotans, to the thrill of watching the Twins unexpected drive to the World Championship in 1987. No longer the owner or directly involved with any of the team decisions, he nevertheless took great personal pride at seeing the success of Hrbek, Gaetti, Laudner, Viola, and Puckett—whose ways to the majors he paved.

"A couple of 'em came up after the World Series and said 'If it wasn't for you we wouldn't be here today.'" Calvin recalls. "That really stimulates your body and your mind. You think, 'Well, damn, you did something good for somebody.'"

After the criticism of the early 1980s, it was almost a more satisfying thrill than the lone American League championship won during his ownership. "It was quite a thrill the first time," he says, remembering that the 1965 pennant came only four years after the hapless Senators had moved from Washington. "But still, this was something, knowing we had to work a little harder. It was more something to prove. When you're proven right then you really feel good."

Calvin would be honored by throwing out the first ball of the seventh game, a fulfillment of a promise he exacted when passed over at the 1985 All-Star Game in Minneapolis. But more typical of his treatment from the Twins organization would be the snub he received on the team flight back from St. Louis during the World Series when he was assigned a seat in the back of the plane while Pohlad and the rest of the Twins officials sat up front. "One of his sons comes back and says, 'Are you all right back there,'" recalls Calvin. "He did that to insult me. I knew it because they're all up front joking and laughing and I'm sitting back there by myself."

But Calvin feels secure that Andy MacPhail and other baseball-savvy Twins officials give him credit for his role in building the foundation for the 1987 glories. "Down in his heart he knows. Championships don't happen overnight."

In Calvin's replay of life, he's always been an actor, if not always on center stage, in baseball's key scenes. "I was in Florida last winter," he says. "And on TV they had a shot of the winning run in the 1924 World Series. And there I am holding the bat. I said, 'Damn, I can't believe it. There I am.'"

How well Calvin and the Griffith family succeeded will continue to be debated. Not a great innovator in strategic or financial aspects of the game, nor a leading political force in baseball circles, he was nevertheless surprisingly often at the center of great controversy. He was able to make a mark, or critics might contend, a blemish, that was larger than his personal role warranted.

Eventually, Calvin's claim to fame may be that he exemplified so much. "He was a guy that the everyday fan can understand,'" says Whitney. "He had trouble with his wife, he had trouble with his kids, he had trouble paying his bills, he had trouble with the high-priced talent around. He tried to run a good business but he had problems just like me and you, just like ninety percent of the people walking down the street. I think they can identify with Calvin. It's hard for them to identify with Carl Pohlad.

"Here's a man totally committed to his work. Everything he had, his dreams, were totally wrapped up with his Minnesota team and Washington ballclub. I think people will remember that when everything else is gone and his Waseca speech and his failure to sign Bostock and his firing of Billy Martin and everything else that people want to rant and rave about. I think Calvin will be remembered with affection."

The years of conflict have perhaps worn down the edge on Calvin Griffith. Or perhaps it is the weight of time. But he has begun to think of his legacy in more than financial or even family terms. "I think I'm a person who looked out for the fan," he says. "I think I was always honest with them. I don't lie. I tell the truth and that's what got me into a lot of trouble . . . . We made mistakes. But my mind has always been open for the betterment of baseball. We always did our best to put a competitive team on the field that wouldn't shortchange the fans. Never."

Calvin's plans after the 1989 season, when he will be almost 78 years old, remain uncertain. There seems little hope for a role with the Twins, though he still hopes for a role in baseball as perhaps a consultant or scout for some Major League organization.

It is a likelihood perhaps less certain than another for which he has already made plans. Calvin has arranged for six gravesites in Maryland, connected to Uncle Clark's mausoleum and the gravesites of other family members such as Joe Haynes and Sherry Robertson. "I'm not worried about it," he says with a laugh. "When it comes I know we'll have some damn good conversations."